Authenticity as an

Routledge Studies in Contemporary Philosophy

Authenticity as an Ethical Ideal

Somogy Varga

Routledge
Taylor & Francis Group
NEW YORK   LONDON

First published 2012
by Routledge
711 Third Avenue, New York, NY 10017

Simultaneously published in the UK
by Routledge
2 Park Square, Milton Park, Abingdon, Oxfordshire OX14 4RN

First issued in paperback 2014

*Routledge is an imprint of the Taylor & Francis Group,
an informa business*

© 2012 Taylor & Francis

The right of Somogy Varga to be identified as author of this work has been asserted in accordance with sections 77 and 78 of the Copyright, Designs and Patents Act 1988.

Typeset in Sabon by IBT Global.

Library of Congress Cataloging-in-Publication Data
Authenticity as an ethical ideal / Somogy Varga.
    p. cm. — (Routledge studies in contemporary philosophy ; 33)
    Includes bibliographical references and index.
    1. Authenticity (Philosophy)   2. Ethics, Modern.   3. Critical theory.
I. Title.
   B105.A8V37 2012
   170—dc23
   2011025813

ISBN 978-0-415-89533-0 (hbk)
ISBN 978-1-138-80978-9 (pbk)
ISBN 978-0-203-14632-3 (ebk)

In loving memory of Ilona Varga

Contents

Acknowledgments

This book is the outcome of a highly inspiring three-year research period at the Goethe University of Frankfurt. The research was funded by the Danish Research Foundation. In addition, I was fortunate to be granted a fellowship at the Institute of Social Research in Frankfurt am Main. I owe a special debt of gratitude to Axel Honneth, who brought me into a highly stimulating research environment and who has encouraged me in this project with comments and corrections over the course of a continuous conversation spanning three years.

I am indebted to a great number of colleagues and friends who have discussed and commented on the central ideas of this book. I want to thank Isak Winkel Holm, Frederik Tygstrup, Martin Seel, Stephan Deines, Hartmut Rosa, and Charles Guignon. Additionally, I thank Alessandro Ferrara, Jacob Golomb, and several anonymous referees for extensively commenting on previous versions of the manuscript, and Thomas D. Robinson and Kelso Cratsley for both meticulous proofreading and valuable comments.

Finally, I owe special thanks to my wife Bettina for steady encouragement, and to my children, for tolerating my time-consuming and useless passion for writing a book without pictures.

Introduction

All concepts of authenticity relate to some extent to the basic meaning of
the word 'authentic,' which is used either in a strong sense of 'undisputed
origin or authorship' or in the weaker sense of 'faithful to an original'
or 'reliable, accurate representation.' This is far from the whole picture
however. A brief look at historical connotations provides a richer range
of meaning. The Greek *authentikos* derives from the noun *authentes*,
"doer, master," which was built from two parts, from *autos*, "self," and
-hentes, "worker, doer, being." It simply meant "authoritative" before
the late eighteenth century when it developed into the modern meaning, which also involves the idea of 'genuine.' The *Oxford English Dic-
tionary* reveals four layers of meaning that still reverberate in current
usage: as being authenticated (thus authoritative or suitably authorized);
as being in accordance with a given fact; as referring to some authorship; or as being 'real' and not a result of replication or pretense. When
assessing the value, authorship or legal status of documents, works of
art, or archeological findings, and generally in situations when an original entity is compared to potential copies, this term appears useful and
perfectly intelligible.

However, distinguishing the authentic and inauthentic is highly context-
dependent. Denis Dutton (2003) argues that the use of the term "authentic"
in aesthetics groups into two categories. In this context, we may speak
of *nominal authenticity* when establishing that a work of art is correctly
identified in terms of origins, authorship, or provenance. Additionally, we
may speak of *expressive authenticity* when discussing the artifact's character being a genuine expression of the author's beliefs or central values in a
given socio-historical context.

Matters are even more complicated when authenticity is used as an ethical characteristic attributed to human agents. What is it to be oneself, or
to be at one with oneself? Any reflection on 'who we really are' discloses
a multiplicity of puzzles connecting to metaphysics, semantics, and epis-
temology. In a straightforward sense, being oneself is inescapable, since
whenever thinking a thought, making a decision, or acting in a certain
way, one is identical with the subject of those thoughts, decisions, and acts.

They are one's own. But in a more sophisticated sense, while someone may acknowledge being identical with the subject of those thoughts, decisions, or acts, she may be inclined to say that some of those are 'not really hers,' thus denying that those thoughts, decisions or acts are expressive of who she really is. At this point, the 'mineness' in question goes beyond the metaphysical sense and acquires its meaning by connecting to a moral-psychological dimension.

While authenticity in this sense is indisputably a slippery concept that is difficult to get a grip on, that is nevertheless what will be attempted here. As a first rough approximation, we deploy the term when describing a person who acts in a way that we think of as faithful to herself and her principles. Such a person acts on impulses and ideals that are not only hers (as bearing her authorship), but that are also expressions of who she really is. It is in this sense that Bernard Williams defines authenticity simply as "the idea that some things are in some real sense really you, or express what you are, and others aren't" (quoted in Guignon 2004: viii).

UNDERSTANDING AUTHENTICITY: MORAL PHILOSOPHY AND CRITICAL SOCIAL THEORY

In this general sense, the concept of authenticity naturally connects with philosophical discussions about autonomy. Autonomy emphasizes an individual's self-governing abilities, and the capacity to reliably follow *self-imposed* principles, which are employed independently of one's position in political and social structures (Schneewind 1998). Kantian 'moral autonomy' is limited to issues of moral obligation and refers to imposing a moral law on oneself, while 'personal autonomy' refers to leading a life according to one's own reasons and motives that are not products of manipulative external forces. In the broad sense, personal autonomy refers to putting one's behavior under reflexive scrutiny and making it dependent on self-determined goals (Honneth 1994: 59), when dealing not just with the strictly moral, but with a very broad variety of aspects of life (Dworkin 1988: 23–47). Beyond referring to leading an autonomous life, guided by non-constrained reasons and motives, authenticity introduces a second normative aspect. The motives and reasons I am moved by and act on should not only be of unconstrained origin, but also be expressive of my personality—of the person I take myself to be. I can act self-determinedly and lead an autonomous life (in the Kantian sense), while my actual actions and indeed my way of living can still fail to express the person I understand myself to be. Authenticity thus involves another ability beyond autonomy or self-determination, namely orientation, in terms of distinguishing between peripheral and core personal commitments, principles, wishes, or feelings that are truly worth following.

Authenticity is also a nexus where the question of the 'good life' and philosophical inquiry connect. In some Greek and Roman traditions, this was considered one of the most important goals in philosophy. With the emergence of modernity, the topic of the good life has lost its central position. On the one hand, such an undertaking was considered much too vague. On the other hand, it became susceptible to the criticism of putative paternalism, seeking to prescribe pre-defined paths of life for individuals. The revival of the concept in philosophical debate is connected to a change occurring in ethics over the last few decades (Taylor 1989; 1991; Nussbaum 1994; Seel 1991; 1993; Cottingham 1998). Elizabeth Anscombe's paper "Modern Moral Philosophy" (1958) marks a turning point in conceptualizing normative theories. Basically, she criticizes the preoccupation of modern moral philosophy with a law-based conception of ethics that operates with terms like obligation and duty. In her view, the approach to ethics which relies upon universal principles (Mill's utilitarianism, Kant's deontology) results in a stiff moral code that does not match modern societies. Instead, Anscombe calls for a return to Aristotelian ideas of the good life. This marks a revival of normative ethics after a period in which modern ethics focused on either descriptive method or linguistic and conceptual analysis of concepts like the 'good' (Steinfath 1998; Dohmen 2003). In discussion with the discourse ethics of Jürgen Habermas, the contract ethics of John Rawls, or recent utilitarianism, authors like Charles Taylor and Martha Nussbaum pose the classical Aristotelian question of the 'good life' once again.

The view that this book will defend is that practical philosophy, and most certainly critical social philosophy, cannot get off the ground without reflecting on the nature of the good life and well-being. Any philosophical undertaking that aims to illuminate the standards by which we pass normative judgments on the quality of self-relations and social relations needs some recourse to an idea of human flourishing, well-being, and thus the good life. Such an idea is necessary in order to explicate the point of social integration and political institutions. However, in order to avoid paternalism such an idea must be formulated carefully and as formally as possible. Therefore, practical philosophy should not involve a particular idea of the good life, but rather focus on the formal and constitutive *conditions* of such a good life. In this formalized sense, even Kant and Habermas make recourse to the constitutive conditions of the good life (for example the particular self-determined participation in social praxis) that provides the reference point for the impartial treatment of others (Seel 1997). Importantly, reaching beyond Kant, Habermas does not focus solely on strict universalizability, but on normative consensus, and goes beyond the idea of pure justice to include "those structural aspects of the 'good life' which can be separated from the concrete totality of particular forms of life" (Outhwaite 1994: 55). My preoccupation with the issue of authenticity has a clear connection to this debate, because the question concerning the formal conditions of the 'good life' can be answered in two ways: in the vocabulary of autonomy and in the vocabulary of authenticity. So, while I share with Habermas the aim of identifying the 'structural aspects of the good life,' I will spell it out not in the vocabulary of autonomy but in the vocabulary of authenticity, which I think is most adequate to contemporary social reality.

In addition, authenticity is also much more than a topic in ethical or moral philosophical debates, and in order to fully grasp it we should not restrict our inquiry to these fields. Besides being a theme in philosophy, authenticity—at least in the Western world—is a ubiquitous *ideal*, a way of conceptualizing the practice of the self to achieve a good life. The rise of authenticity as an ideal is closely connected to the rise of modernity and modern technology. Concerning the authenticity of objects, Walter Benjamin has rightly pointed out that authenticity is a product of modernity, in that it is only against the background of the radical reproducibility of objects and works of art that the modern concept of authenticity becomes intelligible in the first place. Benjamin (1973) describes how authenticity emerges as an ideal, as something we care about and are attentive to in a historical situation permeated by a "loss of the aura." It is in this sense, and in that particular historical context, that this value-laden concept becomes a powerful ideal, something that is seen as worth pursuing. It is not by chance that this question sufaces in late modernity in a particularly powerful manner. Habermas maintains that the processes of disenchantment and the differentiation of value spheres have led to a situation characterized by the plurality of goodness, in which it is impossible to formulate an overarching idea of the human good. In fact, reasonable disagreement regarding ideals of the good life is a characteristic of the modern condition (Larmore 1996; Forst 2007). It is in this context that the ideal of authenticity emerges, embodying a certain individualistic vision of the good that ties in with a particular socio-historical situation.

In his work on American cultural history, Miles Orwell discusses authenticity as a product of modernity and draws attention to the great impact it has had on contemporary societies. At the same time he notes that "we have a hunger for something like authenticity, but are easily satisfied by an ersatz facsimile" (Orwell 1989: xxiii). Importantly, in the second part of the sentence, he addresses the issue of suspicion, which stems from authenticity being a product of modernity and which has been an integral part of the ideal of authenticity ever since. The fear that the 'authentic' might turn out to be a 'fake,' a product of reproduction, has followed the ideal as its shadow. When emphasizing these two sides, Orwell sees authenticity as characterized by the simultaneous experience of desire and fear, which is a formative experience of modernity. Richard Rorty (1989: 24) also notices this intertwinement of desire (for authenticity) and fear (of inauthenticity, self-deception), and quoting Allan Bloom, he points to what he says is one of the greatest fears of modern man, namely the "horror of finding himself to be only a copy or a replica." Still, even with this ambivalent undertone, authenticity has continuously gained momentum and turned into a highly esteemed ideal that has shaped the way we relate to others and ourselves.

Although overshadowed by this intertwinement of fear and desire, authenticity has become a prevalent ethical ideal that tries to give answers to the question of how to lead a good life under the conditions of modernity. It is in this sense that Theodor W. Adorno, in *The Jargon of Authenticity* (1973), deals with authenticity as a problematic way of dealing with the normative gaps caused by modernity. Seeking answers to the question of how to live a good life, the vocabulary of authenticity has in our contemporary cultural context become what the notion of autonomous subjectivity was to early modernity. The "age of autonomy" that emphasized the individual's self-governing abilities is replaced by what Charles Taylor (2007: 472; also Ferrara 1998) called "the age of authenticity." The ideal of authenticity—that one should be *true to oneself and lead a life that is expressive of what the person takes herself to be*—has become a strong and widespread ethical ideal, as contemporary thinkers like Lasch, Taylor, Ferrara, and Guignon have noted. It has become a part of Western thought and practice, and it has contributed to the shaping of the modern worldview. In addition, the ideal of authenticity has also had an immense impact on popular culture, most revealingly and directly manifested in the quest for self-realization in the popular selfhelp movement. Simultaneously with this great impact, many have noted that the ideal of authenticity has deformed and turned into aestheticism and egoistic self-indulgence. As Guignon (2004: 81) eloquently puts it,

> when the older idea of privileged access to a higher truth is abandoned, as it is in our contemporary thinking, what is left is a glorification of intensity and "mineness" as goods in themselves, no matter what their content might be. We are then inclined to think of authenticity as a purely personal virtue, one aimed at firming up the boundaries of one's own self, or at strengthening one's powers of self-assertion, or at affirming one's own worth as an individual, or at some other purely personal end.

This parallel emphasis and deformation of authenticity becomes slightly more intelligible when we consider that due to the differentiation of value spheres, contemporary lives unfold in a social space characterized by a plurality of the good.

THE MAIN IDEA

This book shares a fundamental assumption with these thinkers. There is reason to re-qualify the concept of authenticity and to discern its applicable nucleus from other features that have been subsumed under this label and that now muddle the picture. Therefore, a major aim of this book is to construct *a formal concept of authenticity* that can detect and identify aestheticism and atomist self-indulgence as distortions. However, the aims of the book surpass the ambitions of earlier attempts, since authenticity will provide the normative backbone of a critical social theory that is able to identify not only aestheticism and egoistic self-indulgence, but other and more complex practices of the self and patterns of societal interactions shaped by contemporary capitalism. Additionally, while I share the 'attitude of suspicion' prevalent among these authors, this will unfold more radically, inspired by the critical gesture of first-generation critical thinkers like Adorno and Benjamin.

What I will show is not only that practices of the self rely on a 'deformed' concept of authenticity and therefore 'malfunction.' Rather, by examining contemporary practices of the self on the job market (propagated in the self-help and self-management literature) I will argue that authenticity, far from 'malfunctioning,' actually functions quite well as a 'social technology' that helps enhance production. In fact, contemporary methods of work, organization, and production have adopted authenticity as an important part of their maneuvres, making it an important factor of production in the post-Fordist economy. In this context, authenticity is both an important factor in the context of emerging forms of consumption, advertising, and marketing, and it has also become a factor in the economic utilization of subjective capacities. In this process, there is a reciprocal shaping of capitalism and the ideal of authenticity. To my knowledge, despite the impact of authenticity and some philosophical interest, we do not have an analytical tool that manages this vital aspect. However, given the goal of constructing a concept of authenticity that may provide the normative backbone of a critical social theory, this is necessary.

The concept of authenticity proposed here will be contextualized and normatively embedded within the framework of critical social theory as 'Gesellschaftskritik.' Nonetheless, to work out the core of the concept, I will draw heavily on moral philosophy and discussions on personal autonomy. In this context, the concept of authenticity will be discussed as the *practice of autonomy*.

THE ARCHITECTURE OF THE BOOK

The book is made up of three parts with each providing answers to these questions.

Part I   Chapters 1 and 2

I will start by offering a historical overview of the emergence and development of the concept of authenticity, since insight into the historical scaffolding of ideas from which authenticity emerged will help establish a grip on this concept and to explain its enormous appeal and impact. Rather than attempting a comprehensive review of the history of the concept, which would itself require a book of its own, my approach will be systematic, contrasting authenticity with other related notions such as *sincerity* and *autonomy*. The chapter will culminate in a comprehensive discussion of thinkers who have fiercely rejected the concept and those who have warmly embraced it. In that context, the unique approach of this book will be further clarified.

Chapter 2 raises the question of how a normative account of authenticity can be theoretically framed, which is necessary in order to construct *a formal concept of authenticity* that can serve as a critical concept. I will draw on critical social philosophy that relies on normatively grounded evaluative predicates against which distorted practices become visible. This provides the link between capitalism, authenticity and social criticism. The most important aim will be to find adequate theoretical justification for a critical concept of authenticity. For this I will assess several available models, from Rousseau to contemporary critical social theorists. One of the most challenging issues within this task is to establish evaluative predicates that can legitimately claim some supra-contextual validity and do not embody a particular and historically contingent vision of the good, thereby avoiding paternalism. This will involve taking a critical stand on the foundations of current theories, most prominently Axel Honneth's theory of recognition. While I will draw on the rich sources in this tradition, I will also contibute to sharpening its analytical gaze. I will argue that the concept of authenticity developed here is a needed element at the center of a theory of recognition.

Part II   Chapters 3, 4, and 5

Having clarified the general normative frame within which authenticity shall be reconstructed, I turn to the second problem, namely the question of how such a formal account of authenticity could be made explicit. The issue at hand will be approached from the perspective of moral philosophy and psychology and I will attempt to assess what I will refer to as 'inner sense' and 'productionist' models of authenticity. Roughly, the inner sense model originates with Rousseau and claims that authenticity is about the introspective identification of central inner features that define who we are. In the productionist model, which can be traced back to Nietzsche, emphasis is laid on the aesthetic creation of difference, modeled on the production of art. I will show why such approaches cannot answer the question of who we really are; this is simply not satisfactorily captured in terms of discovery or self-production. This is why I will seek to construct an account that integrates positive features from both models, while avoiding some of the pitfalls. Rather than being about the uniqueness of the self, discovered (inner sense) or created (productionism), authenticity is connected to the (wholehearted) manner in which we engage with our lives, integrating our lives by projects that we wholeheartedly endorse.

Saying that our commitments define who we are and the consequent emphasis upon our agency in the choices of such commitments compels us to embrace the voluntarist position, which basically holds that who we are is a matter of choice. Chapter 4 will deal with this issue, in an attempt to accommodate the constitutive agency of the subject while simultaneously arguing that the relationship between our commitments and the collective background of values (horizon of significance) is of constitutive nature. The decisive take will be to think of agency as inherently 'embedded,' which will allow accommodating both the intuition that the agent has some constitutive power and the idea that authenticity is inherently connected to the articulation of goods from a collective horizon. Similarly, an examination of the structure of our commitments shall provide insights about the normative sources of our commitments. The guiding intuition is that the internal structure of our commitments commits us to more than what merely we happen to care about; it can constrain the manner in which we can pursue our commitment and even determine the mode of our practical deliberation.

Chapter 5 will be concerned with the analysis of those situations in which we make the kind of 'existential' choices that articulate who we are. I shall deploy this term in a non-voluntaristic sense and argue that existential choices are prominent and emblematic when expressing who we are, and that they have an exceptionally complex phenomenology, characterized by a sense of necessity. In such choices, described as 'alternativeless choices,' we articulate who we are, bringing into reality some tacit intuitions that often only take on a gestalt-like formation. We shall also see what inauthenticity amounts to and how those changes or existential reorientations occur in which our fundamental commitments change.

It is in this chapter that the definition of a formal concept of authenticity will be completed. Such a formal concept will neither assume that authenticity is about being at one with some pre-existing and determinate inner norm, nor that it is about the consistency of an aesthetically self-created style of life. The account shall adopt a relaxed universalist method while blocking the charge of paternalism—two characteristics that qualify our concept as one that can be fruitfully deployed in critical inquiry.

Part III   Chapter 6

In the sixth and last chapter, I will attempt to fill a gap that I think contemporary accounts of authenticity leave open. It will be argued that insufficient attention is paid to how the ideal of authenticity and certain practices in capitalism have shaped each other reciprocally. It is at this point that the formal concept of authenticity will be put to work as a critical concept, against which problematic practices become intelligible.

The main concern will be that the ambivalence around the ideal of authenticity, the intertwinement of desire and fear that has accompanied the ideal of authenticity, is today more than justified. The fear connected to the ideal of authenticity is no longer just about the fear that we satisfy ourselves with facsimile (Orwell) or just about the fear that the ideal of authenticity will lose its initial moral dimensions (Charles Taylor). Instead, I will argue that a new kind of fear is justified. Due to the reciprocal shaping of capitalism and the ideal of authenticity, pathological conditions no longer arise from the societal barriers that inhibit authenticity, as Freud thought, but from the practice of authenticity itself. In order to show this, I will examine the popular 'self-help' discourse and point out a recent transformation regarding the concept of authenticity, namely the emergence of a *performative* model of authenticity. As a second step, drawing on Luc Boltanski, Eve Chiapello, and Axel Honneth, a framework will be constructed that renders the emergence of a performative model of authenticity intelligible. I shall argue that this model has made possible what I will call a *paradoxical turn*. Authenticity, once used to question the legitimacy of hierarchical institutions and to target the power of capitalistic requirements, now seems to function as an institutionalized demand towards subjects, matching the systemic demands of contemporary capitalism. As a third and final step, a link will be suggested between this development and a specific form of psychological suffering. The aim is to show that the constant activity of *performing authenticity* exhausts the self and that this may explain some of the preconditions that made possible the rapid rise in the frequency of depression and sales of pharmaceutical anti-depressants. Consequently, the last chapter of this book will attempt to live up to the overall critical social philosophical aim of this book. By using the previously constructed formal concept of authenticity, I will attempt to explicate the pathological consequences of the contemporary practice of authenticity. Hopefully the concept developed in this book can prove to be a measure against which pathological practices of authenticity become comprehensible.

A METHODOLOGICAL REMARK

In the course of this inquiry I will be drawing on different traditions such as critical social theory, phenomenology, and analytical philosophy, using a 'post-analytic' methodological approach to move beyond the analytic/Continental divide. The aim is to retain the rigor that characterizes the 'analytic tradition' while holding on to the hermeneutic-historical strength of the 'Continental tradition.'

Part I
The Sources of Authenticity

1 The Sources of Authenticity

I have already mentioned the great impact of authenticity as an ideal and in this chapter I attempt to explore this in detail. At the same time I provide a historical overview of the idea, its critics, and where we stand today. The appeal of this ideal can be made intelligible if one understands that it grows out of a long tradition of Western thought and practices that have shaped the modern worldview. Due to its long philosophical pedigree and innumerable connotations, authenticity is a difficult concept to handle. I will, therefore, not attempt a comprehensive review of its history. At the same time, I do think that we can only properly assess this central feature of modern culture by gaining some insight into the historical scaffolding of ideas from which it has emerged. Consequently, this chapter is concerned with the history of authenticity in a more systematic way, attempting to review the different forms in which it has surfaced and the different justifications by which it has been defended throughout history. Additionally, to limit and systematize this undertaking, I shall draw the countours of authenticity as it is understood today by contrasting it to other related notions such as *sincerity* and *autonomy*.

One could argue that the idea of authenticity has always been a part of Western thought. Socrates must have had a distinction between the authentic and the inauthentic in mind when he invoked the dictum "Know thyself," which is found on the Temple of Apollo at Delphi. Similarly, both Augustine's and Seneca's work presuppose this distinction between something inner, which is somehow more truthful and 'higher,' and something outer that is false. However, before concluding that authenticity as we understand it today has played a central role from the beginning of Western thought, we must pay attention to the conception of self in question. As Pierre Hadot (1992) has noted, in the Stoic conception of the self authenticity is far from being at one with something inner. Rather, the dimension of the self that is considered to be worthy of discovering and nourishing is exactly that dimension of the self that ultimately points towards something that transcends the self. So the good life is far from merely about being at one with oneself, but also involves transcending oneself towards cosmos. Similarly, Nussbaum (1994) points out that in Stoic spiritual exercises emphasis lies in the connection between the cultivation of 'inner' and 'outer' reason. In the case of Socrates, authentic self-knowledge is not so much a matter of turning inward to detect unique personal traits, simply because Socrates does not operate with the conception of the self as an individual with a personal 'interiority.' Instead, human beings are regarded as parts of a cosmic web of interrelatedness, and individuality is understood as determined by the relation to this wider whole—it is this wider cosmos that determines how things ought to be. In this outlook, self-knowledge and authenticity are not about interiority, but about "excising what is particular and distinctive in yourself in order to be better able to match the ideal that determines your function" (Guignon 2004: 8). So not only are strong inner traits, personal desires, and feelings not considered constitutive of what one really is, but they can even be discarded as personal burdens that endanger authenticity, which is about living up to the place one has in the scheme of things, living up to the position that defines one as an instance of humankind.

Augustine deepens the gap between interiority and exteriority, creating a more profound notion of interiority that according to Richard Sennett has shaped Western culture ever since. Augustine creates a divide between subjectivity and world, self and city (Sennett 1993: xii) and embraces inwardness and spirituality over a worldly oriented life that supposedly turns individuals away from themselves (Ibid.: 6–10). In *De vera Religione*, Augustine's advice on how to live an authentic life reads: "Do not go outward; return within yourself. In the inward man dwells truth" (quoted in Taylor 1989: 129). In Book 10 of his *Confessions*, he uses the symbol of the heart to denote the inner self. At first the symbol of the heart suggests not only a journey towards interiority, but also a privatized spirituality. But instead, for Augustine, interiority is where God dwells, and it is in this interior space that one is truly united with humanity (Augustine 1955; Sheldrake 2003). Therefore, Augustine's pledge to "Return to your heart!" in the *Tractates on the Gospel of John* (18.10) should not be understood as merely an inward journey but one that eventually transcends this interiority towards God and humanity. In all, Augustine clears the path towards the modern duality of outer 'false' self and inner 'true' self, but the inward orientation turns out to be an orientation that exactly transcends interiority. This shows how different Augustine's conception of the self is, when compared to modern and contemporary conceptions of authenticity. The self is not seen as a unified source of agency, but as depending on God as the source of one's being. In the distinction between true and false self, the latter refers to the worldly self. This self only *appears* to be the source of our actions, since for Augustine God is the real source of our actions. Thus, while introspection gets us closer to the hidden force, introspection will always remain unreliable and incomplete, since "there is something of man that the spirit of man that is in him does not know" (Augustine 1955: section 5).

Consequently, we can maintain that authenticity has been a part of Western thought since antiquity, but only if we keep in mind how much the

Greek, Roman, and early Christian views on the authentic self differ from our modern and contemporary conception of authenticity which posits the self as a unified source of agency. What we find in authors like Augustine is really not so much about a pure turn inward. Rather, it is a turn "inward and upward" (Taylor 1989: 134). What is on the inside gains its importance only as a manifestation of something 'higher' that is to be realized. While this 'agent-transcendent' aspect weakens in the course of secularization, the aspect that the realization of something (agent) immanent is at the same time also a realization of something 'higher' remains a feature of authenticity.

Much later, the idea behind the ancient dictums "Know Thyself" and "Return to your heart" is transformed and secularized together with the underlying conception of the self. The emergence of the moral ideal of sincerity, under the dictum of "Be true to yourself," marks a crucial step towards the contemporary idea of authenticity.

1 SINCERITY

In his book *Sincerity and Authenticity*, Lionel Trilling traces the appearance of a new moral idea, putting forward "that at a certain point in its history the moral life of Europe added to itself a new element, the state or quality of the self which we call sincerity" (Trilling 1972: 2). While the moral ideal of sincerity is an important step towards the contemporary shape of authenticity, let me point out some defining characteristics and central differences between sincerity and authenticity. First, let us look at sincerity. Trilling (Ibid.: 3) here points to a moment in Hamlet, where Polonius sends Laertes to Paris with paternal advice:

> This above all: to thine own self be true
> And it doth follow, as the night the day,
> Thou canst not then be false to any man.

Polonius thus conceived sincerity as being true to one's own self, which at first sounds a lot like the contemporary ideal of authenticity. However, a careful look reveals that sincerity is here depicted in a manner that actually corresponds with the 'inward and upward' model that we have seen in the work of Augustine. As with the Greek and Roman thinkers, being true to the self is not an end in itself, but first and foremost an essential condition of virtue. Inward orientation is therefore not valuable in its own right. Instead, it is valuable because it serves the higher moral goal of being true to others. This should make clear that the underlying idea of the true self is very different from the contemporary notion. Sincerity is not essentially a personal but rather a social virtue. Its aim is to avoid being false to others by virtue of being true to oneself. If we look at the defining characteristics of sincerity, we see a particular pattern emerging. Sincerity is defined as the state of the self in which there is equivalence between the statement and the actual feeling that informs behavior. Hence, sincerity refers to the self in its outward manifestation in the social domain, and it can therefore be put to the test by examining whether one's actions actually match one's public declarations. Sincere in this sense means something close to 'honest.' The basic wrongdoing of *insincerity* is about violating the expectations that follow with the position one holds in society, whenever attempting to appear otherwise than one ought to.

Trilling traces how the moral ideal of sincerity transformed into the ideal of authenticity with the evolution of modernity. While the two concepts in the beginning shared common features, they quickly grew apart. In fact, there is today a clash between sincerity and authenticity. The sincere person who seeks to match the requirements of his position in social life is now almost automatically considered inauthentic (Ferrara 1993: 87). For instance, Sartre (1943/1991) discusses the inauthentic waiter who disappears as an individual while trying to fit his professional role. When turning to the question of how authenticity is justified, we see an analogous reversal. Being true to own self is no longer a mere means to a higher moral end, but an end in itself. As Ferrara notes, authenticity is sincerity for its own sake (Ferrara 1993: 86).

In addition, while sincerity does not imply criticism of a given social order, authenticity becomes an implicitly critical concept, which calls into question social order and public opinion. Hegel is among the first to call attention to the fading ideal of sincerity, which he polemically refers to as "the heroism of dumb service" (Hegel 2002: 515). Hegel launches an attack on the sincerity of the bourgeois "honest man," who passively interiorizes a particular conventional social ethos. In the condition of sincerity, the individual is uncritically obedient to the external power of society—a conformity that for Hegel leads to subjugation and a deterioration of the individual (Trilling 1972; Golomb 1995: 9). In the progress of spirit, the individual consciousness moves from this condition to a condition of baseness, in which the individual becomes antagonistic to external power and achieves a measure of autonomy. The loss of transparency that is connected to this process also means that the individual becomes self-alienated, but this is for Hegel a necessary step in progress. As Bernard Williams (2002: 190) has noted, the self-alienated individual "can no longer feel unreflectively at home in its social environment."

Hegel shows this clearly in a comment on Diderot's *Rameau's Nephew*, a story in which the narrator (supposedly Diderot himself) is portrayed as the reasonable, sincere man who respects the prevailing order, and who has achieved bourgeois respectability. In contrast, the nephew is full of contempt for the society in which he figures as a worthless person. Nevertheless, he is in opposition to himself, because he still aspires to a better standing in a society, which he believes has nothing but emptiness to offer (Despland 1975: 360; Golomb 1995: 13–15). For Hegel, Rameau is an example of the sincere, honest soul, while the nephew figures as the "disintegrated," alienated consciousness. The nephew is described as alienated, because he is unable to appropriate and to identify with the social norms of the society he lives in.

But for Hegel this alienation is a step in the progression towards autonomous existence. With Hegel, we see an intellectual atmosphere emerging, in which sincerity becomes suspicious and in which it will later be replaced by the stronger notion of authenticity. Trilling clarifies this development by maintaining that individuals in Hegel's time become aware that society "requires that we present ourselves as being sincere, and the most efficacious way of satisfying this demand is to see to it that we really are sincere, that we really are what we want our community to know we are." And Trilling continues:

> In short, we play the role of being ourselves, we sincerely act the part of the sincere person, with the result that a judgment may be passed upon our sincerity that it is not authentic (Trilling 1972: 10–11).

The corrosion of the ideal of sincerity is an important factor that has made it possible for authenticity to emerge. Another decisive factor was the emergence of a distinctively modern conception of the self that builds on a starker contrast between interiority and exteriority compared to earlier thinkers. One of the intertwining processes that led to such a radicalization of inwardness was the emergence of *religious individualism*, which centers religious life on the individual and stresses the importance of inwardness and of introspectively examining one's inner motives, intentions, and conscience. In *The History of Sexuality*, Michel Foucault calls attention to the origins of the modern subject of inwardness, suggesting that

> Western societies have established the confession as one of the main rituals we rely on for the production of truth . . . The obligation to confess now relayed through so many different points, is so deeply ingrained in us, that we no longer perceive it as the effect of a power that constrains us; on the contrary, it seems to us that truth, lodged in our most secret nature, "demands" only to surface (Foucault 1980: 58. 60).

For Foucault, confession and the look inward to monitor one's interior life and to tell certain 'truths' about oneself has become a part of cultural life, reaching from religious contexts to psychological therapy. The radicalization of the distinction between true interiority and exteriority has led to new possibilities. Inner states, motivations, and feelings can now be objectified and worked upon in different contexts. Also, the focus on the inner paves the way for assessing one's undertakings against the measure of who one essentially is.

2   AUTONOMY

As I have mentioned earlier, understanding the emergence of the ethical ideal of authenticity can be best achieved by describing the context in which it evolves as a contrast to sincerity and autonomy. While the normative grip of authenticity partly stems from its replacing sincerity, the connection of authenticity and autonomy is more sophisticated yet, and even today we find numerous accounts that do not distinguish between the two adequately.

Of course, as ethical concepts there are several parallels between authenticity and autonomy. Most importantly, they both oppose the pre-modern notion of the right, which is justified by recourse to some higher authority like God, the King, or to some good, which can be known a priori (Ferrara 1993: 89). Historically, while autonomy and authenticity to a large extent shape distinct ethical theories, they both come from a common origin. Ethical views, oriented towards autonomy and authenticity, hold that the normativity of ethical norms derives from the capacity of the subject to follow a *self-imposed* principle. Having said this, it is also quite clear that they are distinct. For Kant, norms formed by principles constitute the goodness of moral will. In opposition to this, in an ethic of authenticity, importance is attributed to recognizing (and not denying) the impulses that draw us away us from universal principles. Christoph Menke has convincingly shown that Hegel's discussion of tragedy in fact encircles this particular problem of modernity. The modern ideal of authenticity, where the individual pursues a good life that expresses his identity, clashes with the idea of normatively construed autonomy (Menke 1995: 93). In this sense modernity is divided with regard to these orientations and this division constitutes the "Tragödie der Sittlichkeit." Menke interprets modern social reality in light of this tragic opposition between autonomy and authenticity, between a normative order (that is constructed in prohibitive terms) and individuality.

The idea of autonomy is a legacy of Enlightenment humanism; it emphasizes the individual's self-governing abilities, which are employed independently of position in political and social structures. Autonomy is understood as holding a basic moral and political value, and central to this claim is that moral principles and the legitimacy of political authority should be grounded in the self-governing individual who is set free from various cultural and social constraints. In this sense, the concept of autonomy has these core components: the independence of one's freedom of deliberation and choice from manipulation and paternalistic interventions, and the capacity to decide for oneself (Dworkin 1988: 121–129). Thus, ethical orientations based on the ideas of autonomy or authenticity do not refer to some higher authority, but to the actor's capacity to reliably follow a self-imposed principle. Autonomy was given a key role in philosophical accounts of a person's moral responsibility and in the justification of social political authority. At the core of Kant's moral theory is the idea that rational human wills are autonomous. Like Rousseau, Kant goes beyond the idea of merely 'negative' freedom, the idea of being free from outer constraints. Autonomy does refer to being bound by laws, but by those that are to a certain extent laid down by oneself. Individual autonomy refers to a life led according to one's own reasons and motives, rather than to one that is largely the product of manipulative external forces. In a broad sense, autonomy is about the ability to put one's own behavior under reflexive scrutiny and make it dependent on self-determined goals (Honneth 1994: 59).

In this general picture, 'personal autonomy' is understood as a feature that actors can display when dealing with very diverse aspects of their lives (Dworkin 1988). On the other hand, Kantian 'moral autonomy' is limited to issues of moral obligation and means the capacity to impose the moral law on oneself. In Kantian moral discourse, autonomy is the ideal of self-legislation guided by general principles. But another central issue is that autonomy always entails being responsive to reasons. Thus, for a will to be autonomous it must be unconstrained by external factors, it must emerge from the actor and it must be responsive to reasons—a criterion that excludes, for instance, rigid obsessions.

What authenticity adds to this picture is that it not only refers to leading an autonomous life, guided by one's own non-constrained reasons and motives. Beyond this, authenticity also refers to the idea that these motives and reasons are expressive of a subject's core personality. This points to the conceptual gap between (Kantian) autonomy and authenticity. One can lead an autonomous life, even if this way of living fails to express a person's self-understanding. In this sense, the notion of authenticity accounts for something that lies beyond the scope of autonomy, bringing into play the actor's sense of self-identity. I might act in self-determined in a case where my concrete action fails to be authentic, and thus to fit with who I take myself to be. In an earlier book, Ferrara discusses the relation between autonomy and authenticity, saying that authenticity

> introduces a distinction between deviations which are bound with essential aspects of a person's identity and deviations originating in aspects which occupy a peripheral place in the person's identity (Ferrara 1993: 90).

Authenticity and the expression of the actor's self are difficult to accommodate within the framework of autonomy, since they obviously cannot be reduced to 'self-determined' conduct. Accordingly, Taylor (1991: 90) notes that authenticity entails a "language of personal resonance" in which there is a hightened sense of individuality that cannot be captured within the vocabulary of autonomy. Ethical orientations that build on the idea of moral autonomy seek the coincidence of conduct and ethical principles and the reconciliation of action and reason that involves distancing from immediate, inner impulses. In contrast, the ethic of authenticity does not view right conduct as directly equated with a willingness to abide by these principles, but involves a personal relation *towards* those principles. Consequently, as Menke (2005: 308) says, the ideal of authenticity does not object to the normative content of the self-given law, but disagrees that full freedom consists in making and following such a law. It is not just about being involved in the authorship of such a law, but about how this law fits with the wholeness of a person's life, and how or whether it expresses who the person is. The person is thus not simply located at the intersection of action and principles. A new, second level of normativity emerges, involving taking a stand towards principles. This also means that from the perspective of authenticity, to engage in ethical orientation, we must consider both levels of normativity. We must acknowledge (rather than restrain) the presence of urges that draw us away from self-chosen principles while still taking into account the moral aspects of our conduct.

3   TOWARDS THE ETHICS OF AUTHENTICITY—ROUSSEAU AND HÖLDERLIN

After having drawn some conceptual boundaries between sincerity, autonomy, and authenticity, let us now see how the emerging ethic of authenticity is connected to a specific idea of the self. I will proceed to clarify this issue by turning to Rousseau, who is widely considered one of the most influential thinkers on authenticity. In Chapter 2, I will go deeper into the social-philosophical consequences of Rousseau's turn to authenticity, concentrating on how the 'ethic of authenticity' begins to emerge in Rousseau. In *Emile*, Rousseau presents an example of education that emphasizes the achievement of autonomy, but already here the tension between autonomy and authenticity is visible.

On the one hand, for Rousseau the point of orientation that should guide conduct and shape the path of life one chooses should come from an internal source. In this sense, the interior becomes the most important source of guidance. On the other hand, Rousseau also emphasizes that following the path that is laid down within oneself requires disciplining the self, making it less vulnerable to spontaneous impulses. This of course leads to the problem of detecting central impulses, feelings, and wishes and distinguishing them from ones that are less central. So the space of interiority not only becomes more important as a guiding authority, but must also be divided into center and periphery. While in the ethics of autonomy it is quite clear that *each and every* deviation diminishes the quality of the ethical orientation of the person, in authenticity the picture is not so clear. Interiority is divided and deviations are measured against whether they touch upon essential aspects of a person's identity or upon ones that occupy a peripheral place. From this perspective peripheral aspects can be disregarded and modified, while the neglect of essential aspects of one's self simply adds up to self-negation, betrayal, and annihilation of the self. When these central aspects are in question the normative force of principles can and must be suspended.

Rousseau's *The New Heloise* is partly about the primacy of authenticity over rational and moral principles. Ferrara's interpretation of *The New*

Heloise emphasized this aspect by showing how the novel accentuates the significant costs involved in suppressing one's deepest motivations and traits. Ferrara maintains that through the example of Julie Rousseau "suggests that the attempt to master instrumentally one's affective life always results in a weakening and eventually in the fragmentation of one's identity, regardless of whether it is carried out on behalf of society's or practical reason's demands" (Ferrara 1993: 104; also Anderson 1995a). For Rousseau, societal obligations alone cannot justify a specific behavior. The idea is that I only have good reasons to act in a certain way if this way of acting is in harmony with those 'secret principles' that constitute my core identity. Acting against these secret principles is self-destructive. To get an idea of the great impact of this book it is enough to point out that *Julie* was perhaps the biggest selling book of the century, with at least 70 editions in print before 1800 (Darnton 1984: 242). This success anticipates the dispersion of the ideal of authenticity into popular culture, which was noticeable during the last two centuries and is most striking in our contemporary society.

The idea that every individual displays different traits and is to a certain extent unique is of course not Rousseau's invention. What is important is that Rousseau considers this individual difference as the key to finding out how one should live. The emphasis on individual differences entails that these individual traits are thought to reveal the path that one ought to follow. A similar insight is also laid down in Herder's famous sentence about every man having his own measure that is particular to him. Individuals thus all have their way of being human that is unique to them—a uniqueness that will eventually be revealed to them over the course of their lives.

After briefly outlining the ethic of authenticity in Rousseau, it should be mentioned that such a straightforward account of Rousseau's commitment to authenticity somewhat downplays ambivalences concerning authenticity in Rousseau's work. We should bear in mind that *New Heloise* was published before Emile and another work which was even more ambiguous on authenticity, namely *The Social Contract*.

Another attempt at an ethic of authenticity can be seen in Johann C.F. Hölderlin, who published his translation of Sophocles' *Antigone* in 1804. His translation is infused with his theoretical position that emerged in a dialogue with Kant's philosophy. Hölderlin is critical of Kant's distinction in the *Critique of Judgment* between moral ideas, scientific knowledge, and aesthetic judgment, and most importantly he opposes Kant's view that a single a priori faculty is the foundation of all three types of judgment. Unsatisfied with this hierarchy, Hölderlin brings into play the idea of an "interior intensity" (*das Innige*), which is "the intuition of an all-embracing unity prior to the distinctions of experience and of conceptual thinking" (Rosenfield 1999: 108). He stresses the role of the senses and of feelings in the realm of intellectual pursuit and maintains the existence of a state that is prior to all knowledge and all consciousness, and which is characterized by a complete conformity between imagination, desire, and moral law (Hölderlin 1946–1962: Vol 6: 219, 223). In his translations he gives the dramatic discourse new nuances that increase the scope of its meaning.[1] Hölderlin conveys that self-legislation is not enough to achieve full freedom; instead, full freedom is achieved if the the chain of actions in one's own life adds up to a narrative that expresses who one is. Importantly, Hölderlin's work also displays another feature, which is added to the idea of authenticity during the Romantic period, and which is still a central characteristic in the contemporary culture of authenticity. This is the attempt to recover a sense of wholeness by turning inward—a wholeness that is assumed to have been lost with the emerging modern world. It is the same kind of loss that Rousseau connected to the emerging competitive public sphere.

4   THE AGE OF AUTHENTICITY— DISPERSION INTO POPULAR CULTURE

Some important roots to our current understanding of self, interiority, normativity, and the social sphere emerge in the late eighteenth century. Authenticity stresses the importance of realizing one's own way of being human and defending it against the societal constraints of conformity. A wide array of intellectuals of the nineteenth and the early twentieth century adopted this general outlook on life and even radicalized this ethos by resisting established codes and publicly defending alternative 'artistic' or 'bohemian' modes of life. Some of Nietzsche' work might be a good example of a radicalization in this development, while the 'coming out' of André Gide as a homosexual in the 1920s was not only a direct expression of the growing impact of the ideal of authenticity, it also showed how desire, morality, and the integrity of the self were to be united into a whole.

As Taylor (2007: 475) has noted, the ideal of authenticity did not begin to have a decisive and general grip on society and shape the general outlook until after the Second World War. The 1940s and 1950s mark a turning point on how authenticity is understood. While self-help books used to counsel a form of conformity, with best sellers advocating a full compliance with the obligations of one's adult roles (Taviss Thomson 1997), readers in this period are increasingly warned against measuring themselves against public opinion (Carnegie 1948: 127). The critique of conformity becomes more persistent during the 1950s, when a number of social scientists in widely-read books criticize what they see as widespread conformity and inauthenticity. Among these, *The Lonely Crowd* (1950) by David Riesman and *The Organization Man* (1956) by William H. Whyte received most attention. Riesman basically maintains that the class of other-directed individuals who smoothly adjust to their environment is vital for the effortless functioning of modern organizations. However, for Riesman the other-directed compromise their autonomy, and a society that by and large consists of other-directed individuals will face substantial deficiencies in leadership and human potential. At the same time, in the emerging youth culture there was serious dissatisfaction with the "morass of conformity" of the parental generation—a critique fuelled by the idea that everyone should strive to unfold their authentic identities (Gray 1965: 57).

The impact of authenticity did not stop here. In *The Politics of Authenticity*, Doug Rossinow contends that 1960s politics were centered on questions of authenticity. Following his account, the main driving force towards political and social changes of the New Left movement in the 1960s was "a search for authenticity in industrial American life" (Rossinow 1998: 345). Like James J. Farrell (1997), Rossinow convincingly argues that the New Left partly emerged as a reaction to traditional American liberalism and Christian existentialism, which replaced the negative concept of 'sin' with 'alienation' and the positive 'salvation' with 'authenticity.' Confronted with what they understood as alienation that "isn't restricted to the poor" (Rossinow 1998: 194), New Left activism aimed to reach beyond civil rights and to make possible a sense of personal wholeness and self-realization by curing the institutions of American society.

Since the 1960s this ideal has permeated the whole of Western culture—it has become, as Menke (2005: 309) noted, a "massively used vocabulary." It is however in popular culture that this ideal shows its real impact, becoming something like the "ultimate task of life" (Guignon 2004: 2). The quest for authenticity manifests itself as related to both objects of consumption and to the identities of persons. This is very visible in the way the popular culture of consumption has evolved in the past few decades. In their book *Authenticity: What Consumers Really Want*, James Gilmore and Joseph Pine explain that the consumer's quest for authenticity can be understood as the outcome of a growing commodification in contemporary Western societies. Consumers seek authentic products for self-expression because they feel that everything has become saturated with "toxic levels of inauthenticity" (Gilmore and Pine 2007: 43). It is important to note that even in its manifestation in consumption, the notion of authenticity does not just refer to quality, or to the guarantee that a product lives up to its promises or that it really originates from a special geographic location. Rather, the appeal of this ideal can first be fully comprehended if we understand that some of its compelling force lies in its reference to something 'higher.' In support of this, David Chidester (2005: 10) elucidates the iniquitousness of a concept authenticity in American popular culture, pointing out that it still possesses a dimension that bears traces of transcendence. Thus there is much that connects contemporary understandings of authenticity to the pre-modern versions discussed earlier.

The most revealing and direct manifestation of the quest for authenticity is in the popular self-help movement. While the term 'self-help' originally described an individual or group-based attempt that is undertaken to achieve self-improvement in a vast array of fields (spiritually, economically, socially, or intellectually), today's magazine articles and self-help manuals mostly reflect upon authenticity and offer specific techniques to achieve an authentic existence. The two most successful self-help TV shows, Oprah Winfrey's 'Oprah' (six or seven million daily viewers) and Philip McGraw's 'Dr. Phil', have made authenticity into a central theme. It is also here that we find the idea of discovering the authentic self that is concealed or entirely forgotten under the pressure of daily matters. As McGraw notes, "The authentic self is the *you* that can be found at your absolute core. It is the part of you that is not defined by your job, or your function, or your role. It is the composite of all your unique gifts, skills, abilities, interests, talents, insights, and wisdom. It is all your strengths and values that are uniquely yours and need expression, versus what you have been programmed to believe that you are 'supposed to be and do'" (McGraw 2003: 30). Self-help then is about recovering this lost core of the self, reestablishing it as the gravitational center of life and becoming the person that one already is deep inside. McGraw, like his colleagues, takes the task of being oneself as the primary task in life and a difficult one, since everyday life pulls us away from being ourselves toward what he sees as inauthentic role-playing. This is why self-help, like McGraw's "five-step action plan," contains spiritual exercises that are not unlike ancient religious exercises that aim to transform a 'fictional self' into an 'authentic self.' So from this perspective authenticity has come to mean the successful safeguarding of the authentic inner self "from intrusions of chance, irrationality, necessity, and other persons" (Novak 1976: 39; see also Taviss Thomson 2000: 65). A brief look at the titles of the best sellers in the 1970s—like *Looking Out for Number One* and *How To Be Your Own Best Friend*, for example—suggest this kind of self-indulgence.

All in all, the language of authenticity has become a common currency in contemporary cultural life and not only in popular culture but also in academia. Recent books like Alexander Nehamas's *Virtues of Authenticity* and Geoffrey Hartman's *Scars of the Spirit: The Struggle against Inauthenticity* are indications that the ideal remains strong and that the subject of authenticity is recognized as a valuable object of study. The material referred to in this chapter unmistakably shows the emergence of authenticity as a reigning value in Western societies. As Martin Jay (2004) notes, in a time when relativism appears difficult to surmount, authenticity has become a last measure of value. This may partly be why self-help books and popular cultural discourses reveal an increasing dissatisfaction with what is viewed as the 'inauthentic' comforts of modern life. In all, under the impact of existentialism on American culture, the ubiquitous desire for authenticity has emerged in modern society as "one of the most politically explosive of human impulses," as Marshall Berman argues in *The Politics of Authenticity* (1970: xix).

5   THE CRITICS OF AUTHENTICITY

Of course, this development has its critics. Several critics have expressed serious concerns about the ubiquitousness of an ideal of authenticity that rejects commitments that go beyond the self, like commitments to others or to greater political, social, or environmental issues. Cultural critics have diagnosed the ostensible 'decline' of modern society, arguing that this was not primarily a result of economical or structural transformations but rather the outcome of a pervasive 'culture of authenticity.'

Christopher Lasch's *The Culture of Narcissism, American Life in an Age of Diminishing Expectations*, first published in 1979, stands out as an important work in this context. As the title suggests, Lasch points out similarities between authenticity and the clinical condition referred to as narcissistic personality disorder. Narcissism and the popular understanding of authenticity are both characterized by deficient empathic skills, self-indulgence, and self-absorbed behavior. Allan Bloom criticizes the culture of authenticity even more intensely than Lasch, identifying it as self-centeredness and connecting it to what he describes as the collapse of the public self. Bloom (1987: 61) is persuaded that this movement has made the minds of today's students "narrower and flatter." For Bloom, students both lack the foundation for being able to critically confront the present and to envision alternatives to it.

Due to its self-centeredness and narcissism, the 'culture of authenticity' makes up a serious threat not only to the moral and political coherence of contemporary society, but also to its economic stability. This is exactly the issue that Daniel Bell raises in his *The Cultural Contradictions of Capitalism*. His refections concerning the "Double Bind of Modernity" addresses the growing contrast between the hedonist culture of authenticity and rational economic behavior that slowly loses its traditional legitimacy. What Bell fears is that the "megalomania of self-infinitization" that comes with the culture of authenticity will erode the foundations of market mechanisms that are "based on a moral system of reward rooted in the Protestant sanctification of work" (Bell 1976: 84).

Philip Slater's *The Pursuit of Loneliness*, from 1970, was also critical of the implications of the emerging culture of authenticity and argued that the dichotomies that the ideal of authenticity was built on, like independence vs. conformity, individual vs. society, or inner-directedness vs. other-directedness, are entirely misguided. The underlying assumption that the individual is to be considered separately from the social environment is for Slater an absurd assumption that disregards the bonds between individual and community, which ultimately are the source of the authentic self (Slater 1970: 15). He not only argues that the self-absorbed quest for authenticity is harmful in that society and individuals tend to be acted upon as "manipulable objects" (Sisk 1973: 63). Critics like Slater (1970) and Fairlie (1978) also contend that such a pursuit of authenticity is self-defeating. With the loss of the bond with community, the sense of self is also diminished. In agreement with Slater, Yankelovich (1981) and Bellah et al. (1985) maintain that the culture of authenticity sustains self-indulgence because it is built upon inadequate assumptions about self and sociality. They argue that "we find ourselves not independently of other people and institutions but through them" (Bellah et al. 1985: 84), and that humans cannot be "contained and 'self-created,'"(Yankelovich 1981: 234)—a well-pointed criticism that has since been influentially repeated and elaborated by Taylor, Guignon and others.

A decade before these critical voices were raised, Theodor W. Adorno (1973) launched a polemical attack on what he called "the jargon of authenticity" and the latest version of "the German Ideology." Although published in 1964, the book had close to no influence on the American discussion. In *Minima Moralia*, Adorno notes that the idea of authenticity has filled the normative gap left behind after the end of substantive religious and ethical standards. Instead of identifying this process as a corruption of a sounder notion of authenticity, the whole idea is radically called into question.

> The untruth is located in the substratum of genuineness itself, the individual. If it is in the principium individuationis, as Hegel and Schopenhauer both recognized, that the secret of the world's course is concealed, then the conception of an ultimate and absolute substantiality of the self falls victim to an illusion that protects the established order even while its essence decays (Adorno 1974: 152).

In *The Jargon of Authenticity*, Adorno contends that the "liturgy of inwardness" is founded on the flawed idea of a self-transparent individual who is capable of choosing herself (Adorno 1973: 70). In short, Adorno launches a frontal attack on authenticity, which for him is not only susceptible to criticism as the manifestation of a nostalgic longing for wholeness before the 'fall.' While providing an empty substitute for lost religious and ethical values, it is founded upon on the doubtful picture of the self-possessing individual, a picture that covers up the constitutive alterity and mimetic nature of the self. Interestingly, in contrast to Bell and Bellah and drawing heavily on Benjamin's essay on 'aura,' Adorno goes on to claim that the ideal of authenticity is not an antidote to societal constraints and the leveling tendencies of capitalism, but simply their 'other;' it is itself a function of technologies of reproduction. Therefore, due to the embeddedness of individuals, any attempt to retreat into the authentic inner is not a genuine antidote to contemporary societal power structures but simply a part of them. As we will see in Chapter 6, Adorno's point still has a curious actuality.

Much like Adorno, the strong current of post-structuralism and philosophical post-modernism was enormously hostile to the idea of authenticity. Doubts about pursuing authenticity by gaining access to the innermost self had already been voiced by Nietzsche, who was deeply suspicious about any introspective access to the self. Instead, he viewed the self as a bundle of conflicting desires and possibilities which could only be unified partially whenever taking its own decisions and actions. Nietzsche argued most fiercely against an idea of authenticity, arguing in favor of leaving behind the self-identical subject, which he referred to as "mythology" (Nietzsche 1988: 361). Rather than containing some stable inner core, the subject is depicted as something that must be given form to (Schmid 1992: 654).

More radically, in the concluding part of *The Order of Things*, Foucault maintaines that society is witnessing a crisis, not only of authenticity but also of the whole idea of the subject in its temporary historically contingent constitution, foreseeing that man will be "erased, like a face drawn in sand at the edge of the sea" (1994: 387). Foucault unmistakably opposes the idea of a hidden authentic self that could be liberated. In an interview given to Hubert L. Dreyfus and Paul Rabinow (1983: 266), he clearly distances himself from what he calls the "Californian cult of the self." At the same time, he is eager to emphasize that the ethical approach that he suggests ('care of the self') is not to be confused with the "Californian cult of the self." Instead, like Adorno, he emphasizes the interdependence of autonomy and the destruction of rigid identities fixed by power relations. Like Adorno, Foucault thinks that the ideal of authenticity is simply the mirror image of power-relations. Therefore he proposes an aesthetic selfcreation in which one attempts to shape one's life as a work of art, proceeding without making recourse to any fixed rules or permanent truths. The "aesthetics of existence"—the practice of the self that he proposes—cannot be put in terms of a final result but must be viewed as a process of everlasting becoming. While Foucault emphasized that regarding the ethical concern about one's own existence only aesthetic values should be applied, he continuously refused to provide a more comprehensive description of what stylization amounts to. Instead, he contended that to the absence of universal laws and morality "corresponds, must correspond, the search for aesthetics of existence" (Foucault 1988: 49). The recognition that there is no authentic given self leads him to the practical consequence that "we must create ourselves as a work of art" (Foucault 2000). Since the subject is not given to itself in advance, it must create itself as a work of art (Foucault 1984a).

Some years later Rorty addressed the issue of authenticity in a very similar way, revealing his Nietzschean origins. The idea of achieving the kind of self-knowledge involved in authenticity, thus coming to "know a truth which was out there (or in here) all the time" (Rorty 1989: 27), is simply a myth. Having said this, it is important to note, and I will return to this subject in considerable detail, that despite harsh criticism the idea of authenticity has not been completely given up by the opponents of authenticity.

6   AUTHENTICITY DEFENDED

In recent decades, authors like Taylor (1989; 1991; 1995; 2007), Ferrara (1993; 1998), Guignon (2004; 2008), and Jacob Golomb (1995) have addressed the issue of authenticity from a wholly different angle than the critics discussed above. Unsatisfied with the widespread criticism of authenticity as an adequate ethical orientation, Taylor sets out to prove that authenticity does not necessarily lead to neo-Nietzschean aestheticism or atomistic self-indulgence. According to Taylor, the justified criticism of self-indulgent forms of the ideal does not justify the total condemnation of the ideal itself (Taylor 1991: 56). In *The Ethics of Authenticity* and in the more elaborate *Sources of the Self*, an attempt is made to preserve authenticity by extricating aestheticism, subjectivism, individualism, and self-indulgent interpretations of this ideal from what Taylor (Ibid.: 15) considers an original and undistorted idea that contains an element of self-transcendence (Anderson 1995a; 1996). Restoring an undistorted version, Taylor says, could guard against meaninglessness, which is one of the "malaises of modernity" that Taylor sees connected to trivialized forms of the culture of authenticity. He maintains that the element of self-transcendence, which once was a crucial element in the ideal of authenticity, is practically lost from the contemporary version. This lack gives rise to cultures of self-absorption, which lastly deteriorate into the malaise of absurdity. Already in *Sources of the Self*, Taylor draws attention to how modernism gives birth to a new kind of inward turn that not only attempts to overcome the mechanistic conception of the self linked to disengaged reason but also the Romantic ideal of a faultless alignment of inner nature and reason. Instead, for the modernists, a turn inward did not mean a turn towards a self that needs articulation. "On the contrary, the turn inward may take us beyond the self as usually understood, to a fragmentation of experience which calls our ordinary notions of identity into question" (Taylor 1989: 462). Thus, in modernism, the turn inward still contained a self-transcending moment, reaching beyond the self as usually understood. Instead, the critical point where the ideal of authenticity becomes flattened is when it becomes 'contaminated' by a certain form of 'self-determining freedom' that also contains elements of inwardness and unconventionality (Taylor 1991: 38). Self-determining freedom

> is the idea that I am free when I decide for myself what concerns me, rather than being shaped by external influences. It is a standard of

freedom that obviously goes beyond what has been called negative liberty (being free to do what I want without interference by others) because that is compatible with one's being shaped and influenced by society and its laws of conformity. Instead, self-determining freedom demands that one break free of all such external impositions and decide for oneself alone (Taylor 1991: 27).

Not only is self-determining freedom not a necessary part of authenticity, it is also counterproductive because its self-centeredness flattens the meanings of lives and fragments identities. For Taylor, the process of articulating an identity involves adopting a relationship to the good or to what is important, which is connected to one's membership in a language community (Taylor 1989: 34–35). As he clearly states, "authenticity is not the enemy of demands that emanate from beyond the self; it presupposes such demands" (Taylor 1991: 41). It cannot be up to me to decide what is important, since this would be self-defeating. Instead, whatever is important for me must connect to an inter-subjective notion of the good, wherefrom a good part of its normative force lastly emanates. In this sense, authenticity simply requires maintaining bonds to collective questions of worth that point beyond one's own preferences. Without regard

> (a) to the demands of our ties with others, or to (b) to demands of any kind emanating from something more or other than human desires or aspirations are self-defeating, that they destroy the conditions for realizing authenticity itself (Taylor 1991: 35).

Thus, not only do we need the recognition of concrete others in order to form our identity, but we must also (critically) engage with a common vocabulary of shared value orientations. In other words, Taylor points out that authenticity needs the appropriation of values that make up our horizon of significance without simply being assimilated in them.

Golomb (1995) provides an informative historical overview of the genesis and development of the concept of authenticity, paying attention to both literary and philosophical sources. While continuously reminding us of the inherently social dimension of authenticity, one of the achievements here is the focus on boundary situations where authenticity "is best forged and revealed" (Ibid.: 201). In contrast to the other authors mentioned above, Golomb takes a neutral position on the ethical value of authenticity, maintaining that "there is no reason to suppose that it is any better or any more valuable to be authentic than to act inauthentically" (Ibid.: 202).

Guignon explores both the philosophical roots of authenticity and its contemporary manifestations in popular culture. He thoughtfully criticizes pop-psychological literature that deals with the authentic life by making recourse to the subdued 'inner child.' Since Rousseau, the dichotomy between authentic and inauthentic has often been interpreted akin to the distinction between child and adult (Guignon 2004: 43). Like the inner child, the authentic self is depicted as not yet corrupted by the pressures, competitiveness, and conformity of modern public life. Guignon draws on the psychoanalytic theories of Freud and Jung to remind us of more precise and less romanticized visions of the inner child. Additionally, Guignon (2004: 151) aims to identify the manner in which authenticity can be understood as being at the same time a personal and a "fundamentally and irreducibly" social virtue. Authenticity then involves reflectively discerning what is really worth pursuing in the social context that the agent is situated in (Ibid.: 155).

> If the ideal of authenticity is possible only in a free society with a solid foundation of established social virtues, it would seem that trying to be authentic, if it is to be coherent, must involve a commitment to sustaining and nurturing the type of society in which such an ideal is possible. A reflection on the social embodiment of virtues therefore suggests that authenticity, like many other character ideals, carries with it an obligation to contribute to the maintenance and well-being of a particular type of social organization and way of life (Guignon 2008: 288; 2004: 161).

On the other hand, Guignon (2004; 2008) argues that in a democratic society, in which the authority of government—in setting the political course—stems from the consent of the governed, there is good reason to promote virtues like authenticity that assist such an organization of government.

> To be authentic is to be clear about one's own most basic feelings, desires and convictions, and to openly express one's stance in the public arena. But that capacity is precisely the character trait that is needed in order to be an effective member of a democratic society (Guignon 2008: 288).

In this case it is quite straightforward to maintain that any democratic society should be committed to securing the possibility for the kind of practical reflection that is at the core of the practice of authenticity.

Similar to Taylor's approach, in *Reflective Authenticity* Alessandro Ferrara sets out to defend authenticity as an ideal, but in contrast to Taylor he is interested in the social and philosophical aspects of the relation between authenticity and validity. He insists that autonomy no longer carries the conviction it once did because we recognize that the rules of thought and action derive from a situated understanding of who we are and how we want to conduct ourselves. It does not unfold according to universal principles (Ferrara 1998: 50). This is why, according to Ferrara's diagnosis, we are currently witnessing a profound transition that besides affecting cultures, values, and norms, also touches on the "foundations of validity," thus the "bedrock of the symbolic network through which we relate to reality and reproduce our life-forms" (Ibid.: 1). At the core of this transformation is the reformulation of 'well-being' (eudemonia) as the normative ideal of authenticity. Authenticity, which for Ferrara always contains a reflective moment, can be of help in reconstructing a contemporary understanding of normativity. For Ferrara, it can ground a new ideal of universal validity, "ultimately linked with the model of exemplary uniqueness or enlightening singularity thus far associated with 'aesthetics'" (Ibid.: 10; Ferrara 1994). His account includes a methodological kernel amounting to this point:

> The form of universalism most appropriate to a postmetaphysical standpoint is that proceeding from the exemplary self-congruency of a symbolic whole—two significant models of which are, at the level of life-world practices, the congruency of a life-history and, at the level of expert-practices, the congruency of the well-formed work of art (Ferrara 1998: 10).

Reformulating Aristotle's notion of phronesis and Kant's reflective judgment, Ferrara aims at finding an alternative model of judgment by overhauling a universalism based on principles. Authenticity is then characterized by the "self-congruency" of an individual, collective, or symbolic identity (Ferrara 1998: 70), and is thought of as providing a new universal validity that does not build on the generalizable but rather on the exemplary. Ferrara views Georg Simmel's idea of an individual law as such an anti-generalizing universalism, and it is exactly this characteristic that makes it better suited to the pluralist contexts faced by modern Western societies. He points out that in the light of this change we must revise the idea of universalism. So, universality will not refer to universally binding norms but to an exemplary universalism that is not susceptible to a critique of 'contextuality' that haunts a universalism based on principles. Authenticity thus refers to a kind of normativity which is based on a new sort of universalism.

7 OUTLINE: THE VIEW FROM HERE

The accounts presented above dominate the current theoretical perspective on authenticity. This book shares a fundamental assumption with all these thinkers. The ideal of authenticity should be rescued from turns toward both aestheticism and atomistic self-indulgence. Also, I agree that suitably voiced criticism of self-indulgent forms does not justify total condemnation of the concept itself. Having said this, there are several central issues on which I part ways with these authors.

Agent transcending sources of meaning, central to Taylor, certainly constitute an appealing albeit ambiguous idea. As Anderson (1995a; 1996) points out, Taylor seems to shift between two versions of this claim. It is not certain whether those transcendent demands emanating from beyond the self are thought of in terms of social norms (friendship, loyalty, etc.) or ultimately as transcending the anthropocentric view and appealing to nature or God (Taylor 1991: 91). While it seems appealing that the idea of authenticity must contain a moment of self-transcendence towards "horizons of significance" in order to be meaningful or important to someone, it is questionable and at least unaccounted for why self-transcendence must refer to a non-anthropocentric "wider whole" as a source of value—an aspect that Taylor takes from Rousseau (Ibid. 1991: 91). Thus, while I agree that such an understanding of authenticity can help us understand the malaise of modernity, I find it difficult to see why the horizons of significance would lose their strength as meaning-giving sources if they did not refer to a "wider whole," which seems to involve a strong metaphysical commitment. In other words, I do not see why such a "wider whole" has to make recourse to non-anthropocentric sources of value.

Concerning Ferrara's account, I certainly subscribe to his view that moral reasoning evolves from a contextual, historically situated understanding of who we are. To a certain extent I also subscribe to the criticism of moral autonomy that Ferrara delivers, but I find myself in disagreement on a number of issues. While Ferrara rightly contrasts moral autonomy with authenticity, the account of moral autonomy in question is certainly not one that is widely used today. Therefore, while such choice of contrast is adequate from a historical point of view, from a systematic point of view it does not do much work. For that reason, while acknowledging the historical point, this book will contribute to clarifying the link between authenticity and personal autonomy. Also, it is not really clear to me how Ferrara's methodological approach, which aims at a non-generalizing exemplary universalism, fits with the aim of identifying the fundamental 'dimensions' of an authentic self (coherence, vitality, depth, and maturity). It may be objected that such 'dimensions' really function as context-transcendent criteria for authentic selfhood. Ferrara attempts to deflect such an objection, saying that these dimensions "lack the determinacy that we usually associate with the notion of a criterion" (Ferrara 1998: 106). This is not entirely correct however. I agree that coherence, vitality, depth, and maturity are formal and not *precise* or substantial criteria, but this does not warrant the conclusion that they are not criteria or aspects that form a criteria at all. Saying that these dimensions are necessarily involved in all kinds of conceptions of authentic selfhood amounts to much the same as maintaining that they are criteria—necessary, but not sufficient.

Both of these issues will be considered in Chapters 2 and 3 where I attempt to construct a theoretical foundation for an account of authenticity that is immune to these problems. Unlike Golomb's (1995) approach, the whole inquiry in this book is motivated by the intuition that authenticity has both a certain moral value and critical potential and therefore deserves to be reconstructed. However, there is a significant shortcoming that all accounts share and which makes them less attractive in the context of a critical inquiry into the practices of the self in contemporary life. It is the lack of attention to the reciprocal shaping of capitalism and the ideal of authenticity. It should be mentioned that Guignon's main approach to authenticity—that both encompasses its moral, philosophical dimension and yet remains attentive to contemporary practices informed by pop-psychology—is certainly shared in this book. While I share Guignon's critical impetus, I also claim that if we want to understand the current transformations of this ideal, and if we want the notion of authenticity to function as a useful critical concept that avoids the pitfalls of paternalism, we must consider recent and fundamental transformations in the relation between capitalism and authenticity. In Chapter 6, I will attempt just that.

2 Authenticity and Critical Social Philosophy

In the introduction I mentioned that one of the central tasks of this book is to re-qualify the concept of authenticity. This involves both discerning an applicable nucleus from other superfluous features that have come to muddle the picture, but also adding components so that it can be used to diagnose contemporary practices. As we shall see, such critical role is not alien to the concept. In fact, authenticiy has continuously served as a *critical concept*, as a measure against which particular self-relations and patterns of societal interactions can be considered distortions. In order for such critical inquiry to be possible, we must embed the concept of authenticity in the framework of critical social theory. This will enable us to broaden the reach of our investigation and to critically scrutinize contemporary practices of authenticity that are shaped by capitalistic requirements. No existing account of authenticity has paid attention to the reciprocal shaping of capitalism or embedded the concept of authenticity in the framework of a critical social theory. This makes them less attractive as tools for critical social-philosophical inquiry.

In the present chapter I shall begin by arguing that authenticity—as a critical concept—is closely tied to a particular mode of addressing 'the social,' as *Gesellschaftskritik* (1.). In this branch of philosophy, a normative and critical concept of authenticity—or related concepts implying a concept of authenticity—have long been employed in order to assess and criticize capitalist practices. In the following, central ideas from *Gesellschaftskritik* will inspire the restoration and actualization of authenticity as a key concept for critical social philosophy. The concept will be normatively founded and will assist in identifying deformed practices of the self. However, it is not merely the case that our undertaking benefits from recent work in critical social theory. Contemporary critical social theory would also benefit from a detailed concept of authenticity to sharpen its theoretical gaze and further its aims. These initial steps will raise further questions about how such a critical undertaking can be normatively grounded (2.) and whether such grounding involves recourse to a particular notion of the 'good' that would make it vulnerable to accusations of paternalism (3.).

1 CRITICAL SOCIAL PHILOSOPHY AS GESELLSCHAFTSKRITIK

The emergence of social philosophy is connected to the work of Thomas Hobbes, who, motivated by the social and political disintegration of his time, sought to discover rational principles for the construction of social and political stability. In other words, social philosophy emerged at a point when philosophers no longer aimed at providing the criteria for how government should proceed to attain the 'good life' but solely focused on how to construct a stable and consensus-based political order. In Hobbes's account, the "natural condition of mankind" is a state of relentless violence, uncertainty and threat. It is a "war of every man against every man," where "the notions of right and wrong, justice and injustice have no place" (Hobbes 1968: 188). The transition from the state of nature to civil society can only be effec-tuated if some "right of nature" is given up in favor of the sovereign. Therefore, in the closing section of his "Review and Conclusion," he emphasizes "the mutual relation between protection and obedience" (Ibid.: 491). This is the only foundation upon which contractual conditions can be established and on which an absolutist state could establish any kind of peace, stability, or civil order.

In the span between Hobbes and Rousseau social philosophy went through a radical change, adapting to altered social and political circumstances. According to Habermas, concurrent with the process of capitalistic modernization, a bourgeois public sphere emerged with new patterns of interaction which reflected that the focal point of public discourse was no longer a "homogenous," but a more "differentiated" individual (Habermas 1989: 37–56). By the time Rousseau entered the debate these new historical circumstances fundamentally changed the questions that guided social philosophical investigations. The focus of social philosophical inquiry shifted from exploring the conditions of a stable civil order to exploring the conditions of a good life and self-realization within such an order.

> With this theoretical change of stance, Rousseau paved the way towards the development of a new approach to social philosophy. Unlike political philosophy, such social philosophy would no longer seek out to determine the conditions of a correct or just social order, but instead would attempt to identify the limitations that new forms of sociality imposed on human self-realization (Honneth 2007a: 5).

Consequently, Rousseau's social philosophy makes recourse to a concept of human self-realization or authenticity as a normative backdrop. Rousseau's particular way of addressing the social field comes together with the inauguration of an idea of authenticity which functions as the measure against which developmental processes of society can be regarded as processes of distortions, or in stronger terms, pathologies. In our context, Rousseau has an important role in social philosophy. Not only was he the originator of a specific social-philosophical way of reasoning, as Honneth (2007a) notes, but he was also the "originator of the modern authenticity discourse" as Taylor (1991: 45; 1995: 232) and Trilling (1972) argue. The concept of authenticity or human self-realization becomes the normative core in his approach to a critical social-philosophical inquiry, against which societal practices and self-relations can be assessed. What is also characteristic of Rousseau is that his concept of authenticity involves (agent-) immanent and transcendent aspects. The self-realization of the agent is at the same time also realization of something 'higher' that is genuinely expressive of mankind. This aspect had proved influential.

1.1 Rousseau and Critical Social Theory

Rousseau's version of social philosophy continues in the tradition of *Gesell-schaftskritik*, which was established by key figures among first and second generation critical theorists. This tradition of social philosophy distinguishes itself from Anglo-Saxon, analytic traditions of social philosophy in terms of the scope and aims of investigations into the realm of the social. The Anglo-Saxon tradition has to a significant extent developed into research on normative questions that arise in cases where civil society necessitates intervention from state institutions. The most prominent of these investigations deal with crime, private property, and healthcare (McPherson 1970; Feinberg 1973). This means that the domain of social philosophy becomes narrower and addresses social issues by restricting itself to the normative vocabulary of moral and political philosophy, using concepts like 'justice' and 'injustice.' Not only has addressing social questions in the vocabulary of justice narrowed the domain of social philosophy, but the very notion of social justice has also been narrowed and it is now mainly understood in a distributive manner. Partly due to the influence of Rawls's work, this understanding of social philosophy is very widespread and has successfully resisted the communitarian critique (Honneth 2004a: 213–214).

Such a narrowed focus has its advantages of course, but also precludes certain pertinent questions from being asked. Therefore, Honneth argues that we should not lose sight of the distinctive contribution that a Gesell-schaftskritik could make to the domain of normative ethics, and also to social and political philosophy. Central to the idea of critical social philosophy is the diagnosis of social pathologies.[1] Honneth (1998: 37) states this unequivocally in an interview with Simon Critchley: "The only chance we have to keep the tradition of Critical Theory alive is to continue the social-philosophical enterprise of a kind of diagnosis of our present culture, the pathologies of that culture, of a certain capitalist culture." Here, Honneth also argues that the idea of social pathology is necessary as the normative justification of a critical undertaking (see Cannon 2001: 155).[2] Thus, instead of focusing on issues of individual obligation, right action (moral philosophy) or law, and equal distribution (political philosophy), critical social philosophy focuses on questions at a more fundamental level. It attempts to address the structural conditions which are necessary for authenticity and self-realization, and to identify the social constellations that obstruct them. From such a view, it is insufficient to invoke the notion of (in)justice without attempting to highlight the distortive social pathologies that might have led there in the first place.

2   THE NORMATIVE FOUNDATION OF CRITICAL SOCIAL PHILOSOPHY

Criticizing pathologies of self-relations and of social life only makes sense in light of specific assumptions about what a 'full' and 'non-distorted' condition amounts to. In other words, in order to substantiate this critical, social–philosophical approach, it is necessary to rely on a theoretical framework that makes social pathologies and successful forms of social life intelligible. Detecting the social etiology of those pathologies requires normatively grounded and subtle evaluative predicates. Also, the evaluative vocabulary that critical social philosophy has to apply to achieve its goals must reach 'below' the principles of justice, in order to detect distortions and forms of suffering related to social practices that do not infringe the principles of justice (Zurn 2000). In other words, critical social philosophy requires a concept of authenticity, in the sense of an undistorted self-relation that is embedded in social practice. This generates the central question: how can such a notion be underpinned?

In order to answer this, let us assess the different and opposing possibilities in which critical social philosophy is underpinned. Following Honneth's (2007a) distinction, the normative backdrop of such critical inquiry has been attained either anthropologically, as referring to some original state (Rousseau), or historical philosophically, as referring to the anticipation of a presumed future conclusion to human history (Hegel). In other words, a normatively grounded theoretical framework can be achieved either *retrospectively*, referring back to some original state, or *prospectively*, by anticipating a fulfillment of human history.

2.1   Prospective, Historical-Philosophical Justification

In opposition to Rousseau, for whom the process of socialization inescapably leads away from an original state, Hegel's pattern of theoretical justification is taken from his philosophy of history. Authenticity, or the realization of true human characteristics, is to be found at the end of historical progress. In order to understand the full scope of Hegel's theoretical reflections, we need to look at the way he, in comparison with Rousseau, builds on fundamentally different ideas about the self. The authentic self-relation, which Rousseau depicted as the manifestation of the self to the self as a particular entity, is for Hegel a deficient notion of the authentic. Instead, Hegel emphasizes the constitutive inter-subjective dimension of the self. Rousseau's particular individual is isolated and cannot attain any stable sense of self because he is only connected to the public sphere in a negative way, as something that cannot be contained in the 'general' (Allgemeinen) (Hegel 1970: 161). In order to argue this, in a famous chapter in the *Phenomenology* Hegel sets out to examine recognition as the inter-subjective condition necessary for any form of stable "consciousness." He attacks the concept of a self-contained subjectivity existing in the space of self-enclosed interiority, and instead he depicts the subject as necessarily involved and embedded in the cultural and historical contexts that shape his ways of relating to objects, others, and to himself. Hegel denies the so-called 'problem of other minds' on the grounds that the subject is necessarily linked to his social environment and usually does not have to bridge a gap between himself and the 'other.' As Habermas (1999: 134) notes, the Hegelian subject

> is at the same time inside and outside of itself. Speakers and actors find themselves in the course of established performances and practices, while conceptual networks in advance shape their perceptions and judgments. A subject cannot be with itself before being with an other, so that self-awareness emerges only from encounters with others.

Prior to any relations that subjects engage in, there is "Geist" that structures all relations and opens up a field of intelligibility. This is why Hegel urges us to "speak neither of such subjects, nor of such objects, but of *Geist*" (Hegel 1986: 205). The subject does not understand itself through practices of introspection but through externalization via the symbolic media of language and through work that distances the self from empty particularity (Ibid.: 153). Hegel calls attention to the subject, understanding it both as a person that shares the constitutive features of subjects and as a unique individual that forms and is formed by a particular life history. This double understanding of the self is essential for achieving full selfhood and it only comes into life when engaging in the practices of a community.

It is based on such a conception of the self that Hegel argues that the solution given by Rousseau's 'Social Contract' is deeply ambiguous. Such a contract relies on an account of negative freedom expressed in terms of rights, which for Hegel brings the danger of destabilizing the community that in return undermines the possibility of the self-realization of individuals. He argues that the autonomy and the nature of man is not only "not relinquished in the state, but it is actually in the state that it is first realized. The freedom of nature, the gift of freedom, is not anything real; for the state is the first realization of freedom" (Hegel 1963: 402).

In Hegel's work the theoretical justification for his account of authenticity is ultimately grounded in his historical-philosophical idea of the '*Bildungsroman*' of the spirit, which after an evolving series of 'shapes of consciousness' will arrive at an end state. Far from being merely about individuals, authenticity also concerns the dynamic self-manifestation of 'spirit.' For Hegel, authentic subjectivity is not adequately described in individual manifestations—not even in those of important historical figures. Instead, authenticity is reached when these 'heroic' individuals act as individual 'agents of world-spirit'[3] and thus realize something 'higher'. The idea of authenticity as the realization of something 'higher' than particular individuality is therefore a feature that is shared by Hegel.

After Hegel, the rather speculative historical-philosophical attempt to ground authenticity faded away and only resurfaced rarely, e.g. Oswald Spengler's influential *The Decline of the West* and partly in the work of Lukács.[4]

2.2   Retrospective, Anthropological Justification

The second pattern of theoretical justification, which goes back to Rousseau, makes recourse to an anthropological idea of what we are as humans. In Rousseau, the normatively grounded theoretical framework for social philosophy is achieved *retrospectively*, referring back to some original state.

Rousseau criticizes the impact of modernization in terms of social competition and differentiation. He questions whether society is able to provide the setting for a well-lived life. The struggle for esteem, role-playing, and false appearances reduce humans to "specters and phantoms, which strike the eye for a moment and disappear as soon as one tries to touch them" (Rousseau 1968: 197). In the light of the social transformations that Rousseau witnessed, he begun to not only question the possibility of human flourishing under these circumstances. He went even further in his *Discourse on the Origin of Inequality* of 1755 and argued that societal structures caused most of the suffering and corruption in human existence. His way of formulating the problem illustrates his commitment to authenticity. Socially induced deficits are not primarily depicted in terms of injustice but in terms of alienation. What is harmed is not primarily the justice and equality between men. Rather, inequality is merely a consequence of failing to realize inherent human capacities.

For Rousseau, much is destroyed in this process of transformation. He observes that "most of our ills are of our own making" and notes that they could have been avoided by preserving "the simple, regular and solitary lifestyle prescribed to us by nature" (Rousseau 1992: 22). For instance, the physical health of modern, social man is compromised, since the competitive relations require a mastery of role-playing that is an "excessive labour" leading to "fatigue and mental exhaustion," and innumerable other maladies (Ibid.: 22). The ongoing calculation of outcomes to social relations and roles also causes inequality and injustice, since they destroy the immanent moral understanding, which humans are hard-wired with. According to this line of reasoning, the artificial character of society is responsible for a loss of authenticity, which causes the 'inner voice' of existence to fade. This not only results in 'wrong' living or inauthenticity, but a mode of living that undermines the very basis of social cohesion and morality. The loss of the 'voice of existence' reaches even deeper than ethics and morality to the deepest levels of the self where it causes pathological effects that manifest themselves in various forms of psychic suffering.

As Ernst Cassirer (1932) has pointed out, Rousseau finds a way of solving the theodicy problem without having to place the origin of evil in God or natural man. It would however be too hasty to condemn such an anthropology of the natural human state as too optimistic. Indeed, Rousseau emphasizes the ideal nature of such a state "which no longer exists, which perhaps never existed," and "which probably never will exist" (1992: 12–13). Nevertheless, having said this, Rousseau's position is that pathological aspects were not immanent in man but were produced by the dynamics of modern society, which is characterized by a competitive way of relating to others and striving for acknowledgement in the public sphere. Jean Starobinski (1971: 33) rightly calls this an "external condition" and he points out that Rousseau externalizes the origins of societal evil and alienation from the original nature of man. Rousseau is well aware that living in the state of nature humans are independent of one another, but with their *amour de soi* ensuring their self-preservation, the potentially problematic *amour-propre* does not get the upper hand. In speeding up interactions oriented at status gains, this is exactly the kind of self-relation that becomes dominant. The natural *amour de soi* becomes perverted, reshaping social relations into dependency, inequality, and consequently oppression. This is because the undistorted *amour de soi* also inspires sympathy and considerate relations with others, sensitive to "seeing any sentient being, especially our fellow-man, perish or suffer, principally those like ourselves" (Rousseau 1992: 14). So the instinctive concern with self-preservation in the state of nature was moderated by a direct and non-reflective identification with the sufferer. For Rousseau, natural man lived in the 'state of nature,' enjoying a political, moral, economic, and most of all psychological independence, experiencing the 'sentiment of existence' and thus 'living within oneself.' With the emergence of society and mutual dependence, social man becomes deformed and unhappy, because he derives his "sentiment of existence" from the judgments of others (Cullen 1993: 38).

Overall, implicit in his notion of 'state of nature,' Rousseau's account of authenticity makes recourse to a rather substantial idea of what human nature amounts to. Such an account faces a number of insurmountable difficulties and surely the idea of the inherent nature of men does not ring true to our ears. Also, adding to the problems in Rousseau's anthropology, there is an inherent contradiction. If the arena of the social is character-ized by dishonesty and hostility, we must ask how this situation could have emerged from supposedly 'pure' individual minds. It seems that Rousseau must admit the existence of at least the possibility of an unruly and poten-tially evil mental configuration within the state of nature, which would run counter to his overall claim.

On the other hand, simply maintaining that Rousseau's anthropology is too substantial and too individualistic misses an important point. One should note that in Rousseau, as in Hegel, authenticity is not sufficiently described in terms of an individual's self-relation, but it involves a moment of tran-scendence, in the sense of a parallel realization of something 'higher' than the self. This higher element is not the self-manifestation of 'spirit' through the individual, as in Hegel, but the realization of the 'natural' in man. As Muchnik (2000: 54) notes, in Rousseau, "The *natural* in *man* . . . remains operative as an *ideal*: namely, as an *ought* en-tangled in an is." We could say that authenticity in both Roussau and Hegel involves the co-realization of two aspects: the immanent and the transcendent. It clearly involves the realization of some 'inner' motives, plans, etc. of the individual, but impor-tantly, the realization of these aspects also realizes something that is agent-transcendent, be it either historical–philosophically or anthropologically conceptualized. Now, in these accounts, the agent-transcendent component is substantial, defined retrospectively or prospectively. Note however that the immanent, agent-internal component is less determined and quasi-formal. It does not involve an attempt at defining the explicit aims of human self-realization but merely the more modest attempt at showing the conditions of possibility for an ethically authentic orientation to emerge.

As noted earlier, both approaches harbor some difficulties. The formal-ized concept of authenticity in Rousseau rests on the idea of a self-contained self that—after Hegel—had become untenable, while in Hegel it involves highly speculative ideas about the unfolding of 'spirit.' As I shall argue in the following, being indebted to both Rousseau and Hegel, Marx devel-ops these ideas further in a way that avoids these problems. On the one hand, he follows Rousseau's anthropological manner of securing normative foundations, while formalizing anthropology and abandoning the idea of anthropological constants that are independent of the social and material conditions of society. On the other hand, following Hegel, he underscores the social dimension of the self and rejects the idea of a self-contained self.

2.3 Non-Retrospective and 'Formal' Anthropology

Marx actualizes many of Hegel's thoughts and reformulates them so that his social philosophy is able to address economic issues and those seemingly impersonal forces that govern society. In a genuine *gesellschaftskritisch* manner, Marx discusses the consequences of capitalist development as *alienation*, which he finds alarming not because they are manifestations of legal or moral injustice, but because they are hindrances to human self-realization. For Marx, human kind develops itself and its profound understanding of the physical world through the means of labor. Human self-realization and thus authenticity can therefore be achieved only through self-determined labor. His main argument is that capitalist modernization obstructs this process because it destroys the conditions for this kind of labor. Alienation is not rooted in religion, as with Feuerbach, but in the material world, and could thus not be eliminated through rational argument. It is no longer man's eternal condition, but the product of a specific form of labor that has a historical point of emergence, which will cease when capitalism is replaced by socialism (Gouldner 1980). Marx (1975: 324) argues that the product of work becomes alien to the subject that produced it: "It exists outside him, independently of him and alien to him, and begins to confront him as an autonomous power; that the life which he has bestowed on the object confronts him as hostile and alien." The necessary step towards human self-realization, which involves the objectification of human capacities, becomes the means of capitalistic production, a process that leads to alienation (Marx 1990: 517). The human capacity of subjects to objectify themselves through labor is put to work in a manner that hinders the realization of human characteristics, alienating subjects from the product of their labor, from their own person, and from other humans. As Terry Eagleton (1997: 27) notes, such development drives a wedge between individual and communal dimensions of the self. Although this is strongly reminiscent of Rousseau, Marx is generally anti-Rousseauian, because he opposes the idea that humans have an unchanging nature, independent of the social and material conditions of their society (Callinicos 1996: ch. 3). In his sixth 'Thesis on Feuerbach,' Marx (1976: 4) questions the existence of such a thing as 'human nature': "The essence of man is no abstraction inherent in each single individual. In its reality it is the ensemble of the social relations."

Marx rejects the idea of an unchanging human nature as the backdrop against which failed self-realization becomes intelligible. This is why, in the *Economic and Philosophic Manuscripts*, he takes over Feuerbach's anthropological ideas on the nature of man but formalizes their content: For Marx (1976: 333), "Labour (is) the essence of man." Similarly, in *Capital*, he clearly states that by "acting on the external world and changing it, he at the same time changes his own nature" (Marx 1974: 177). Thus, in Marx, the anthropological feature is formal, limited to the idea that humans are creatures that realize their nature in a specific, non-estranged form of labor. However, this does not mean that he rejected the idea that formal conditions for human self-realization may be constant, even in divergent societies.

Marx's account also involves what we have referred to as the co-realization of something agent-immanent and agent-transcendent or 'higher.' Nonetheless, in opposition to Rousseau and to Hegel, Marx avoids substantial ideas pertaining to the transcendent aspects. The agent-transcendent component in this account is not substantial and not defined retrospectively or prospectively. Rather than invoking an original state of being, Marx merely refers to the 'formal' societal conditions that should be present. By this he means the possibility of non-alienated labor. The philosophical-historical element of his reasoning about the conditions of authenticity is also formal. At the point in time when capitalism is replaced by socialism the conditions of possibility for unobstructed human self-realization will be given. Even if the later Marx still relies on "systematic reference to anthropological determinations" (Honneth 2007a: 15), he replaces the concept of alienation with reification and carefully avoids referring to explicit, non-formal anthropological characteristics.

Importantly, while authenticity in Marx remains a critical concept against which pathologies can be detected, the focus is on the formal societal conditions under which it can be achieved. In Marx, authenticity neither arises introspectively from a mysterious inner realm, nor prospectively through the self-manifestation of world-spirit in individuals, nor retrospectively by being at one with unchanging human nature. Instead, human nature is about an ongoing process, in which human kind changes the external world whereby it simultaneously changes its own nature. Human nature is to change human nature. While human nature is not fixed, the adequate manner of interchange between man and man and man and world is. The adequate manner of interchange is non-alienated. Thus, self-realization does not entail being at one with an unchanging human nature, but is about the realization of agent-immanent and agent-transcendent aspects through non-alienated labor and social interaction.

With Marx, we have arrived at a notion of authenticity that is justified in a formal anthropological manner. It is not about being at one with an unchanging human nature but refers to a self-relation that springs from specific patterns of inter-subjective interaction with others and the environment.

2.4   Critical Social Theory Today: Recognition

In contemporary critical social philosophy, it has become mainstream that any stable self-relation and personal identity (that is a necessary precondition for the pursuit of a good life) depends on participation in various inter-subjective practices. For Habermas and Honneth, there are two ways of coming to terms with these practices: participation and recognition. The formal anthropological idea that we have seen in Marx is taken further in the work of these authors.

In Habermas, the key to a stable personal identity is non-constrained participation in forms of social practice that enable socialization and in which actors reciprocally attribute communicative freedom to each other (1996, 361). Therefore, securing the conditions for the possibility of active participation in such processes in the public sphere must be seen as an essential duty of modern societies. Such participation is not restricted to ordered discussions that find a place in formal settings but describes "every encounter in which actors do not just observe each other but take a second-person attitude, reciprocally attributing communicative freedom to each other, unfolds in a linguistically constituted public space" (Ibid.). Thus, participation and the second-personal, socially embedded encounter provides the point of reference for a critical social philosophy.

While the focus on second-personal interactions remains of theoretical interest in critical social philosophy, Honneth shifts the emphasis from 'participation' to 'struggles for recognition,' which take place at various levels. With this shift, Honneth aims to ground and normatively justify social philosophy with recourse to the threefold constitutive role of recognition for the formation of a firm self-relation and personal identity. There is an inextricable link between the formation of a stable identity and practices of social recognition, and processes of identity formation are endangered by a lack of recognition or when experiencing different forms of disrespect (Anderson and Honneth 2005). Honneth (1995a: 172) parts ways with the attempt to ground ethical life in the moral autonomy of human beings and instead focuses on "the conditions for their realization in general."

The threefold structure of recognition refers to three different facets of ontogenetic development *and* to three different self-relations, which they ideally enable. The stages of identity development in individuals depend on three forms of inter-subjective recognition, which are partly enabled by societal institutions and forms of organization. Identity is formed in a permanent inter-subjective struggle for attaining recognition in interaction, and the three distinctive forms of self-relation are ideally achieved in three different categories of interaction. 'Primary affective relations' like love and friendship allow the achievement of a measure of self-confidence in the most basic developmental sense, as the trust in the stability of their selves and the world. 'Self-respect,' the second form of self-relation, is gained through the legal acknowledgment of one's universal and equal rights, legal responsibility, and moral capacity. The third form of self-relation, 'self-esteem,' emerges from being acknowledged as a distinct individual that contributes to the shaping of a community oriented around a set of shared values.

These three forms of self-relation entail relating to oneself as a concrete unique individual (self-confidence and self-esteem) and relating to oneself as one among the many (self-respect). Although these forms of recognition are different, they are hierarchically intertwined. Without self-confidence one cannot gain undistorted self-respect, and without self-respect the chances for self-esteem are significantly diminished. Three forms of disrespect match the three stabilizing functions of recognition which make up the moral source of struggle for more inclusive relations of recognition. Self-confidence is endangered by various violations of physical integrity and results in loss of trust concerning the stability of self and world. Self-respect is undermined by the denial of universal rights as an equal citizen. Self-esteem is endangered when the life of an individual is degraded and not acknowledged as providing a unique contribution to the community. So, disrespect is not only understood as an injustice, as a harm done to the freedom of an individual, but as an injury with regard to her positive self-understanding (Honneth 1995a: 131).

Since these inter-subjective processes of recognition represent both the means through which individuals develop a stable sense of self and world and the means through which the reproduction of the social world is achieved, they may function as the normative foundation of a formal conception of ethical life, against which pathological societal constellations that undermine these universal features can be identified. In other words, the normative foundation is secured in an anthropological manner, by reflecting on the formal inter-subjective conditions that serve as indispensable preconditions for non-pathological self-relation and individual self-realization (Honneth 1995a: 173).

There is some common ground between the theory of recognition and neo-Aristotelian ideas in moral theory. The emphasis upon developing a good life, highlighting a stable personal identity as a crucial aspect of a person's capacities to be a moral agent, the resistance to detach issues of justified moral agency from the personal motives of the agent, and the emphasis upon the importance of being embedded in a shared horizon of significance for moral agency are all reliable indications for such a proximity (Zurn 2000). Also, rather than relying on universal principles that can be applied regardless of motivational sets and cultural embeddedness, focus is on furthering an infrastructure for social forms of life that will promote individual authenticity (see also Siep 2010). On the other hand, as the title of Honneth's paper "Between Aristotle and Kant: Recognition and Moral Obligation" (2007c) reveals, Honneth wants to retain certain aspects of what Kantian thought has to offer. As in Kant, and in opposition to Nietzschean-Foucaultian critical thought, Honneth's recourse to a "weak, formal anthropology" aims at constructing normatively evaluative standards that are universally valid, thus not restricted to certain types of life or culturally contingent social settings. As in Habermas, Honneth (1995: 172) isolates in the patterns of recognition 'structural elements' that are universal, in the sense of being extricable from all forms of life and at the same time sufficiently abstract and formal to deflect the criticism of being articulations of specific and substantial understandings of the good life (Ibid.: 174). Thus, without extricating critical social theory from social experience, the justification of normative ambitions in such a theory is achieved not via recourse to formalist proceduralism, but to a formal anthropological feature that characterizes the nexus of self-realization or authenticity ("realizing, without coercion, one's self-chosen life goals" [Ibid.]) and patterns of interaction.

2.5   Authentic Selfhood: At the Core of the Theory of Recognition?

Clearly, Honneth's recognition-informed approach has the enormous advantage of being able to account for the complex interconnectedness of not only authentic self-relation and concrete second-personal interactions, but also social struggles among groups. But we may ask: What is at the positive center of gravity in his theory of recognition if the inter-subjective patterns of recognition are only the conditions of individual self-realization? While the notion of recognition seems to be the center of interest, its normative significance is derivative, since it only gains importance as the precondition of self-realization or authenticity, which really is the normative core (Hardimon 1997; Zurn 2000). In that case, it would be more precise to refer to the relevant struggles not as struggles to achieve recognition but as struggles for 'undistorted self-realization' or authenticity. This is clearer when Anderson and Honneth (2005: 144) emphasize the "intersubjective conditions for being able to lead one's life as one's own." Thus, the center of gravity of the theory of recognition is occupied by an implicit idea of authenticity. The good that is to be protected against violations through various forms of social exclusion does not merely refer to the possibility of acting autonomously but to the realization of the self. Violations that endanger the capacity for self-realization cannot be adequately articulated in terms of social justice based on rights and just redistribution of resources.

If it is true that authenticity provides the normative core of the theory of recognition, then one may wonder why such a notion is not worked out in greater depth. If this is not achieved, then the analytical gaze of such a critical inquiry remains somewhat blurred. Let me mention three aspects here. First, there may be a plurality of contradicting conceptions concerning authenticity that would be impossible to differentiate and assess from within the theoretical framework of recognition. Secondly, if authenticity remains unspecified, then it also remains unclear if patterns of recognition are the only or even the most relevant structural features that enable it. Thirdly, individuals who fail to achieve non-constrained self-relation while being granted all relevant forms of recognition cannot be accounted for.

Thus, at the normative center of gravity in Honneth's critical social theory there is a gap that needs to be filled by a more advanced concept of self-realization or authenticity. A major goal of this book is to provide such a concept of authenticity that can serve as a core concept for critical social philosophical inquiry. While such a contribution could sharpen the focus of critical inquiry, it certainly does not pretend to provide a comprehensive solution to all the challenges that a theory of recognition faces. Having said this, I should nevertheless emphasize that in the next part of the book I will add aspects that are necessary for self-realization while not being intelligible from within a framework of recognition.

3   TOWARDS A 'RELAXED UNIVERSALISM'

It seems safe to say that, *in principle*, authenticity can function as the normative core of a critical, social theoretical approach. Yet we must rethink the scope of the claim and confront what is one of the greatest challenges in critical socio-philosophical approaches. As mentioned, Honneth seeks to retain certain appealing aspects from Kant, and—via recourse to a "weak, formal anthropology"—to construct normatively evaluative standards that are universal in the sense of not being valid only in certain types of life or in certain culturally contingent social settings. The claim is that patterns of recognition are both universal and at the same time sufficiently abstract and formal to deflect the charge of being articulations of specific and substantial understandings of the good life. As I will argue in the following, this cannot really be the case. In order to see the depths of this problem, I suggest that we first investigate whether more abstract, procedural approaches can proceed without making recourse to some particular understanding of the good. If they fail, then it is reasonable to assume that the criticism targeting universalist approaches also works against the Honnethian approach to critical social theory. Thus, the two interlocking questions will be: can a critical inquiry avoid making reference to the good (3.1), and if so, does this good embody a particular view? (3.2).

3.1   Critical Inquiry Without the Good?

A central question at the center of Habermas' approach is how to construct an ethics "that will not succumb to the distortions of a potentially destructive cultural tradition" (Rasmussen 1990: 57) and that avoids the suspicion of paternalism. In this view, any theory must remain abstracted from particular views of the good, since this could lead to various forms of exclusion and paternalism. Habermas' discourse ethics aims at determining normative validity and seeks to explore the mutual respect needed for autonomy and a sense of personal identity. In his framework this is constituted by the possibility of autonomous and non-coercive participation in social praxis.[5] Hence, what are to be identified are "structural aspects of the good life which it is possible to abstract from the concrete totality of specific life forms when we look at them in terms of the formation of communicative communities" (Habermas 1991).

Habermas' formulation reveals that the goal of mutual respect is made explicit as a condition for the possibility of a good, self-determined life. Non-coercive participation in social praxis, mutual respect and moral acknowledgment are not goals in themselves but are conceptualized as means of protecting the conditions of possibility of the good. The nature of the question pertaining to the moral good is in itself already a higher-level question, referring to the question of what is good for someone (Tugendhat 1979; 2007; Seel 1991). Thus, the epistemological priority of the right presupposes the ontological priority of the good. Prior to deontological considerations, we find a hypothesis about a form of life that is good for a human being (Seel 1993: 315). Further, even the very fear of antipaternalism cannot get off the ground without recourse to an idea of the good. As Seel (1997: 47) convincingly argues:

In a word, the whole idea of democratic welfare states securing the conditions for a good life for their citizens, as opposed to providing for a good life for them, goes back to a particular notion of a good life, namely to the idea of the advantages of a self-determined life. The anti-paternalism of a universalistic morality and a democratic constitution can therefore be grounded only in a formal theory of the good life.

We may have reasons to think that the goal of 'respect' (or 'recognition') can only be explicated through recourse to some more or less formal understanding of the good, but does this mean that such understanding of the good is one that is valid only in specific cultural, historical and social settings?

3.2   The Particularity of the Good

Rawls' immensely influential theory concerning egalitarian liberalism aims to establish principles that are independent of any specific idea of the good. Abandoning substantive ideals, a neutral and fair framework is to provide a structure within which persons are able to pursue their visions of the good. But, as in Habermas, the goals of justice in Rawls make recourse to a formal idea of the good (Sandel 1982). What is more, ethical neutrality is violated, as particular individualistic and secular values are smuggled into the supposedly neutral description. Both Michael Sandel (1982) and Martin Seel (1993; 1997) question whether such accounts are truly protected against accusations of paternalism. Rawls' understanding of equality as a neutral procedural requirement disregards the fact that equality is a substantive value. Additionally, as feminist and multiculturalist thinkers have objected, equality is a substantive value that far from always constitutes a defense against domination and can in fact actually support the social pressure to assimilate to specific gender or cultural norms.

Moreover, equal rights are given normative priority over the 'good' at the price of an atomistic concept of subjects as isolated, solipsistic, pre-societal subjects who choose individual paths through the rational calculation of their particular interests (Sandel 1982: 21). If this atomistic idea is corrected and replaced by a notion of the self that seeks to fulfill life goals not in a void but through interaction with others, then the whole priority of 'rights' and 'values' must be inverted. To understand oneself as an agent seeking freedom from external constraints and as pursuing a good life, one must be engaged in a community of shared values. Both Sandel (1982) and Taylor (1989) have argued that the self must to some extent be seen as constituted by its ends (goods), and that identity-generating ends, however individually distinct, are only acquired in cultural processes of socialization. In short, individual self-interpretations spring from the sources of an inter-subjectively constituted 'pool' of value orientations. The idea is that moral judgment is dependent on local 'vocabularies' and frameworks of understanding that enable moral agents to hold a view (Taylor 1985).

Therefore, it makes little sense to build an account of morality in abstraction from the interpretive horizons and practices that make moral agency possible in the first place. The liberal idea regarding the priority of equal rights forces a wedge between moral subjects and inter-subjectively shared value orientations, and this ambiguity leads to an account that is blind to the social preconditions required for the subjects to effectuate their liberties in practice. The liberal description does not take into account the need for a substantive common good and shared virtues and ties required for conserving a cultural community.

3.3 'Formal Anthropology' and the Strength of the Universality Claim

On the background of the last two paragraphs we can establish two issues. First, a critical social theory that aims at identifying particular self-relations and patterns of societal interactions as distorted processes needs subtle, evaluative predicates that rely on a concept of 'the good.' Second, such understanding of the good, however formal, is to a certain extent never completely neutral—it always embodies a particular and historically contingent vision of the good.

The same goes for Honneth's approach to 'formal anthropology.' First, even an inquiry limited to the *formal conditions of possibility* under which a good life can emerge is not completely neutral on what a good life amounts to. Whenever we maintain that x is a *formal condition of possibility* for y (the good life), we inescapably say something about what y amounts to. If x is a constitutive *condition, no matter how formal*, then it cannot but be shaped according to what it is a condition *for*. Claiming that there are certain formal structures of human existence that make up the *conditions of possibility* of a good life is to a certain extent already discussing some features of a non-neutral idea of the good. Second, as we have seen in Chapter 1, it is quite clear that the idea of authenticity emerges out of a specific historical context in which Europe witnesses a change of moral vocabulary. Trilling, Taylor, and Ferrara point to particular historical contexts in which authenticity materializes as a normatively loaded concept that with time comes to appear superior to notions such as sincerity and moral autonomy. Even if there are similarities between that notion of authenticity and Greco-Roman conceptions of self-knowledge, we have also seen how deep the gaps are between the notions of self that underlie various accounts of authenticity.

In light of these problems, we must deal with the issue concerning validity. We need to ask: how universally applicable is an account when it relies on a concept of authenticity and 'formal anthropology' that embodies a particular and historically contingent vision of the good? Can such an approach legitimately claim any supra-contextual validity? It seems like we have several viable options in order to avoid these risks and they will be considered in the following.[6] May we engage in critical social philosophical inquiry, while at the same time abolishing any recourse to a concept of authentic selfhood (3.3.1.) or any anthropological underpinning (3.3.2.)? Alternatively, we may confront the problem head-on and engage in critical social-philosophical inquiry while acknowledging that authenticity as formal concept is not entirely neutral and has therefore limited supra-contextual validity (3.3.3.). Let us now assess these alternatives.

3.3.1   Abolishing Authenticity

Authors like Nietzsche and Foucault are usually understood to reject any idea of authentic selfhood as the normative backdrop to their critical stance. In the common view, these authors maintain that authenticity at best builds on flawed assumptions about the self and is therefore not applicable to any critical, socio-philosophical undertaking. But is this picture entirely adequate?

Nietzsche is usually considered to fiercely reject the concept of authenticity. In his social critique, he (1988: 361) departs from the idea of the self-identical subject, calling it a "mythology." His *Untimely Meditations* (1997) reveal some of his most transparent reflections on what constitutes one's 'true self' and his rejection of the claim that authenticity is about something 'inward':

> But how can we find ourselves again? How can man know himself? He is a thing dark and veiled; and if the hare has seven skins, man can slough off seventy times seven and still not be able to say: "this is really you, this is no longer outer shell." Moreover, it is a painful and dangerous undertaking thus to tunnel into oneself and to force one's way down into the shaft of one's being by the nearest path. A man who does it can easily so hurt himself that no physician can cure him (Nietzsche 1997: 129).

Nietzsche thus rejects the idea of some underlying fixed core of selfhood that we can posit as the real origin of behavior. When ascribing mental states to ourselves, we illegitimately posit a self that stands behind them as the source. From the notions of substance and efficient causality we illegitimately infer a unitary self, which affects that causality and unifies the plurality of mental states (Whitmire 2009). The way our language works may lead us to suppose that the world is made up of individual entities and selves that can be ascribed certain attributes. "The assumption of one single subject is perhaps unnecessary; perhaps it is just as permissible to assume a multiplicity of subjects, whose interaction and struggle is the basis of our thought and our consciousness in general? . . . My hypotheses: The subject as multiplicity" (Nietzsche 1992: par. 17).

While the passage reveals Nietzsche's hostility towards the idea of a united self that we can access introspectively, the point is not to simply sit back and passively view oneself as a battlefield of blind forces, where different selves simply appear and vanish as the relevant context demands. Rather, the goal is to limit this chaos by giving form to oneself. How this form-giving and the unification of the manifold self is to be achieved is developed in *The Gay Science*:

> *One thing is needful.*—To "give style" to one's character—a great and rare art! It is practiced by those who survey the strengths and weaknesses of their nature and then fit them into an artistic plan until every one of them appears as art and reason and even weakness delights the eye (Nietzsche 1974: § 290).

One should develop a style (or taste) that gives form to one's self. Wholeness of the self is therefore reminiscent of the wholeness of a work of art, which is able to fuse contradictory aspects into a single unity (Nehamas 1985: 185, 221). In this process, originality is the most important criterion: "whether this taste was good or bad is less important than one might suppose, if only it was a single taste!" (Nietzsche 1974: § 290).

For Nietzsche, the process of becoming one's true self (or 'what one is') is not about living and acting in accordance with some knowledge of the 'inner' that one has established introspectively. Instead, what lends unity to the self is a *style* that appears in various manifestations. The method for achieving authenticity is by transposing the aesthetic creation of unique masterpieces to the self. While this is arguably not the case in works of art, style pertaining to the self involves a perpetual movement of self-overcoming. Consider this passage dedicated to the notion of self-overcoming in *Thus Spoke Zarathustra* (Nietzsche 2006: 90):

> That I must be a struggle and a Becoming and an end and an opposition to ends . . . Whatever I create and however much I love it, soon I must oppose it and my love; thus my will wills it.

Nietzsche resists the idea of an authentic style that is self-identical and that may ultimately be fully completed. The important virtue of 'self-overcoming' underscores that constructing the self out of chaos is a perpetual project that can never be completed. In this context, the constant self-overcoming means that the emergence of a definite style is already pregnant with its own abolition.

In all, contrary to post-structuralist readings of Nietzsche, there is evidence that Nietzsche does not completely eradicate the idea of authenticity. As Golomb (1990; 1995) notes, instead of abolishing the whole idea of authenticity, Nietzsche radically transforms it: the 'real' self is something that one has to give a form to. It is important not to underestimate the radicalism of Nietzsche's concept. This is why I tend to disagree with Rorty's (1989: 65) view of aesthetic selfcreation in Nietzsche (and Foucault) as "attempt(s) at authenticity and purity." Such a view would downplay the central idea of constant self-overcoming.

As in several variants of Nietzsche-inspired, post-structuralist thought, Foucault launches a powerful critique of not only authenticity but also of humanist ideas that underlie much liberal and political thought. In many cases, and certainly in Foucault's, concepts such as autonomy and authenticity, once believed to have emancipatory potential, are now revealed at best to build upon erroneous assumptions of the self, and at worst as subtle, repressive instruments of control. The culture of authenticity that he refers to as the "Californian cult of the self" might very well be such a repressive instrument. Rather than embracing who we are, Foucault therefore proposes self-creation as a means towards 'refusal of the self' (Varga 2009). We should struggle against the notion of the true self and even the very notion of self-identity, which in modern societies turn into tools of the "government of individualization" (Foucault 1983: 221). The point is that such a notion suggests some stable truth about us that we ought to conform to, and this effectively hinders us from envisaging radically different forms of identity. For Foucault, we should not attempt to recover our 'lost' identity and discover the deepest truth about ourselves, but rather change who we are and move towards something 'radically Other' (Foucault 1991). The aesthetical dynamization of existence is supposed to lead to the erosion of 'rigid identities' which allow for 'not-normalized' selves and forms of existence.

In this way, reminiscent of Nietzsche's position, the aspect of active self-transformation and self-overcoming is at the center, paired with the idea that such 'techniques of the self' are adequate means for combating forms of subjection and for breaking open fixed identities and power relations.[7] Another strong parallel to Nietzsche is that this self-overcoming is modeled on artistic practice.[8] The recognition that there is no unified inner self leads Foucault to the same conclusion that Nietzsche reached, namely that one must create oneself as a work of art. In an interview with Dreyfus and Rabinow he declares: "from the idea that the self is not given to us, I think that there is only one practical consequence: we have to create ourselves as a work of art" (1983: 237). The authentic self is the self that is created like a work of art, leading to "full enjoyment of oneself or the perfect sovereignty of self over self" (Foucault 1985: 30, translation modified SV).

Thinkers who are usually taken to abolish the idea of authentic selfhood in their critical inquiries, rather than completely rejecting it, radically reformulate what an authentic self amounts to. Also, it could be objected that there is inherent tension between the heteronomy of the subject on the one hand and the idea of the sovereign individual, capable of aesthetic self-fashioning on the other.[9] What is important here is that both Nietzsche and Foucault embrace the idea that the self *is to be realized* in a certain way, albeit in a radically fragmented and aesthetic way. Authenticity no longer refers to the realization of something given, but to the creation of an aesthetic 'Stimmigkeit.' The realization of the self is still connected to leading a life that we see as the fulfillment and expression of ourselves. What is different is really the 'mechanism' of how authentic selfhood is achieved, not by introspection, but by continuously reworking and recasting the elements of one's life into an aesthetic whole. It is not authenticity as such that is revealed as faulty, but a certain way of achieving it. The point to be emphasized here is that authors usually considered hostile to the idea of authentic selfhood, instead of rejecting it, reformulate it in the vocabulary of aesthetic creation. In a sense, a concept of authenticity is inevitable in such critical and normatively loaded inquiries. Defending the creation of the self as a work of art involves ideas about why such a life is better, 'higher,' or worthier than others. As we will see in the next section, a solid account of authenticity must be able to incorporate important aspects addressed by these authors.

3.3.2 Abolishing Anthropological Underpinning

Our previous passages revealed that an approach to social inquiry which takes a critical stand on practices of the self must employ some evaluative idea of what authentic selfhood amounts to. With this in mind, let us assess the second alternative, which proposes a manner of doing critical social philosophy while eliminating recourse to any philosophical anthropology as a foundation.

We may start by discussing relevant aspects in Nietzsche and Foucault. The aesthetical dynamization of existence that both authors embrace is supposed to lead to the erosion of 'rigid identities'—a process that is thought to result in the *right sort of identities*, namely 'non-normalized' selves and forms of existence. At this point a question arises: on what grounds is it established that these non-normalized selves are those that we should strive for? Here, Nietzsche and Foucault part ways. Nietzsche is elitist and limits his claims to certain strong individuals; not everybody is to achieve this ideal. In Foucault however, the case seems to be that it is *good for everybody*, and not just for certain strong individuals that make up an elite. Everybody should resist pre-formed identities and create themselves within an aesthetic paradigm. It is something valuable, something we should embrace because such self-fashioning fits who we are, namely non-pre-given selves that are able to give shape to our existence.

Defending such 'artistic' construction of the authentic self, Foucault—in spite of his radical epistemological critique and hostility to any universalism—implicitly relies on anthropological reflection. While rejecting validity claims concerning normative rightness about identity, he nevertheless draws on formal anthropological assumptions. There is no radical rejection of the normative beliefs about what it is to be human, but rather a rejection of certain historically specific normative ideas. In addition, these historically contingent normative rules (like 'rigid identities') are criticized by making recourse to formal anthropology. Due to such a strategy, Foucault is prevented from offering a normative underpinning for his own position (see Fraser 1989).[10] What is really important in our context is that such prominent approaches to a critical social theory also appeal to formal assumptions about the 'nature' of man. To speak of authentic selfhood, then, does not mean realizing ourselves by being true to something personal within. Instead, it involves the realization of some agent-transcendent aspect of human nature, which in this case is depicted as heterogeneous and chaotic. This is an important aspect that binds all accounts together. What is to be realized in authentic self-relations is not something that is exclusively internal to a particular agent.

The point is not merely that Foucault's critical social inquiry, albeit resistant to philosophical anthropology, relies on formal anthropological assumptions. Rather, my point is that such a critical undertaking must make a similar move. In order to provide the backdrop for such a critical inquiry, it is simply not enough to refer to an understanding of the self or the good embedded in a particular tradition. The mere fact of our being rooted in a particular tradition does not by itself give adequate justification for a particular notion of the self or the good life.

In his recent work Tugendhat (2006; 2007) understands anthropology as *philosophia prima* (replacing metaphysics), arguing that the way in which we understand ourselves as humans constitutes the root of all philosophical questions. Very roughly, Tugendhat argues that as a consequence of the structure of propositional language, every instance of human self-understanding—including questions about the good and justice—is open to questioning (Tugendhat 2007: 42). The resultant gap is filled in everyday life when we justify our motives and our self-understanding in dialogue with others. The gap or tension makes it inevitable that self-understanding ultimately finds place in a broader horizon. Through this dynamic every particular normative stand finally refers back to a 'we,' which is to be understood as the "broadest understanding of us as humans" (Tugendhat 2007: 38–39).[11] The justification and the practice of giving reasons pertaining to our self-understandings only makes sense if it involves reflection on how we see ourselves both as embedded in a particular tradition and as humans in the widest sense. Consequently, any inquiry into 'the good' is only meaningful if it explicitly or implicitly touches on these levels of justification and thus involves some anthropological considerations.

While the discussion in (3.3.1.) revealed that a critical social inquiry that aims at taking a critical stand on practices of the self must make recourse to some evaluative idea of what authentic selfhood amounts to (3.3.2.), we may add that there is a double reference to evaluative ideas at the heart of authenticity. Besides non-distorted selfhood, authenticity also demands that the practice of such non-distorted selfhood is in accordance with certain structural features that characterize us as humans. Therfore, the idea is that with the realization of ourselves, we simultaneously co-realize non-substantial anthropological aspects.

3.3.3 Relaxed Universalism

Let us now summarize. A critical social theory that aims at identifying particular self-relations and patterns of societal interactions as processes of distortions needs subtle evaluative predicates that rely on an understanding of the good and the self. However, such an understanding, however formal, is never completely neutral and always embodies a particular and historically contingent vision of the good. Not only is this true for the concept of authenticity (which emerges out of a specific historical context), but it is also true for a critical socio-philosophical inquiry limited to the formal (anthropological) conditions of possibility under which a good life can emerge.

Considering these potential difficulties, we have assessed whether we can engage in critical inquiry without a concept of authentic selfhood (3.3.1.) or without any anthropological assumptions (3.3.2.). Neither of these alternatives was satisfying. Therefore the question remains: how strong a universality claim can we actually make? For this reason, I have argued that we must opt for a third alternative. This option means relaxing the universalistic ambitions and admitting that our account of authenticity is not completely neutral on the good life, since the norms that underlie 'participation' or 'recognition' themselves refer back to deeper norms that concern authenticity. These again are intelligible as guiding values in a particular modern and Western setting. Consequently, we may apply authenticity as a formal concept that relies on a formal anthropology while acknowledging that it is not entirely free from particular ideas of the good life. Such a relaxation of the claim would also have the advantage of not needing to assume that some relevant formal structures are somehow immanent in the complete range of cultural life forms—which seems to be an empirical issue. Thus, bearing in mind some indebtedness to a particular idea of the good, this book attempts to avoid the charge of paternalism, by constructing a concept of authenticity that is as formal and minimal as possible while still substantial enough to be applicable as a *critical* concept.

4 CONCLUSION

In the course of Chapter 1, I pointed out that while I share fundamental assumptions with contemporary accounts of authenticity, they all have significant shortcomings as critical accounts against which contemporary 'distorted' practices can be identified. While the central aim of this book is to construct *a formal concept of authenticity* that can serve as a critical concept, the question in this chapter was how such a concept can be theoretically framed. For this, we turned to a branch of social philosophy in which a broadly conceived notion of authenticity has long been connected to social criticism. The view is that identifying pathological social practices and their social etiology requires normatively grounded evaluative predicates. In this context, critical social theory requires some formal notion of authenticity, against which reified practices become visible and against which social pathologies can be measured. Within this tradition, we have assessed two different and opposing possibilities of how such a notion of authenticity could be underpinned. While the historico-philosophical underpinning was found less appealing, Rousseau's account of authenticity attempted to define the explicit aims of human self-realization. We found that in Rousseau the concept of authenticity builds on a questionable assumption that claims the existence of constant anthropological features, independent of societal practices. Opposing such an idea, Marx's account is not susceptible to the charges of assuming constant anthropological features. Marx simultaneously formalizes his anthropology and abandons the idea of anthropological constants that are independent of the social and material conditions of society. Following Hegel, he rejects the idea of a self-contained self. In Marx, the idea of human self-realization and authenticity (as a critical concept against which pathologies can be detected) no longer refers to the inner realm of a self-contained self but to specific *patterns of intersubjective interaction*.

Honneth's recognition-informed approach continues and develops this line of reasoning and it can therefore account for the complex intertwinement of authentic self-relation, second-personal interactions, and social struggles of groups. However, the notion of authentic selfhood that is at the positive center of his theory remains underdeveloped. This book will provide a concept of authenticity that may fill this gap and that sheds light on aspects that are necessary for self-realization, while not being intelligible from within a framework of recognition.

The chapter also addressed one of the greatest dilemmas of critical socio-philosophical approaches. On the one hand, a critical social theory needs a normatively substantial evaluative vocabulary that does not rely on a particular understanding of the good. On the other hand, we must also accept that such vocabulary, however formal, is never completely neutral and always embodies a particular historically contingent vision of the good. There is no easy way out of this dilemma; the alternatives (3.3.2.) have not been satisfactory. This is why I opted for relaxed universalism with a modest validity claim.

Critical social philosophy provides an appealing theoretical framework in which we can situate our notion of authenticity that is yet to be fully defined. This way of situating the concept is adequate to the specific focus of critical social philosophy. Beside this, we have made some progress concerning the overall argument. First of all, we have achieved a normatively situated concept of authenticity and uncovered some of its indispensable preconditions. While current accounts of authenticity neglect the reciprocal shaping of capitalism and the ideal of authenticity, the concept to be constructed here should be able to deal with this inter-twinement. While this contextualization was mostly about the 'outer' framing of a concept of authenticity, it nevertheless has some conse-quences for the preliminary definition of the concept. First, we have seen that authenticity is not sufficiently described in an individual's self-relation. It involves a moment of transcendence, something 'higher' than simply inner motives and urges, thus the co-realization of immanent and agent-transcendent aspects. Yet, for now, the nature of authentic sel-frelation and the characteristic co-realization of (agent) immanent and (agent) transcendent aspects remain unsaid. This will be one of the tasks of the second part of the book.

Part II

Towards a 'Formal' Concept of Authenticity

3   Models of Authenticity

Following the inquiry into the historical sources of the idea of authenticity, we must now complete the picture and assess some established accounts of authenticity. In this chapter I will establish a distinction between what I will call the 'inner sense' and the 'productionist' models of authenticity. According to the inner sense model, authentic inner traits, projects, wishes, etc. are stable and *given* entities that one can access introspectively. The practice of authenticity is then bound to the introspective identification of these individual features. In striking contrast, the productionist model emphasizes the (aesthetic) self-constitution of individuals, often modeled on the production of art. Who I really am is not a matter of discovery then but of a matter of creation or production.

The critical assessment of these two models of authenticity should bring us closer to the overall goal of the next three chapters, namely the construction of a formal account of authenticity. Let us now look at these models while using the famous example of Martin Luther. As is well known, after Luther questioned certain church practices, an official sent by the Archbishop of Trier, named Eck, confronted him, saying that he had no right to teach contrary to the Church or to question its authority. Eck gave Luther a last chance to renounce his teachings and publicly reject their content. Luther resolutely replied: "I cannot and will not recant anything, for to go against conscience is neither right nor safe." Although not entirely documented, Luther continued with the renowned sentences: "Here I stand. I can do no other. God help me. Amen" (Bainton 1950: 142–144). The aftermath of this confrontation was the Edict of Worms, issued by the Emperor on May 25, 1521. It banned his work and declared him a heretic and an outlaw.

1   THE 'INNER SENSE' MODEL

Rousseau appropriated the literary medium of autobiography in order to discover the particular traits that constitute him as a unique individual.

Using this medium helped him introspect, which lastly brought about an "accurate knowledge" of his "inner being" (Rousseau 1782/1957: 148), which he considered to be a decisive feature of authenticity. Importantly, for Rousseau, the only reliable source of orientation that should inform the person's choices in life comes from an 'inner' source. With this elevation of introspection as the path to authenticity, the picture is roughly as follows. Who one really is is a matter that can be settled by introspection best be pursued in a solitary manner, disengaged from one's public activity and political commitments that alienate the self from the self. In Rousseau's view, Luther's choice must take the 'interior' as the single and most important source in guiding his judgment. Using the distinction made by Williams (1981b) between 'internal' and 'external' reasons, we can say that Rousseau's position is internalist. It maintains that those in Luther's position can only be said to have reason to act if they believe some motives are best served by engaging in that action. In this picture, 'external' reasons and justifications cannot justify how Luther should live and act. Rather, he has only good reasons to choose or act in a certain manner if that action is in harmony with those stable and given inner properties ("secret principles," as Rousseau says) that constitute his core identity. In order to attain such knowledge, Rousseau (1782/1957: 148) notes that he needs nothing else but to "enter again into my inner self"—what one discovers there will reveal the path that one ought to follow.

This raises two issues to be taken up in the following. First, we should look closer at how Rousseau answers the central question of authenticity: "How should I live my life, so that it expresses who I truly am?" Here, the response is that an answer can only be achieved by looking into the self in order to detect and discover the deepest motivations. Second, Rousseau implicitly assumes some 'inner sense' mechanism, as Derrida has noted (1997: 17). This is the mechanism that must be in place if we are to detect those inner states, motives, and motivations that truly make up who we are. To put this in more contemporary terms, his model of authenticity relies on the assumption of an inner-directed mechanism whereby we have 'privileged' perceptual access to our inner states. In this view, Luther makes his decision by introspectively detecting and discovering his deepest motivations, a task that is achievable through an 'inner sense,' or inner perception.

To presage the content of the following, I am going to argue that while the inner sense model helps us clarify central issues, it nevertheless fails to provide an adequate account of authenticity. First, the presupposition of an inner mechanism is inherently problematic. Second, even supposing the existence of such a mechanism that could provide the relevant data, one would still fail to answer the question of authenticity.

1.1 'Inner Sense' and Introspection

At first sight, the inner sense story accounts for our intuitions about the sense of intimacy and privileged access we have to our inner states. In most cases, introspection (deriving from the Latin *spicere* and *intra*, look and within) is a term used to refer to this faculty of looking inward upon conscious states, much like an inner *sense*. Most prominently, John Locke held that introspection is "the Perception of the Operations of our own Minds within us"—a sense that has "nothing to do with external Objects; yet it is very like it, and might properly enough be call'd internal Sense" (1689/1975: II.1.iv). In this account, to make his choice, Luther used a faculty somewhat like perception to 'look inward.' This process provided him with a good view of his relevant mental states, motivations, wishes, and so forth, which made available the necessary information to make the right decision. Luther discovered the relevant entities through a kind of 'inner' perception, utilizing a perceptual faculty dedicated to the detection of beliefs and intentions.

David Armstrong has defended a more contemporary view of introspection as a kind of self-scanning process in the brain, in which the connection between the introspective state which does the scanning and the introspected state which is scanned is causal and contingent (1981: 124). As with Locke, Armstrong's model regards introspection as something that is fundamentally similar to perception by involving a monitoring and representative mechanism. As he notes, by outer directed perception, "we become aware of current physical happenings in our environment and in our body. By inner sense, we become aware of our current happenings in our own mind" (Armstrong 1968: 95; also Hill 1991). Also, the inner mechanism functions as a kind of internal scanning device and does not deviate significantly from the way in which one discovers external objects through perception. In all, be it by traditional introspection or some brain scanner, the basic idea is that one's beliefs about inner states, dispositions, etc. are justified by this inner mechanism and its monitoring capacity (see Shoemaker 1968; 1994). In a prominent version of this idea, the inner mechanism provides the agent with something like perceptual evidence.

1.2 Perceptual Evidence

In such a view, the special authority which Luther has when speaking about his own mind exists due to an inner sense mechanism that enables inner observation and makes it possible for Luther to detect his inner states. Also, it is intuitively appealing that Luther is the person in the world with the best possible position from which to speak with authority about those states, because he has the only or at least the most reliable epistemic access to his mental states.

However, a closer look reveals that the inner sense account is susceptible to a range of objections. The first objection could be that even if we admitted the existence of such an inner sense it could not be neatly modeled on externally oriented perception. It is possible to lose a perceptual faculty such as vision or hearing, smell, or taste and continue living with a diminished access to the surroundings without damaging the self or its rationality. This is where the two 'senses' part ways however. If we for a moment imagine the existence of such an inner sense, we quickly see that one cannot lose it without also losing something that is constitutive of personhood, agency and even experience. Sidney Shoemaker (1994) has compellingly argued that no rational agent can suffer from such "self-blindness," since this would amount to being deficient in the skill of sharing beliefs and of all agency that entails higher-order deliberation.

One of the main problems with the perception analogy is brought up by John R. Searle, who notes that the "doctrine of introspection is a good example of what Ludwig Wittgenstein calls the bewitchment of our intelligence by means of language" (Searle 1992: 105). In Searle's account introspection differs essentially from perception. While perception involves a clear distinction between subject and object, this distinction is fuzzy in introspection. At least, in order to maintain the model of inner inspection we need to posit a clear distinction between that which inspects and the object that is being inspected. But this very distinction obscures the special relation we entertain with our mental states and dispositions. Besides this issue, Searle goes on to argue that this model of introspection, implying the existence of a particular inner sense mechanism, ultimately leads to an infinite regress. This is simply because the awareness of a mental state is gained through an inwardly directed perceptive act, which also constitutes a mental state. If this is true, then the same procedure also has to apply to this second state: this is also a mental state that we must access through another higher order act of perception, and so on. It is not difficult to see how this leads to an infinite regress. Acknowledging the limits of introspection modeled on perception, Searle rightly instructs us to understand introspection in a metaphorical sense.

In the inner sense model, the irreducible distinctiveness and intimacy of the first-person position is guaranteed through the mind's access to itself. It is considered privileged and in some cases infallible. Nonetheless, the account is problematic insofar as it maintains that Luther's knowledge of his own state of mind, attitude, or commitment is based on observation and consulting evidence via the mechanism of inner sense. The idea is flawed, because in introspection one cannot simply detect an *independently obtaining* state of mind.

1.3   Behavioral Evidence and Inference

There is a way of working around the problems described above. There are ways of avoiding the vicious regress that threatens the inner sense account while holding on to its intuitively positive features, for instance its capacity to explain the special acquaintance and authority we have concerning our mental states.

A radical version of this idea is found in Gilbert Ryle, who tried to show that the there is no fundamental difference between our awareness of internal states and of objects in the world, or in other words between intro-spection and ordinary perception. Ryle's famous formulation partly reveals his behaviorist rejection of privileged access: "John Doe's ways of finding out about John Doe are the same as John Doe's ways of finding out about Richard Doe" (Ryle 1967: 156). Privileged access simply stems from the commonplace fact that I am the one who has the best opportunity for constantly observ-ing my behavior. While this view also involves adopting an observational stance on oneself, it is simultaneously immune to obvious counterexamples that touch on the issue of infallible self-knowledge. In other words, it is in better harmony with the fact that we are sometimes not the best judges of whether we are angry, annoyed, or jealous.[1] Ryle assumed that the only viable alternative to the 'inner-sense' model of self-knowledge is that all knowledge of mental states must have an inferential basis (Zimmermann 2008).

Altogether, the similarities of the 'inner sense' to perceptive faculties can be brought into doubt and the whole existence of an inner detection mechanism can be questioned. Ryle's attempt to solve this problem is how-ever bought at the price of wholly giving up the idea of a special, qualitative acquaintance with the self. In principle, it would be possible for someone to know your mind better and to speak about it with greater authority than yourself. Such a view has wide-reaching implications; for our purposes it is sufficient to note that the consequence would be denying our constitutive role or agency in regard to our 'inner life.'

1.4   Making Up Our minds—Agency and Transparency

In that case, without buying into the idea of an inner sense mechanism, how can we hold on to our intuitions about intimate self-relation and self-knowledge while simultaneously maintaining our constitutive agency towards our mental life? The solution involves a fundamental departure from the inner sense account that can be achieved in two steps that connect to the issues of (a) agency and (b) transparency.

(a) John McDowell has attempted to retain the idea that the agent has a constitutive role pertaining to her states of mind while keeping some of the aspects that characterize the inner sense approach. Just as perceptual judgments are rationally constrained by experiences of the outer world, our judgments about inner states are constrained by experiences of the inner world. McDowell therefore constructs a model that includes introspection and outward perception but at the same time tries to account for the par-ticularly intimate relation we have with our own mental states. He recom-mends that we should "think about 'inner sense' in parallel with 'outer sense' to the fullest extent that is possible" (McDowell 1996: 22). While this may initially sound very much like the standard inner sense (mechanism) account, McDowell introduces an important difference between inner and outer sense. In fact, McDowell consistently puts "inner" in scare quotes, reminding us that the inner is not to be understood literally as referring to something in our heads. He notes that while the objects of outer sense have an independent existence, the objects of inner sense cannot exist independently of our awareness of them (Ibid.: 21). For instance, without some awareness of my pain, I cannot be said to be in pain. Therefore, in such cases we cannot make out a clear distinction between the inner impression and what it is an impression of. McDowell (Ibid.: 36) notes that in many cases the object of inner experience "has no existence independently of the awareness that the experience constitutes." Thus, unlike the 'outer sense,' awareness of mental states to a certain extent constitutes the states in question. The advantage of McDowell's account is that it explains the special authority we have over our mental states—sometimes, it is simply the case that our awareness of our mental states is constitutive of them.

Both Gareth Evans (1982) and Richard Moran point out that bringing mental life to consciousness involves a "stance of agency beyond that of being a kind of expert witness" to one's internal states (Moran 2001: 4). Bringing into play both the issue of the constituting agency of the person and the dynamic relation between first-person reflection and mental states, Moran holds that acquiring knowledge of our inner life is not a neutral epistemic undertaking, since it involves a self-reflection that has certain "specific consequences for the object of consciousness" (2001: 28). With this move, we leave behind the inner sense account. Mental states cannot just be thought of as stable entities that await introspective discovery and they are not independent *objects* that can be detected by an inner-directed quasiperceptual act.

(b) The second step towards a solution involves another departure from the inner sense (mechanism) account. In some cases, rather than looking inward, we acquire knowledge of inner life by looking *at the world*. Ryle doubts whether coming to know ourselves (and our states of mind) involves turning inward at all; he rather focuses on semi-privileged observation of our behavior. Others have suggested opting for an even broader view of self-knowledge, which focuses not only on self-directed observation, but also on how the world is presented. Jean-Paul Sartre (1957: 31) held that the known self "is outside, in the world. It is a being of the world, like the ego of another." For Sartre, the way we establish knowledge about some thoughts, motivations, and feelings is by looking *outward* to the world. More recently, Evans has spelled out what such a view can amount to. Evans (1982: 225) maintains that when making a self-ascription of belief, instead of looking inward, "one's eyes are, so to speak, or occasionally literally, directed outward—upon the world." Evans continues: "If someone asks me 'Do you think there is going to be a third world war?' I must attend, in answering him, to precisely the same outward phenomena as I would attend to if I were answering the question 'Will there be a third world war?'" This look 'outward' refers to what Moran calls "transparency." To be able to decide whether one holds the belief 'that *x*,' one must also, to a certain extent, attempt to decide whether the case really is *x*, and this involves 'looking outward' and examining evidence regarding *x*. This also means that the belief 'that *x*' involved is open or 'transparent' to outer evidence regarding *x*.

At this point, we can connect these two issues of agency (active reflection) and the 'look outward.' Thus, we do not just discover our inner states but to a certain extent constitute them by a process that also involves a deliberative look 'outward,' focusing one's attention not to the belief itself as the object of knowledge but to states of affairs in the external world. In this view, first-person authority is sometimes a matter of looking 'outward' and determining our beliefs, which is not simply the discovery of a pre-existing belief, but a process of its constitution. Consequently, while with McDowell we established that far from being passive observers of our independent inner, our agency has a unique role to play in understanding our mental states, with Moran and Evans we can now hold that this agency involves reflection, weighing reasons and looking 'outward'. Of course, one could reasonably object that the looking 'outward' is a far cry from really permitting us to detect pre-existing mental states. Instead, such a look 'outward' may simply function as an incitement to bring into being new mental states. Even if this were the case, the interesting dimension here is the aspect of outward looking deliberation. When I am asked, "do you want a glass of wine?" I not so much look inward to seek advice from a set of pre-existing desires but instead direct attention towards the wine as the object of knowledge while trying to deliberate on its attractiveness. This amounts to passing a judgment.

We have thus come far from the initial fundamental assumptions of the inner sense model on authenticity. Introspection as depicted in the inner sense view cannot represent the path to authenticity. Discovering inner traits and the deepest motivations of the self through a kind of 'inner' perception, utilizing a perceptual-like faculty begins to look untenable when considering the vast amount of plausible counter-arguments. Luther's example cannot be adequately described within the model of inner sense.

1.5 Inner Sense and Authenticity: Epistemic Access or Practical Deliberation?

Let us now, for a second, disregard these arguments and imagine that Luther was somehow able to detect what he was really about as the inner sense (mechanism) model suggests. The point I want to make through this experiment is that even in that case Luther would still fail to answer the question concerning authenticity.

Martin Heidegger (1998: 30) warns us not to confuse how we understand objects with the way we understand ourselves, maintaining that the meaning of our *being* is not accessible by means of inner perception or any observation. Adopting an observational stance towards oneself in order to answer the question of who we are and how we should act would mean confusing two kinds of 'is.' Heidegger differentiates between 'the sense of is,' (Seinssinn) and 'the sense of existence' (Existenzsinn). "When it has the sense of 'is,' the sense of being (*Seinssinn*) has developed from objectively oriented experiences that have been explicated in 'theoretical' knowledge, and in which we always somehow or other say of *something* that it 'is something'" (Heidegger 1998: 30). However, when it comes to knowing ourselves and seeking orientation in life, the sense of 'is' that arises from detached observation cannot be of any help. Rather, the relevant sense of 'is' arises from "*what is of significance to us* in our experience of the environing world, the social world we share with each other, and also the world of the self" (Ibid.: 30). This other sense of 'is' is what Heidegger terms the 'sense of existence': "When the sense of existence is investigated in terms of its origin and our genuine basic experience of it, we see that it is precisely *that* sense of being that cannot be obtained from the 'is' we use to explicate and objectify our experience in one way or another when we acquire knowledge about it. The sense of existence is to be obtained rather from its own basic experience of having itself 'in an *anxiously concerned* manner'" (Ibid.: 26).

It is worth noting that Heidegger has been accused of being an adherent of both an inner sense approach and productionism. Ferrara (1998: 53) accuses Heidegger and existential philosophy of taking up an inner sense approach and thus of holding the view "that every human possesses an essential core, a kind of psychological DNA." In contrast, Habermas (1978: 141) argues that Heidegger falls prey to a kind of productionism. This is what he terms "the decisionism of empty resoluteness." In opposition to these charges, Heidegger distinguishes between a *theoretical* and a *practical-deliberative* route to knowledge about the self. The point is that a theoretical stance involving observation and inference, however privileged or 'inner,' will *in principle* not allow us knowledge about who we are 'deep inside' and what is of true significance to us. I say 'in principle' because the case would not be any different if we assumed the actual existence of a particular inner sense mechanism that detects such states. Even if we counterfactually imagine Luther as somehow able to observe, detect, and discover his deepest motivations and attitudes, with the relevant knowledge in hand, he would still be unable to answer the question pertaining to authenticity, which is something like "How should I live my life so that it expresses who I truly am?" This question cannot be answered by a look into the self in order to detect inner states, because when we look into ourselves we find a vast amount of interlocking and conflicting wishes and motivations. If the inner sense model were right, then we could simply detect which of these wishes is the strongest and most pertinent. This would not however be able to help us settle the original question. *The fact that a particular wish (desire, etc.) is stronger than others does not warrant regarding it as more expressive of ourselves than any of the other less resilient ones.* Luther may have had a strong wish to live a calm life in which he would not be deemed an outlaw. In fact, it may have been his strongest wish at that time. The strength of a wish can of course sometimes be the source of valuable knowledge about ourselves. For example, it can retrospectively explain an action that one has undertaken. However, both in general and in Luther's case, the strength of a wish or motivation can never by itself explain why one should follow it or even endorse it. So even if Luther detects a strongest wish to live a calm life, it does not mean that he really endorses it as his and as something that is good for him to follow (Menke 2005: 315). As Korsgaard argues, we are able to turn our attention to our own mental activities but also distance ourselves from them.

> I desire and I find myself with a powerful impulse to act. But I back up and bring that impulse into view and then I have a certain distance. Now the impulse doesn't dominate me and now I have a problem. Shall I act? Is this desire really a reason to act? The reflective mind cannot settle for perception and desire, not just as such. It needs a reason. Otherwise, at least as long as it reflects, it cannot commit itself or go forward (Korsgaard 1996: 93).

In other words, even if one gains epistemic knowledge of such an extremely strong wish, desire, or motive, it does not mean that one *reflexively* conceives of this wish as one's own, as expressive of who one takes oneself to be. It does not mean that one *authenticates* it as truly belonging to oneself. Before we can act on a desire, we must authenticate and reflectively endorse it, which involves treating this fact about oneself as a justifying reason (Bratman 1999: 197–198). In Kantian terms, we are compelled to make it into a maxim to act on the wish, desire, or motive in question.

Clearly the inner sense model fails to answer the question it set out to answer: who am I really and how should I act? These questions cannot be answered by detecting the strength of inner entities. In other words, who we are is not an epistemological issue that we settle by gathering evidence about ourselves, be it through privileged or less privileged routes. To be more precise, the question is inherently practical and involves deliberation about whether an attitude of mine really is one that I endorse and thereby *authenticate*. For this reason we must think of the relation between detection and what is detected, not in epistemic terms, but in inherently practical and normative terms. Who we are is partly constituted by what we value, aspire to, respect, care about, and admire. To paraphrase Taylor (1989: 27), to know who we are is simply a matter of knowing where we stand. Heidegger (1998: 26) goes further and maintains that if I base my judgment of how I should act to express who I am on what my theoretical gaze (inner sense, observation, inference, etc.) reveals to me, "all my explications will then have an objectifying nature, but they will put me at a remove from existence and from a genuine having of it (anxious concern)." Instead of authenticity, we would have a case of self-alienation.

The inner sense model simply fails to identify the self-evaluation and authentication involved in dealing with one's states: 'mineness' is not about detecting a mental entity like a wish and registering its strength, but about the agent's active avowal or disavowal of that wish. Whenever

I ascribe attitudes to myself in the normative way, it is the outcome of an evaluation. This means that I must regard myself as committed to those attitudes. If I would simply detect inner objects and maintain that they are expressive of me without evaluating them then I would lose any kind of agency or authority over my 'inner.' If these states, beliefs, motivations, etc. were simply objects of knowledge for me, then my usual sense of authority would be replaced by a sense of self-alienation. This suggests that the authority involved is not passive and epistemic but active and normative. We take a deliberative stance toward our own states of mind and thus play an active role in constituting ourselves. Another appealing feature of this view, which this account of authenticity will build on, is that evaluation involves openness to the outer world, in both an epistemic (as deliberating about evidence regarding the state) and a normative (as deliberating about whether it ought to be the case) sense. This means that to be mine, to be expressive of myself, I have to conceive of a belief or intention of mine as open to change by external factors like evidence or moral considerations. In other words, the authenticity or 'mineness' of my belief involves some commitment to its truth which transcends any descriptive identification of my inner state.

Before working out what this involves, let us consider a rival, non-inner sense model that emphasizes self-constituting agency, producing completely different conclusions.

2   THE "PRODUCTIONIST" MODEL

In contrast to Rousseau, Nietzsche can be viewed as a proponent of a wholly different model that focuses on the active component of self-relationships and rejects the idea of an 'inner sense.' I will refer to this as the 'productionist' model of authenticity, since it emphasizes active involvement in constituting who we are through wishes, desires, and motivations; we somehow produce or create them.

The idea of self-creation in Nietzsche is an aesthetic modification of an idea that is found in Greco-Roman thinkers. Nietzsche (1974: 335) clearly opposes the inner sense model and emphasizes the element of active self-production. Authentic individuals "want to become those we are—human beings who are new, unique, incomparable, who give himself or herself laws, who create himself or herself." Similarly, Foucault describes the turn-of-the-century figure of the metropolitan dandy who creates himself and shapes his life as a work of art. Such an individual is far from being the inner sense individual "who goes off to discover himself, his secrets and his hidden truth; he is the man who tries to invent himself" (Foucault 1984a: 41–42). Foucault argues that since the subject is not given in advance, it has to create itself as a work of art (Foucault 1984b: 392). Regarding the ethical concern about one's own existence, only aesthetic values should be applied. To the absence of morality "corresponds, must correspond, the search for aesthetics of existence" (Foucault 1988: 49). The recognition that there is no such thing as an authentic self given to that very self leads him to the conclusion that we ought to craft ourselves as works of art.

Another contemporary and prominent version of this idea is defended by Richard Rorty. His early work was critical of Ryle's radical assessment of introspection, but suggested that

> our knowledge of what we are like on the inside is no more "direct" or "intuitive" than our knowledge of what things are like in the "external world." For knowledge to be "direct" is simply for it to be gained without going through an introspectible process of inference—so that we know with *equal* directness that we feel nostalgic, that something before us is brown, that it is a table, that it is the table that used to stand next to the fireplace in our childhood home, and so on (Rorty 1982: 330–331).

Thus, while Ryle is taken to be wrong to throw out the whole idea of introspection and introspective events, Rorty argues that there is nothing truly exceptional about self-knowledge. At the same time, he is clearly sympathetic to a kind of nominalism about the mind, noting that beyond the vocabulary of natural science "there are the vocabularies of our moral and our political life and of the arts, of all those human activities which are not aimed at prediction and control but rather in giving us self-images which are worthy of our species. Such images are not true to the nature of species or false to it, for what is really distinctive about us is that we can rise above questions of truth or falsity" (Rorty 1982: 346). In the same paper, we find a first indication of his commitment to what I have called productionism: "We are the poetic species, the one which can change itself by changing its behavior—and especially its linguistic behavior, the words it uses" (Ibid.).

In line this with his earlier work, he later maintains that the kind of self-knowledge involved in the idea of authenticity, the idea of coming to "know a truth which was out there (or in here) all the time" (Rorty 1989: 27), is simply a myth. In his account, authenticity is not a matter of discovering antecedent facts, validated by a detected correspondence, and he declares the "final victory of metaphors of self-creation over metaphors of discovery" (Ibid.: 40).

More radically, he also questions the legitimacy of distinguishing between authentic and inauthentic modes of existence. In the process of private self-creation, privilege cannot be given to any specific self-definition. Instead, and it is here that Rorty democratizes Nietzsche, the complete range of methods in self-creation must be viewed as expressive of human nature. Rorty describes the ideal modern intellectual as a "liberal ironist," a person who accepts the contingency of the vocabulary that constitutes selfhood. This is a person who is "ironic, playful, free, and inventive" and who moves freely between different vocabularies as tools, while knowing that they all fall short of conveying a final truth about the self. Therefore, the ironist can only be committed to an ironic stance on stances. For the liberal ironist, authenticity is achieved through the emancipatory re-creation of existing vocabularies that come about in creating an 'own vocabulary.' This process inevitably starts from the collective vocabulary that we are born into, but the goal is to develop one's own unique vocabulary and new descriptions of the truth about oneself. The liberal ironic is "the person who uses words as they have never before been used" (Rorty 1989: 28). Rorty does not deny that self-production and the production of a unique vocabulary becomes possible only against the background of a shared vocabulary and an intelligible web of practices. But importantly, the crucial point is that since one cannot assume to discover a veracious or 'objective' answer to the question "who am I," no particular vocabulary of oneself can be embraced as more true than any other. According to Rorty, this is simply impossible, since we do not have a neutral standpoint from which such an assessment could be accomplished.

Like the inner sense model, this approach also relies on the existence of certain capabilities and a mechanism that allow for an authentic self-relation. While the inner sense model implicitly assumes some kind of mechanism through which we detect those inner states that make up who we are, the productionist model must imply the existence of some mechanism that allows us to produce or create states, but also traits and dispositions. As with the previous case, I am going to treat this issue on two levels and argue that even though this model helps us clarify aspects about agency, it nevertheless fails to account adequately for authenticity. First, the presupposition of the relevant mechanism is inherently problematic. Second, even supposing the existence of such a mechanism, the productionist model would fail to answer the question which authenticity is about.

2.1   Productionism: The Mechanism

As noted in connection with the brief discussion of 'transparency,' the knowledge of one's beliefs and mental states should—in particular cases—be viewed as a kind of production or constitution rather than discovery. In some cases, acquiring knowledge about whether one holds a belief that *P* is not achieved through the same kind of observational stance towards the inner life that one would adopt when aiming to gather knowledge about states of affairs in the world. In such cases we simply get to 'make up our minds,' or to put it differently, facts about our mental lives are in such cases simply fixed by self-ascription. As David Finkelstein (2003: 28) describes this position, "typically, what I say or think about my own mental state plays a constitutive role in determining what it is. Mental self-ascriptions are unlike observation reports in that they constitute, to some significant extent, the facts to which they refer." In this account the agent possesses non-observational, non-inferential, and authoritative knowledge, and in the case of a sincere and competent agent, one's psychological avowals cannot be challenged rationally (Coliva 2008). On the mechanism-level, Crispin Wright has defended a version of 'productionism' concerning propositional attitudes, but he has delimited his case to what he calls 'phenomenal avowals,' such as 'I have a headache' or 'I am tired' (1998, 14). The point is that some beliefs like the self-ascriptions of 'I believe that P' simply bring into being the matching first-order mental state, namely the belief that P. If we accept that our knowing any kind of truth is achieved via either inference or observation, the conclusion that Wright embraces is that such instances of self-knowledge are not really based on anything.

While Wright admits that such constitutive agency does not apply to all self-knowledge and mental states, this mechanism-level idea is generalized in the productionist model of authenticity. A person's own stipulation (or interpretation) of his mental state being in a certain way is sufficient for its being that way. McDowell's modest point that our awareness of our mental states to an extent constitutes the state in question is radicalized here. The productionist point is that whenever we think and describe our inner states with our vocabulary we simply determine their quality; our agency, our deployment of a conceptual vocabulary simply determines 'the inner.'

2.2 Productionism II

In a way, productionism faces the same difficulties as the inner sense account. The inner sense idea holds that we come to know ourselves through an inwardly directed (perceptive) act and thus fails to acknowledge the non-objective nature of mental states. In contrast, the productionist conception falls short because it overemphasizes the non-objective nature of mental states and therefore does not acknowledge the disruptive, spontaneous, and uncontrollable character of mental states. We are sometimes surprised by the power with which our emotions, intentions, and feelings overwhelm us, as it often is the case in for instance jealousy. We are here passively exposed to the emotion, often without being able to attain an interpretative distance to it. It is therefore very difficult to square the everyday phenomenology of mental states that surprise us and pop out of nowhere with Rorty's description of inner states. These do not always possess the kind of flexibility that one would need to adequately describe them within the productionist model. The seemingly endless capacity for self-attribution clearly fails to account for the phenomenology of a wide range of inner states that catch us by surprise.

Also, the transparency of certain kinds of self-knowledge is lost in productionism. Rather than being open to issues in the world or to reasons, the truth criteria for self-descriptions are now only relative to personally chosen vocabularies. This has some immediate and problematic consequences, because it means abandoning the independent backdrop against which different self-descriptions can be assessed.

Additionally, one might suspect that identifying selves as self-weaving webs of beliefs and desires comes at the price of incoherence. On the one hand, Rorty departs from Nietzsche and does not embrace the strong concept of the sovereign self that simply creates itself *ex nihilo*, independently from a cultural background, or as Rorty prefers to say 'vocabulary.' On the other hand, it is obvious that the same idea of the sovereign self (that executes this self-weaving) is smuggled in through the backdoor. A good part of this criticism also applies to Foucault and Nietzsche. The idea of life as a material for an aesthetic piece of art, and the underlying assumption that one can relate to the self as to objectively given materials that one can manipulate leads to a fundamental terminological problem. When grasping a self-relation in these terms, the unobjectifiable and performative dimension is not taken into account. In other words, it is simply wrong to say that life *has* material. Instead, it is lived material and there is therefore no outside, no neutral place that is not a part of the *material* of life, from where the self could shape its life like an artist. Applying the idea of aesthetic production would presume a distance between material and artist, which is not the case. On a more general level, we can say that the conduct of life is a performative process, in the sense that the material of life cannot be separated from its execution. It is therefore misleading to conceptualize 'bios' as material for a work of art. The fact of authoritative agency, which entails that awareness of mental states is to a certain extent constitutive of them, does not mean that we simply create mental states or lives as works of art. Both versions overstate their point and fail to take into account the constitutively dynamic and somewhat opaque nature of self-relation.

It is not difficult to understand the motivation for embracing productionism. For instance, in Rorty's case, his account based on a concept of irony—as a central feature of the ideal liberalist—takes on the difficult task of both critically addressing life in modernity while at the same time remaining safe from accusations of paternalism. This gesture may be seen as an inheritance from French thinkers like Foucault, whose attempt to address such issues without being prescriptive had a political motivation. The idea is that if nobody claims to have the 'right' interpretation of how a good life should be led then no one could be pressured into adopting a certain lifestyle. This is of course a worthy motivation, but in the end the emphasis on irony erodes the foundation of the whole project. If the ironic liberal has deep-seated doubts about the entire range of vocabularies, then the same radical doubt must also apply to the vocabulary of irony within which these doubts are understood. In other words, to be ironic necessarily involves being ironic about being ironic, and thus not taking this vocabulary seriously either. The ultimate consequence is that the ironist would not have any reason to adopt one vocabulary over any other.

This also sheds light on a weak point in Foucault's argument: if the self is not *somehow* given, what should then justify Foucault's normative verdict that we *must* create ourselves as a work of art? (see also Taylor 1986). Similarly, Richard Shusterman (1992: ch. 9) questions the logical adequacy of this statement. If the lack of an essence of human nature precludes a *particular* ethical approach then it cannot be taken to support this *particular* (aesthetical) ethical approach. In an attempt to avoid such difficulties, Rorty has provided another argument in favour of the ironic life. He contrasts two antithetical forms of authenticity in an essay on Heidegger, "a search for purity" and "a search for self-enlargement" (Rorty 1991: 154), and clearly supports the idea of authentic self-enlargement, a "life that seeks to extend its own bound rather than find its centre" (Ibid.). With this, Rorty not only leaves the inner sense model behind, but also Nietzsche. Authenticity is not about discovering some basic core self, nor is it about the artistic integration of the raw material of life into a whole that must then be defended against leveling and disintegrating societal forces. One should adopt the ironic vocabulary not because it adequately integrates the self around central motivations, but because it is an expansive vocabulary that allows for more forms of self-weaving. This runs into similar difficulties however. Being decisively ironic must also involve being ironic about the idea of self-enlargement, leaving the ironic without reason to choose such a life.

If we—for the sake of argument—ignore these problems for a moment, we could ask what the self-enlarging life of such an ironic intellectual would be like. The ironic would try out new vocabularies, but declaring none of them more expressive of her then any other. Understanding oneself as a mere placeholder for shifting vocabularies cannot give rise to a wholehearted identification with any single vocabulary. Arguably, completely lacking any wholehearted identification with a vocabulary, the ironist would experience herself and the narrative she is weaved into as arbitrary. She would lack a center around which experiences can become intelligible and she would be left in a disorienting ethical void; she would not know whether the life being led really is one that is hers to lead (Jopling 2000: 132). This would bring about a sense of not owning her life, because being a devoted ironist involves conceiving one's life story as something that happens 'outside' in an object-like manner. It is difficult to imagine how such a detached and ironic agent should actively engage in life and develop a sense for a particular path of life really belonging to her.

To sum up, the ironic liberal is correct to be skeptical about any idea of the substantiality of the self and about a 'final vocabulary' that reveals the objective truth about the self.[2] However, she confuses the third-person description with the first-person aspects of experience. From the third-person perspective, it is indeed untenable to appeal to the idea of a final vocabulary revealing the ultimate truth about oneself. But from the first-person perspective one has to regard a particular vocabulary to be true, in the sense of being more expressive of oneself than other vocabularies. What is more, it is necessary to have this center that we create by authenticating and identifying with a single vocabulary. This is simply, as Frankfurt (2006: 19) also notes, what integrates the self over time. It is only by having such a (however fictional from a third-person perspective) center that we can make judgments and choose to identify with or disavow our mental states, weaving them into a more or less coherent whole.

2.3   Inner Sense and Productionism

Both the inner sense and the productionist models fail to provide an adequate account of authenticity. Of course, both accounts have appealing features in their favor. The inner sense account is strong in accounting for the strangeness and overwhelming quality of our feelings and motivations, while the productionist account makes our everyday experience of having some authority over our inner life intelligible. However, neither is able to answer the question of authenticity: How should I live my life so that it is expressive of who I truly am? The inner sense model builds on the idea of privileged introspection, implying the existence of a particular inner sense mechanism. The idea of introspection as a (quasi)perceptual *act* of becoming aware of an independent *object* ultimately leads to problems. Mental states are not simply stable entities that await introspective discovery. Productionism overemphasizes this, maintaining that far from being something substantial or pre-given, selves are incessantly self-weaving webs of intentions and desires. From this outlook, we are familiar with ourselves not because we are in a privilegded position to discover ourselves but because we 'produce' or invent ourselves through our own vocabulary. This however implicitly involves the problematic idea of some sovereign agent that executes the weaving.

In this chapter the inner sense model of authenticity was also called into question from another angle. Recall that the reason for engaging in introspection is to seek guidance for our actions, and in this case we have to think of the relation between detection and what is detected not in epistemic, but in normative terms, entailing deliberation, reflection, and lastly, identification. The inner sense model simply fails to see the dimension of self-evaluation that is present when we deal with our feelings, wishes, and motivations. The 'mineness' of a wish does not spring from its persuasiveness or strength, but from my active avowal of it. The productionist model of authenticity is strong on emphasizing the creative agency of the self but ends up overemphasizing it. In order to have a sense of ourselves as agents, we must understand ourselves as more than placeholders for random configurations of vocabularies. Ironism makes it impossible to identify with particular vocabularies, which is central to the emergence of a sense of ownership. Lastly, both inner sense and productionist selves would be paralyzed selves, lacking basic existential orientation and lacking a unified sense of agency. The inner sense self would lack an understanding of the self as at least partly constituted by actions upon that self. The productionist who does not make recourse to any self-transcending framework to evaluate the possible vocabularies would have difficulties choosing a vocabulary from the limitless array of possibilities, and that deficiency would simultaneously render the chosen identity random and meaningless. Later I will elaborate more on this issue and argue that authenticity depends on the embeddedness in a collective, inter-subjective horizon of significance.

Moreover, both inner sense and productionism fail to acknowledge the issue of normativity. While I am going to deal with this issue at length in the next chapter, there is an important point that needs to be mentioned. When I identify with an introspectively achieved or self-constituted aspect of myself, my motivation to identify with this aspect is contingent on whether I am able to see this as something *good*. To a certain extent, even the ironic liberal must also assume that the ironic way of life is something good, something to be followed, and something that it is of higher value than others. If not, the ironist faces something like a value version of the transparency condition in Moore's paradox: "Who I really am, what I really identify with is *P*, but *P* is not good or valuable in any way." Now there would be something inherently wrong with this. Such a stance would involve dissatisfaction with P, which would prevent me from identifying with *P* in the first place. Of course, from a third-person standpoint the fact of me identifying with P does not answer the question of whether *P* is good. But from the first-person perspective it is inevitable. If I identify with *P*, I must also hold *P* 'true' in the sense as something better, higher, or more worthy, something I ought to follow. In this version of the transparency condition, it is not the case that my identifying with P is amenable to reasons as such, but to values. As already noted, this issue will be further explored and underpinned in Chapter 4.

3 AUTHENTICATION AND IDENTIFICATION

The notion of identification is central to the account given here and it must be further clarified to understand the sense in which it is deployed. In the following I am going to draw on this notion as it has been discussed in contemporary theories of personal autonomy.

In Chapter 1, in the context of our tracing the historical sources of authenticity, I used the Kantian concept of 'moral autonomy' as a contrast. As we have seen, both moral autonomy and authenticity share the view that normativity in the relevant sense derives from the capability of the subject to follow a self-imposed principle free of manipulative external forces. Also, both emphasize the individual's self-governing abilities that she utilizes independently of her position in political and social structures. However, while in the Kantian account moral autonomy is characterized by its being formed by principles, the concept of authenticity accommodates some of our more affective impulses that may conflict with principles.

As a first rough approximation, the concept of personal autonomy can be situated somewhere between moral autonomy and authenticity. Very roughly, actors can be said to be personally autonomous when they engage with a very diverse selection of life aspects that goes beyond moral obligation and the ability to impose the moral law on oneself (Dworkin 1988). Of course, it also emphasizes the capacity to decide for oneself, the independence of one's freedom of deliberation and choice from manipulation and paternalistic interventions by others, as well as the ability to critically examine one's own behavior. But as Joseph Raz (1986: 370 fn.) has noted, personal autonomy also involves a specific notion of the good, an ideal of individual well-being, and "should not be confused with the only very indirectly related notion of moral autonomy." So while personal autonomy also refers to a capacity for self-governance, it is more broadly conceived as encompassing our choices of commitment to personal projects, relationships, and ideals. On such an understanding, Anderson (2008: 8) maintains that "being autonomous is a matter of being competent to guide oneself in such a way that what motivates one's actions are the considerations by which one genuinely wants to be motivated, rather than (ordinarily, at least) by unconscious prejudices, compulsive obsessions, or the like." So some aspect of authenticity is at stake in the notion of personal autonomy. As John Christman (1988: 108) asks: "After all, can a person be said to be free or acting freely if the desires which produce those actions do not bear the pedigree of authenticity—the person's 'true desires'?" Again, the Kantian may approve such a position, maintaining that autonomy can be rightly ascribed when the behavior of the agent is determined by his 'nature.' But in a Kantian context, this would mean acting guided by practical reason, which places every agent under universal laws (Velleman 2006: 332).

Our motives are not always transparent to us, and we often simultaneously have multiple and incompatible standards of evaluation. In this sense, personal autonomy also involves the practice of negotiation and integration between different motives and standards of evaluation, and this is why it is so closely tied to authenticity. Now the question is what exactly is meant by personal autonomy and how does it tie in with our discussion of authenticity and identification?

3.1 Personal Autonomy and Identification

According to classical compatibilism, two conditions have to be met for an agent to act freely. First, the agent must act in accordance with his motivations. Second, it must be the case that the agent could have acted otherwise had he wanted to do so—the so-called condition of alternative possibilities. As Harry Frankfurt and many others have pointed out, this account cannot explain a case like that of an unwilling addict who is moved against his own will. In theory the addict would meet the two conditions set by compatibilism. For Frankfurt, to whom this is counter-intuitive, this account also fails because it has nothing to say about the freedom of the will, which is about being free to have the will one wants to have or being able to endorse the will that one is moved by. Frankfurt emphasizes our competence to form reflective judgments about our beliefs and desires. His hierarchical, two-level account is based on this distinction. For instance, one might have a first-order desire that urges one to smoke a cigarette, while at the same time one may form a second-order desire that one does not really want the urge to smoke a cigarette to guide one's actions. So I act freely whenever the desire that guides my action is one that I endorse and identify with and therefore want to guide my action. This is in contrast to the addict, whose action of using drugs often stems from a desire that he does not reflectively endorse (Frankfurt 1988b: 34).

The formations of second-order volitions are put in terms of identification (Frankfurt 1988a: 18). Whenever I want a particular desire to shape the will that I act on, I identify with it. So in an important sense second-order desires express the "real self" (Dworkin 1989, 59), while first-order desires express only the "superficial self," as Cuypers (1998: 46) puts it. With this distinction between the 'real self' involving second-order desires and identifications, we are clearly discussing a matter that is at the heart of the concept of authenticity. Nonetheless, it has been objected that the idea that identifications reveal who one really is inescapably leads to several problems.

First, the question that immediately arises is why second-order, rather than first-order, desires reflect the 'true self' of the person in question. Gary Watson (1975) and Marilyn Friedman (1986) have questioned whether second-order volitions are more indicative of the person than any first-order desires. Watson argued that first-order phenomena should be granted this status. Recalling our criticism of the inner sense model, we may reasonably doubt whether Watson's strategy would work. First-order entities are sometimes just brute facts of our inner life. They seem to come out of nowhere and force themselves upon us. The sense of 'mineness' that also autonomy theorists take to be central is simply not settled by detecting such inner impulses. Instead of being theoretical-epistemological, the question is inherently practical. In this sense 'mineness' is not intrinsic to any state, but the outcome of my deliberation and, lastly, identification. It is a practice, something that we do. I shall later use the term authentication to underscore particular aspects connected to this matter which 'identification' may not always convey.

Second, it has also been argued that second-order identifications lead to a vicious regress (Watson 1975; Thalberg 1978). If one claims that the authority granted to a given first-order desire (say order x) relies on a second-order desire $(x + 1)$ in which the person identifies with x, then the question is what establishes the authority of the second-order desire in question, if not the appeal to a third-order phenomena $(x + 2)$. But in that case, it is difficult to see how a regress can be avoided. Frankfurt answered his critics and reinforced his view by further narrowing the issue of second-order desires. His point is that we should only consider *wholehearted* second-order desires (desires that come in absence of any inclination to change them) as really belonging to the 'real self' and as being genuine signs of autonomy. Identification counts as wholehearted when it is "made in the belief that no further accurate inquiry would require (the person) to change his mind" (1988c: 169). Accordingly, it is not a certain higher level of reflection or identification that blocks the threatening regress, but a certain quality the identification displays, namely wholeheartedness. This is characterized by a certain sense of certainty and satisfaction, which is not an additional attitude (Frankfurt 1999c: 105).

3.2 Wholeheartedness

Often we do not have a single wish or desire, but several at the same time. This may lead to conflicts. Which desire do we then prioritize as the one that should guide our actions? Frankfurt distinguishes between two sorts of incoherence. There may be a conflict between what is the most powerful desire and the desire that one most wishes to be moved by (Frankfurt 1988c: 164–166). Luther may have been in a situation where his desire for a calm life effectively motivates his behavior, while he really would have preferred not to act upon it. The incoherence would then be between two levels of the will. The first-order desire of tranquility and peace clashes with higher-order volition. The negative outcome of this conflict could be that he is unable to do what he truly wants in terms of higher-order volition. In that case, he would not identify with the will that actually guides his actions and he may feel that his will is imposed on him by something that feels like an external force.

Another and more serious incoherence can arise when a discrepancy appears between two entities on the level of higher-order volitions. As Frankfurt maintains, such conflict "does not concern the relation between volition and will. It is a matter not of volitional strength but of whether the highest-order preferences concerning some volitional issues are *wholehearted*" (Frankfurt 1988c: 165). Such a person has no unequivocal answer to what he really wants and thus there is an incoherence within his volitional complex. In other words, the division is not between him and what seems to him to be a brute 'alien' force. Rather, the division runs *in* him. Frankfurt conceptualizes this conflict as a lack of wholeheartedness rather than a mere abundance of higher-order volitions. The problem is therefore not that Luther has two equally strong higher-order volitions that contradict each other, but that neither of them is wholeheartedly identified with. When Luther does not wholeheartedly and unequivocally endorse and identify with a motive, it cannot appropriately be said that he really wants it.

> Being wholehearted means having a will that is undivided. The wholehearted person is fully settled as to what he wants, and what he cares

about. With regard to any conflict of dispositions or inclinations within himself, he has no doubts or reservations as to where he stands. He lends himself to his caring and loving unequivocally and without reservation. Thus his identification with the volitional configurations that define his final ends is not inhibited in any way. Such wholehearted identification means that there is no ambivalence in his attitude toward himself (Frankfurt 2004: 95).

In contrast to identification, where there may only be a synchronic coherence between first- and second-order entities, in wholehearted identification there is a diachronic coherence that, for both Frankfurt and Korsgaard (1996; 2006; 2009), is important for the unity of the self. Wholehearted, second-order desires come in absence of any inclination to change them, and they are endorsed while believing that no further reflection would lead to changing one's mind. When wholeheartedly identifying, we take responsibility for them as "authentic expressions of ourselves" (Frankfurt 2006: 8). Yet the concept of wholeheartedness needs to be more specific. There are two dimensions of wholehearted identification that I want to emphasize in this regard:

a) *Centrality.* A wholehearted commitment to a project involves serious dedication of a certain kind. Such commitment concerns the project being so central to one's self-understanding that betraying it would also mean betraying oneself. There is no buffer zone between self, practical identity, and the project that one wholeheartedly cares about. In Luther's case, caring about a certain way of understanding religious practices and institutions is a kind of wholehearted engagement or commitment. He could have abandoned his wholehearted caring about this matter only at the price of being disloyal to something fundamental that defines him as a person. Had Luther contradicted this fundamental concern, he would most likely not have been able to continue living as the same person. He would have had to rethink his life.

b) *Continuity.* Another characteristic that wholehearted caring involves is what we could call continuity. When wholeheartedly caring, we commit both to the actual goal or content of our desire and to having and entertaining the desire itself. In other words, besides wanting to reach the specific goal, we simultaneously want to continue wanting it. In the case of Luther, had he felt that his crucial commitment is losing its strength and motivational power, he would have attempted to revive the commitment in question (Frankfurt 2006: 18–19). He would have attempted to remind himself of the value that he once ascribed to the commitment in question, trying to trigger the fascination and identification with that commitment. Thus, wholehearted caring entails some commitment that surpasses the object of desire. I care about acting on my wholeheartedly endorsed commitment, but I also care about continually having this desire (Korsgaard 2006; 2009). If someone would tell us that he wholeheartedly cares for, say, a commitment, we would expect him to want to attempt to refresh his commitment, should it begin to fade. Otherwise, we would say that he simply does not wholeheartedly care at all. Put differently, when I form a 'maxim' out of caring about something, my commitment is weakly universal. I feel obliged to will it as a law that I should act on under all similar circumstances. If this is not the case, if I am ready to give up this caring of mine because I regard momentary wishes and impulses as valid reasons to abandon it, then I clearly was not genuinely committed from the start. To wholeheartedly care, such that it somehow gives life a diachronic unity, is central to authenticity. I cannot just allow any momentary desire to guide my decisions but must will this maxim as a universal law in this weak sense.

In all, wholehearted identification that displays the two features of centrality and continuity can be said to be at the heart of the kind of diachronic coherence that we would expect authenticity to exhibit. While in 'simple' identification a synchronic coherence between first- and second-order entities arises, only the deep engagements of the wholehearted kind can ensure the diachronic unity of the self. Such unity may very well be conceptualized as a narrative unity (see Christman 2004).

As a last remark, while the discussion here of personal autonomy is certainly an aid in clarifying those of our commitments and identifications that make up who we are, it should nevertheless be pointed out that the practice of personal autonomy does not amount to the same thing as authenticity. Nonetheless, some personal autonomy theorists hold this view. Raymond Geuss (2005: 74) notes that while in his early work Frankfurt deals with traditional problems of the mechanisms of autonomy, in the later work centered on identification and wholeheartedness he begins to deal with authenticity. Diana Tietjens Meyers (2005: 46, 49) has argued that in exercising the skills of autonomy a person simultaneously constitutes and enacts her authentic self. In my view, such an approach runs the risk of lumping together two distinct concepts, resulting in concepts with diminished trajectories. One should be generally careful when applying a strategy that defines a difficult concept such as personal autonomy, while at the same time altering it to encompass another difficult concept such as authenticity. Now I do think that the work on personal autonomy that takes seriously the dimension of identification is exceptionally relevant for a concept of authenticity. But authenticity is also more than the practice of personal autonomy as it is depicted by authors like Frankfurt, Dworkin, Velleman, Christman, Tietjens Meyers, etc. Neither internalist accounts nor those that de-center autonomy bringing in social and relations aspects (Anderson and Honneth 2005; Oshana 2007) are able to account for important elements that we connect to authenticity. As we shall see in more detail, authenticity has a wider reach that goes beyond the concept of personal autonomy. It also captures the manner of our embeddedness in a collective horizon of significance, the complex relation of what we wholeheartedly care about, to agent-transcending goods that may restrain what we care about, and a sense of responding to something 'higher' whenever responding to what is fundamental to us.

Having said this, we must emphasize that personal autonomy, the ability to act from within a framework of beliefs, desires, etc. that one identifies with, is clearly needed for authenticity. This is why it is wrong to assume that authenticity may involve acting in a non-autonomous fashion or losing authority and practical control over one's life. Raz (1986: 375) argues that autonomy is not the precondition for self-realization "for one can stumble into a life of self-realization or be manipulated into it or reach it in some other way which is inconsistent with autonomy." Both Raz and Oshana (2007) argue in this manner, but their argument rests on a very narrow and impoverished concept of authenticity, connected to some kind of honesty towards the self. It is only on such a definition of authenticity that their argument works. Such impoverished notions of authenticity often figure in the debate on personal autonomy. Bracketing off the historical origins and "particular philosophical baggage" (Christman 2009: 134) of the concept, it is used in a purely *procedural* sense. In this context, the adjective 'authentic' is usually employed to describe those parts of a person's psychology that are part of or produced by this true or real self (Noggle 2005: 88). In opposition to such an approach, this book attempts to show the advantages of taking seriously the 'particular philosophical baggage' of the concept of authenticity.

4 CONCLUSION

Based on our discussion in this chapter, it is safe to maintain that authenticity neither arises from the congruence between detection and what is detected nor from the self-congruence of an artistically created whole. It arises not from the uniqueness of the self, be it found (inner sense) or created (productionism), but from the 'resoluteness' or 'wholeheartedness' with which an individual is engaged in life. This seems to avoid the pitfalls of the inner sense and the productionist model. We may steer clear of the 'myth of the given' and be able to give an account of the constitutive activity of the subject, without going down the same road as the productionist by overemphasizing this aspect. In this account, authenticity is about wholeheartedness concerning the commitments one is involved in. Unlike the dispersion of the productionist model, authenticity is about the integration of one's life over time through projects one wholeheartedly endorses.

Wholeheartedly engaging in life in this manner is of course not the whole picture. While such an account steers clear of the problems found in the other two models, it remains empty in the sense that it does not say anything about how we choose our commitments or whether we are free to choose our commitments. I will turn to this difficult issue in the next chapter. If our wholehearted commitment to certain projects defines who we are, and if we define ourselves as the kind of creatures that are able to choose our projects in life, then it seems that we are forced to accept something like the productionist assumption that we are able to choose ourselves. In this chapter, however, I have argued against such a position. On the other hand, it can neither be the case that our commitments simply sneak up on us, leaving no room for choice—a problem that we found unattractive in the inner sense account.

Before going further, it is important to notice that the account of authenticity emerging here avoids the pitfalls of paternalism. Rather than saying something substantial about the content of projects and commitments, which may be contingent, it only emphasizes the *manner of commitment*. What one is committed to is ontically contingent (at least for now), because authenticity is a question of *how* we relate to those commitments. The notion of authenticity is therefore decisively *formal*. The analysis of authenticity does not say anything about concrete life orientations, but about the circumstances and formations of the will under which such an orientation can emerge.[3]

4 The Embedded Practice of Authenticity

In the last chapter we assessed two different models of authenticity, namely the inner sense and the productionist models. Our conclusion was that both models fail to deliver an adequate account of authenticity. Authenticity is neither about gaining introspective access to pre-existing inner traits, projects, wishes, nor about the (aesthetic) self-constitution of individuals, often modeled on the production of art. 'Who I really am' is not adequately captured in terms of discovery or production but is rather about the (wholehearted) manner in which I relate to my commitments. In other words, who we are is defined or constituted by our wholehearted commitments to what we really care about. I have defined wholeheartedness as engagement in a 'project' that is central to one's self-understanding, such that betraying it would also mean betraying oneself (centrality). Also, I have said that wholeheartedness involves being committed not only to the project itself, but also to entertaining the desire that fuels our commitment (continuity).

While laying down these characteristics of wholeheartedness, I have remained neutral on the issue of how we choose our commitments or whether we actually can be said to be free to choose our commitments. This is a thorny issue. We usually understand ourselves as human agents who are the authors of our lives. In other words, we take ourselves as beings that constitute an important part of who we are through the choices we make. We take ourselves to have constitutive agency when it comes to defining what we care about. However, if we claim that wholehearted commitment to certain projects defines who we are, while simultaneously claiming that we are the kind of creatures that are able to choose projects in life, then it seems that we are required to accept something like the productionist assumption—that we are able to choose or create ourselves. Thus, if who we are is a matter of what we are wholeheartedly involved in, and if we are able to choose the things we wholeheartedly care about, then who we are may be little more than a matter of choice. For Sartre, this characteristic condition of our being comes about because we do not have any pre-established human nature. Since our existence precedes our essence, "choosing oneself," making one's own essence as one lives is simply what it means to be free (Sartre 1943/1991: 440). It is well known that Sartre takes the radical freedom of choosing ourselves as illustrating humanity's fundamental condition of "forlornness".

> Freedom is simply the nothingness which is made-to-be at the heart of man and which forces human-reality to make itself instead of to be. As we have seen, for human reality to be is to choose oneself, without any help whatsoever, it is entirely abandoned to the intolerable necessity of making itself be—down to the slightest detail (Sartre 1943/1991: 440–441).

At first sight, this may seem exactly like the productionist position. While we have rejected such an account, we have also denied that our commitments are simply 'there' as brute facts, or that they sneak in on us leaving no room for choice—a problem that we found unattractive in the inner sense account. Again, it looks as if we need something in between. I will provide a substantial reinterpretation of Sartre's idea of fundamental choice and suggest that we need to consider how we rely on collectively constituted contexts of significance in order to constitute ourselves. This is an important issue that we have not touched upon so far when discussing the parameters of wholehearted engagement in terms such as centrality and continuity. As we shall see, being embedded in a culturally shaped horizon of significance is necessary to constitute ourselves by making up our minds on what we wholeheartedly care about. What we care about and where we situate ourselves in such a context becomes intelligible in relation to goods that qualitative distinctions of worth are based on.

The investigation into the structure of wholehearted care, to be provided in the last part of this chapter, will show that it is constitutive of our personal commitments to involve a commitment to public goods that provide the normative sources for our commitments. While this will give additional support to the core claim (regarding the constitutive embeddedness of wholehearted engagements in collectively constituted horizons of significance), it also critiques the widely held view that authenticity and public goods and values are antagonistic or, at best, pleasantly coincidental. It will be shown that the internal structure of our commitments may actually commit us to public values that we take our commitments to embody and that this structure may constrain the manner in which we can coherently pursue our commitment. Therefore, while we explored authenticity from a standard point of view in the last chapter—mostly as being responsive to what we wholeheartedly and personally care about—it will be argued that the responsiveness to our concrete particularity goes via our responsiveness to inter-subjectively constituted values and orientations, without which we would not be genuine moral agents.

1 DISPOSITION AND FUNDAMENTAL PROJECTS

According to Sartre, one's actions express a 'fundamental project' that helps define one's being. To illustrate this, Sartre describes the relation between the fundamental project and individual actions as akin to the relation between a painting and the individual brush strokes. While the significance of a brush stroke is only intelligible when framed by the painting as a whole, the painting itself merely consists of the sum of brush strokes (1943/1991: 491–492). While this is quite unproblematic—and in harmony with both Frankfurt and Korsgaard's thoughts and with Williams' concept of 'ground projects' (1981a)—Sartre's more radical claim is that the fundamental project is itself a product of a choice. Interestingly, in *Religion Within the Limits of Reason Alone*, Kant's discussion of the problem of evil has several affinities with Sartre's work (Baldwin 1979; Lieberman 1997). Kant's analysis of radical evil makes recourse to a particular way of describing character as a 'freely chosen disposition.' The idea—that maxims determine particular actions and spring from an ultimate disposition, which itself is a product of a free choice—unmistakably foreshadows the Sartrean talk of the original choice of a fundamental project (Sartre 1943/1991: 563). The following discussion of Sartre's and Kant's views on this subject should help us make sense of whether we are capable of choosing what fundamentally matters to us. The aim of the comparison is not to establish a historical link but to elucidate important facets of such a position and thereby to advance the overall argument.

Kant argues that we should understand evil as stemming from the free adoption of certain kinds of maxims that give priority to natural inclinations instead of morality. A man performs evil acts on grounds of evil maxims (1998: 16), but these maxims rest upon an "underlying common ground" (Ibid.), which is itself something like a fundamental maxim that Kant subsequently classifies as a 'disposition.'

> We call a human being evil, however, not because he performs actions that are evil (contrary to law), but because these are so constituted that they allow the inference of evil maxims in him. . . . But we cannot observe maxims, we cannot do so unproblematically even within ourselves; hence the judgment that an agent is an evil human being cannot reliably be based on experience. In order, then, to call a human being evil, it must be possible to infer a priori from a number of consciously evil actions, or even from a single one, an underlying evil maxim, and, from this, the presence in the subject of a common ground, itself a maxim, of all particular morally evil maxims (Kant 1998: 46).

Such an underlying maxim is for Kant "the subjective ground . . . of the exercise of the human being's freedom" (Kant 1998: 46) that is the necessary antecedent to any act. In order for man to be accountable for this underlying disposition, Kant argues that this is not a pre-given part of human nature, established by a natural incentive, but rather acquired through free choice.

The subjective ground must be thought of as the outcome of an act of freedom, "for otherwise the use or abuse of the human being's power of choice with respect to the moral law could not be imputed to him, nor could good or evil in him be called 'moral'" (Kant 1998: 21; Guyer 2003: 79). The subjective ground is thus taken to explain why an individual may adopt a particular maxim over another. Kant says that the subjective ground is itself acquired in free choice, and he attempts to block the threatening regress by saying that this ground is "inscrutable" (Kant 1998: 47). The ultimate subjective ground that shapes the adoption of maxims serves to account for disposition, which is "adopted through the free power of choice, for otherwise it could not be imputed" (Ibid.: 50).

We begin to see a clear parallel with the Sartrean theme. The disposition of an agent refers to a fundamental maxim that is something like a guiding principle that governs the adoption of specific 'local' maxims. Allowing for individual accountability, the fundamental maxim does not merely reflect a pre-given aspect of nature but is itself an outcome of choice, by which we become the authors of our dispositions. One could say, evoking Sartre, that by choosing the fundamental maxim we choose ourselves.

Like Kant, Sartre points out that we understand the actions of our fellow humans by reference to an underlying 'project,' which we take to inform that agent's act. More importantly, Sartre also maintains that one's wishes, desires, and intentions become intelligible only as elements within a single project that provides life with a unique volitional structure (see also Baldwin 1979). Sartre (1943/1991: 563) calls this the 'fundamental' or 'original' project, which reflects the totality of a person's "impulse toward being his original relation to himself, the world, and to the Other." A fundamental project unifies the agent by providing the framework within which mundane intentions and motives become comprehensible and in which the world becomes intelligible by affording certain actions rather than others. The fundamental project is active on the basic level of non-reflective self-consciousness, which for Sartre is a part of every act of consciousness (Ibid.: 463). A short clarification is needed here. Sartre argues for a non-dualistic approach to understanding consciousness (Ibid.: 12).[1] He differentiates between non-reflective and reflective self-awareness, arguing that "consciousness has no need at all of a reflecting consciousness in order to be conscious of itself. It simply does not posit itself as an object" (Sartre 1957: 45). A central point is that reflective awareness presupposes a ubiquitous, non-reflective self-consciousness, which is a condition for reflection. Thus, in every conscious state, there is what Sartre calls a non-positional (or non-thetic) self-awareness, which is *not separate from* the world-directed mental state.[2] It is at this basic level of consciousness that the fundamental project is active. It discloses the world as meaningful, not so much through a reflected, theoretical perspective, but through the practical approaches that characterize our lives much of the time. Usually we are presented with a meaningfully disclosed world, which does not appear as the sum of objects, but rather as imbued with significance and structured by *affordances* (usefulness or uselessness, proximity or distance, etc.), particular potentialities for action that are specific to our intentions and desires (Sartre 1943/1991: 463). Objects, events, plans, etc. within an atmosphere of implicit familiarity become intelligible as affording certain types of actions. It is at this deep level that there is constant reference to a fundamental project that allows for one's present to appear as valuable, inadequate, etc.: "choice and consciousness are one and the same" (Ibid.: 462). How one acts is only intelligible against the background of a fundamental project, which constitutes the identity of the person (Ibid.: 468).

Like Kant, Sartre considers the fundamental project—and thereby the self—to be chosen, albeit not in a completely straightforward act. Both authors want to emphasize the issue of responsibility and avoid the impression that a fundamental project is merely pre-given as a brute matter of fact. Clearly, the claim that a project that grounds individual choices is itself acquired through choice is problematic. Let us first see how the similarities go deeper than merely the claim that the fundamental project or disposition is achieved through an act of choice.

2 TRANSFORMATION AND SELF-KNOWLEDGE

Kant and Sartre agree that a transformation of one's fundamental project (or disposition) is not something that can be achieved voluntarily. For Sartre, this more or less follows directly from the voluntarist conception of value implied in his account. With the fundamental project that we choose, we simultaneously create the values that guide any further choice, but since our values are thereby fixed, we are no longer in a position to find reasons that have enough impact on us to allow us to change our project. This is not to say that it is not possible, but it is not a possibility that is in the power of our will (Sartre 1943/1991: 475–476). Kant similarly argues that if we accept disposition as the fundamental basis for acts of will, then we cannot expect to transcend such ground to gain access to disposition–changing normative forces. Such changes do not occur gradually, but through a "revolution in the disposition of the human being" (Kant 1998: 68). Clearly in both cases, from such a revolution, a new person ("new man," Ibid.) emerges.

Additionally, an aspect that almost follows from the above-mentioned issues, both Kant and Sartre hold that we cannot ever have self-knowledge in the sense of knowing our fundamental project (Sartre 1943/1991: 570). Due to its transcendent nature, the project cannot turn into an object of knowledge for its possessor (Ibid.: 463). Such a view of one's fundamental project would require that one steps out of the fundamental project that shapes the whole of one's life, which is impossible. There is no such view from 'nowhere' on the project itself, since it serves as a ground against which everything becomes intelligible.

3 OBJECTIONS

The concept of choosing the fundamental project is notoriously ambiguous and many have doubted the possibility of it. Habermas (1978) detects a problematic and unfounded decisionism in such an idea, while David Velleman (1989) views it as building on a mischaracterization of our decisions and actions. There are two points I want to emphasize here, relating to the question of (a) agency and to the issue of (b) ends.

(a) Choice necessitates the agency of an individual that is somehow integrated. To be able to go through with an act of choice, one must already display some vital characteristics of an integrated self, which in Sartre is taken first to arise by choice. Rejecting the idea of a human agent prior to acts of choice entails denying that the act of making choices requires a self-aware individual competent of bringing such choices under will. A choice requires an agent upon whom we can attribute at least some authorship of the choice in question. Without authorship, no choice. A choice only counts as truly mine if I acknowledge it as an expression of my self, rather than as a product of a random force in me. Consequently, it would be incoherent to simultaneously hold that choice is dependent on a self-aware and competent agent, and that the self is entirely constituted through choices.

(b) Additionally, choice is only intelligible as always necessitating antecedently possessed ends that ground such a choice (Cohen 2008). Sartre makes use of the example of the young man who must decide between joining the Resistance and caring for his ill mother at home. Sartre takes this example to demonstrate (among other issues) that it is sometimes impossible to reach a decision by simply reflecting on ends. Instead, pointing to the arbitrary nature of such a choice, Sartre argues that the young man simply 'throws' himself in one direction. But this does not convince. The very initial fact that the young man experiences the situation as a dilemma with two possible options is itself based on some antecedent ends and reasons and thus cannot be the result of a radically free existential choice. If this were not the case, the young man could dissolve the grievous nature of the dilemma by simply declaring one of the rival claims as neutral or by declaring that the situation is not even a dilemma (Taylor 1985: 30; Cohen 2008: 93). Frankfurt invites us to imagine a case where someone is not restricted by antecedent ends and can choose from an almost unlimited field of conceivable courses of action. "It will be possible, then, for him to change those aspects of his nature that determine what choices he makes. He will be in a position to redesign his own will"

(Frankfurt 1999a: 109). In such a case, without a definite set of ends and stable volitional constraints, the person would not be able to engage in careful deliberation about his actions. What we can add here is that in the lack of ends and motives that propel him into the future this person would have no reason to engage in deliberation (see Williams 1981a).

Taking (a) and (b) into consideration, in the following I will argue for understanding fundamental projects in a different manner. I will present a way to navigate the difficulties that such an account faces, while maintaining that a group of choices—'existential choices'—are ones in which we constitute ourselves, while they can be correctly referred to as choices within the reach of personal responsibility. Existential choices are not indeterminate free choices that are not based on anything. We neither have to throw ourselves in a random direction, nor to detach ourselves from all ends to make such a choice.

4   A SUGGESTION

Before that however, the idea that I am going to spell out here is that fundamental choice at this level really refers to being immersed in a meaningfully disclosing world. At this level, especially considering the critical points mentioned above, it is untenable to speak of a 'choice.' In fact, this position is to a certain extent compatible with Kant's account. Henry E. Allison (1990) and Marcel Lieberman (1996) argue that Kant attempts to solve the problem of disposition constitution by distinguishing between intelligible and sensible acts. The original choice of disposition is an intelligible act cognizable by means of pure reason alone, while our everyday actions that are performed in accordance with maxims are sensible acts. These are obviously very different ways in which freedom is exercised, and this distinction has no counterpart in Sartre. One may be little satisfied with Kant's solution that to a large extent pushes the problem further (towards the noumenal realm) without really solving it. There is a sense in which Kant recognizes that we must allow for qualitative difference between ordinary choices and acquiring our fundamental dispositions or projects. Allison argues that we should understand 'disposition' not in an ontological but in a *regulative* sense (1990: 140–143). Regulative means that instead of being the product of an act, a disposition is understood as obtained through an act (Lieberman 1996). This could then also explain why Kant thinks that such an act is to be placed outside the phenomenal world and thus space and time.

In opposition, Sartre's account cannot really be read in this way and it is difficult to see how he could accommodate a qualitative difference between making choices and attaining a fundamental project. We could however understand the latter more like a background, a 'framework' or horizon of intelligibility, but not really a project. For this reason, instead of regarding the meaningful disclosure of the world as the outcome of a choice, we should instead follow

Merleau-Ponty, who proposes that "free action, in order to be discernable, has to stand out against a background of life from which it is entirely, or almost entirely, absent" (1945/2002: 507). At this fudamental level, we should not speak of choice, but rather about "signification" and about the meaningful appearance of a "field" (Ibid.: 509–510), within which we locate ourselves. It is in such an inter-subjectively constituted background that we may begin to speak of choices though which we constitute ourselves. As in the example of the painting given by Sartre, we can say that individual actions, choices, and life paths are embedded in and become meaningful by relating to other narratives that unfold within a certain historical-cultural context. To discover and to take a stand on who we are, therefore, involves grasping how our narrative is placed compared to both stories of concrete others and to what we could call 'meta-stories': backgrounds against which individual narratives become comprehensible and significant. If we want to say that the disclosure of the world as inherently meaningful takes place on this basic level *and* that such disclosure is somehow the outcome of a project (and thus reducible to acts of choice), then we must acknowledge that such a 'project' cannot be reduced to the inner life of a single person. It is rather the product of an inherently collaborative process of communication and meaning-making. When we deliberate upon our goals and about who we are and who we want to be, we are always already a part of such a 'project' that constitutes a meaningful context in which such questions can arise. We should therefore no longer speak about meaningful disclosure of the world following from one's choices, but rather of something that reflects being embedded in a 'field' or collectively shaped background of a particular historical-cultural context. It is within such a framework that we make the choices through which we constitute ourselves. This context within which our lives unfold is not to be thought of as a rigid container of a set of pre-fixed values, but more as a dynamic field that hosts a permanent negotiation about what matters.

5   AUTHENTICITY AND THE BACKGROUND

Such an understanding of being immersed in an inter-subjectively constituted background or 'field' can be brought into interaction with Heidegger's account of authenticity in *Being and Time*. Admittedly, in Heidegger the internal relationship between authenticity and inauthenticity is painstakingly ambiguous. In addition, the term is used in both evaluative-normative and purely descriptive senses that can lead to quite dissimilar interpretations. In the descriptive use of the term, mainly in the first part of *Being and Time*, Heidegger sees two possibilities for being. These are authenticity and inauthenticity, where inauthenticity is simply the default condition of everyday life. We are inauthentic because our self-relations are mediated by others. This mode is how we 'zunächst und zumeist' are aware of ourselves. In a sense, we are lost, since we are not aware of ourselves in terms of our 'ownmost' possibilities of existing. In this way, authenticity involves no judgment about which mode of being is superior for Dasein. But then Heidegger's language changes (Carman 2003), turns normative, and the seemingly neutral inauthentic form of relating transforms into something negative. Inauthentic Dasein is now "not itself," loses itself (Selbstverlorenheit), and becomes self-alienated (Heidegger 1927/1962: 109 and 166). If one is not aware of this sudden shift, then the conclusion is inevitably that for Heidegger it is inherently wrong to relate to oneself in mediation by others. Nonetheless, a careful reading reveals that when introducing the normative-evaluative sense at the beginning of part II, Heidegger presents a third possibility: "but this potentiality-of-being that is always mine is free for authenticity and inauthenticity, or for a mode in which neither of these have been differentiated."[3] In other words, there are three modes of life: authentic—average(ness)—inauthentic. The authentic and inauthentic modes are existential modifications of average everydayness (Dreyfus 1991; Blattner 2006: 130). If we use the term 'ownedness' to describe authenticity, we could say that an authentic way of life is owned, an inauthentic disowned, and the middle one—which is how we live much of the time—is simply one that is unowned.

> Dasein must not be interpreted at the outset of the analysis in the differentiatedness (Differenz) of a particular way of existing, but that it should be uncovered (aufgedeckt) in the undifferentiated character which it has proximally and for the most part. This undifferentiatedness of Dasein's everydayness is *not nothing*, but rather a positive phenomenal characteristic of this entity. Out of this kind of Being—and back into it again—is all existing, such as it is. We call this everyday undifferentiated character of Dasein, "averageness" (Heidegger 1927/1962: 69).[4]

In this model, everyday life is not inauthentic per se and Heidegger here displays a more differentiated view of the everyday immersion in life than Kierkegaard and Nietzsche (see Dreyfus 1991: 283–293). The picture that emerges boils down to this: for Dasein to appear to itself in an intelligible way, the everyday undifferentiatedness serves as a necessary background, or 'field.' Dasein and authenticity emerge in contrast to this background and out of this background, so that the primordially indifferent mode is the condition of possibility for authenticity or inauthenticity. Throughout our lives, we move back and forth between this undifferentiated mode of being and the differentiated modes. It is from this basis that one can 'own' life or become existentially disorientated and lose one's sense of self-understanding.

Consequently, instead of regarding the meaningful disclosure of the world as the outcome of an act of 'fundamental' choice, we should speak of the meaningful appearance of a historical-cultural 'field' of significance within we can locate ourselves, and within which making choices becomes meaningful in the first place.

We began by addressing a dilemma that arises from claiming that our wholehearted commitment to certain projects defines who we are, while simultaneously claiming that we are able to choose our projects in life. If this is the case, it seems that we are required to embrace production-ist assumptions that were rejected in the last chapter. Sartre's and Kant's accounts helped advance the overall argument. An admittedly radical rein-terpretation was given of the basic level of consciousness, upon which Sar-tre locates the unfolding of the fundamental project. If the fundamental project is the source of a meaningfully disclosed world, in which entities appear within an atmosphere of implicit familiarity, not as neutral, but as imbued with significance and affordances, then this level of 'disclosure' is better referred to as being embedded in a culturally shaped horizon of sig-nificance. With such an interpretation, we can hold on to idea that such a background is something that can neither be altered voluntarily, nor turned into an object of direct knowledge, while rejecting the underlying volun-tarist conception of value. Heidegger's account of authenticity also lends support to such a view, when given a less standard reading.

6   INTERACTION AND THE BACKGROUND

It is important to note that such a cultural framework is not one that we are 'thrown' into as solitary creatures, but one that we are raised within. It is not that we individually create meaning within such a cultural out-look, but it is rather that meaning and the specific significance of objects, acts, relations, etc. come to us through second personal interactions with significant others. In them we are introduced to a cultural context within which objects, facts, relations, and possible projects that we may care about come to appear as meaningful, valuable, interesting, dangerous, and so on. Hence, there is a close connection between being immersed in a field and concrete forms of second-personal interactions. On the one hand, second-personal interactions build on a shared context of social life, in which indi-viduals form a community through aiming towards shared conceptions of the good (Honneth 1995a: ch. 5). On the other hand however, and this is of particular interest, the ability of individuals to commit to whatever they find valuable in such a cultural outlook, can only be guaranteed through a process of socialization that involves specific, second-personal interactions characterized by recognition (Ibid.: 173). Processes of recognition have a constitutive role in the formation of stable self-relations that are necessary for engaging in commitments. The threefold structure of recognition refers to three different facets of ontogenetic development, as well as the three different self-relations they enable. Such 'practical relations-to-self' are self-confidence, self-respect, and self-esteem.

Self-confidence arises from the sphere of intimacy that is made up of emotional relationships of loving acceptance. Honneth argues that through this loving acceptance the child learns about mattering to others. It is also learned that his or her desires and commitments are valuable and worth pursuing. Consequently, the fulfillment of early affective demands provides the subject with self-confidence needed to form commitments and participate in the public life of a community.

Self-respect arises from being able to see oneself as an equal among others, for example before the law. This 'egalitarian' sphere of recognition has emerged with the rise of modernity and has led to the egalitarian idea of granting autonomous individuals equal legal standing and rights. Honneth refers to this universalism as "respect," while Taylor uses the term "politics of universality," because recognition is here understood as non-sensitive to individual identity. In terms of practical self-relation, the experience of being considered an equal and autonomous person by others supports one's sense of self-respect. Self-respect does not merely mean having a good opinion of oneself but has to do with a sense of "possessing of the universal dignity of persons" (Anderson 1995b: xiv).

Self-esteem is a positive relationship to one's particular capacities and achievements within the context of a community. So while a self-respecting person is entitled to the same kind of status as every other person, self-esteem comes through the recognition of unique contributions to collective issues. In this sense, self-esteem differs from self-respect, by involving the recognition of something unique—some valuable contribution that distinguishes that person from others.

These three self-relations and their corresponding relations of recognition are—as rightly seen by Nancy Fraser—all central ingredients and preconditions of the good life (Fraser and Honneth 2003: 235–236, fn. 15).

While many thinkers like Heidegger emphasize being 'thrown' into such a cultural context as solitary creatures, it is necessary to point out the second-personal interactions through which we find meaning in such a cultural 'map of mattering.' We are introduced into a cultural context and grasp the significance of projects in actual or imagined second-personal interactions. In this sense, we are always in *dialogue* about what really matters to us (Taylor 1994: 32). Roughly speaking, being immersed in a 'field' and being in specific forms of second-personal interactions cannot be separated. This is true in more than one sense, since the individual capacity to engage in commitments and existential reflection depends on patterns of interaction that we have described in the vocabulary of 'recognition.'

7 STRONG EVALUATIONS AND ARTICULATION

As noted earlier, one condition of our ability to make choices through which we constitute our selves is being embedded in a culturally shaped horizon of significance, in a 'field' or collectively shaped background of a particular historical-cultural context. We can now refine this by adding that such background is—at least partly—constituted by qualitative *distinctions of worth*. Who we are and where we situate ourselves in such a context become intelligible in relation to what we view as having or lacking worth. This is the frame within which we get to make up our minds about what really matters to us and about what is truly worth pursuing. In other words, we make up our minds on where we stand in regard to a 'map of mattering' constituted by qualitative *distinctions of worth*. In the following, I shall explore this issue together with an investigation of the manner in which we make up our minds. As argued in the last chapter, such choices are to be described as being located on the level of second-order volitions. In order to deliver a more precise description of our practice of authenticity, we need to consider a specific kind of second-order phenomena, namely 'strong evaluations.'

Taylor draws an additional conceptual distinction pertaining to our reflective attitudes towards first-order states. Our practice of evaluating first-order wishes, motivations, etc. can proceed in a weak or a strong sense (Taylor 1985a; 1989; 1991). In weak evaluation, we simply calculate options without questioning the intrinsic worth of the desire that motivates us.

> A subject who only evaluates weakly—that is, makes decisions like that of eating now or later, taking a holiday in the north or in the south—might be described as a simple weigher of alternatives. And the other, who deploys the language of evaluative contrasts ranging over desires, we might call a strong evaluator (Taylor 1985: 23).

In strong evaluation the person assesses what is desirable by a further qualitative characterization of options as higher and lower, noble and base, virtuous or vicious, more or less refined, profound or superficial, etc., thus by qualitative distinctions concerning the worth of an option. When making such qualitative distinctions, we not only evaluate our motivations but also express our ambition to be a specific kind of person and hope for our acts to express this. While in weak evaluation "for something to be judged good it is sufficient that it be desired" (Taylor 1985: 18; 1991), in strong evaluation that relies on qualitative distinctions of worth, "there is also a use of 'good' or some other evaluative term for which being desired is not sufficient" (Ibid.: 9).

Hence, while for Frankfurt second-order volitions express preferences that are merely quantitatively different from other preferences, Taylor introduces a useful qualitative distinction concerning the basis upon which they are made. Such identity-constitutive orientation toward the good compels us to distinguish between "right or wrong, better or worse, higher or lower, which are not rendered valid by our own desires, inclinations, or choices, but rather stand independent of these and offer standards by which they can be judged" (Taylor 1989: 4).

With this we return to the issue of transparency from the last chapter. My endorsement of a commitment of mine (be it introspectively achieved or self-constituted) is contingent on me being able to understand this commitment as something *good*. Even the ironic liberal must assume that the ironic path of life is something *worthy* to pursue and of higher value than other alternatives. If not, the ironist would be confronted with a modified version of Moore's paradox that concerns value: "who I really am, what I really identify with is *P*, but *P* is not good or valuable in any way." Recall that from a third-person standpoint my commitment to *P* is neutral concerning the question of whether *P* is good. However, from the first-person perspective, the case is different. If I am wholehearted about *P*, I must also grasp *P* as 'true' in the sense of something higher or worthier to pursue. Of course, in such case of transparency, my identifying with *P* is not amenable to the state of facts, but to values. Now, further developing what we have established in the last chapter, namely that authenticity is essentially about our being committed to certain projects, ideals, relations, etc., we may add that such commitments also involve some reflection on our commitments in a qualitative vocabulary.

While Taylor has been criticized for constructing a far too 'moralistic' and 'intellectual' approach to the self, in our context we need not be worried about these issues. There is no need to understand 'worth' in a limited 'moral' sense, referring to being altruistic, dutiful, or benevolent (see also Smith 2004). Additionally, we need not understand strong evaluation in each case as the outcome of explicit reflection. Such evaluations may (and often do) guide choices non-reflectively, since they exist both as implicit understandings and as explicit judgments. What is important is that such evaluations constitute a personal horizon that provides the "horizon within which I try to determine from case to case what is good, or valuable, or what ought to be done, or what I endorse or oppose. In other words, it is the horizon within which I am capable of taking a stand" (Taylor 1989: 27). Now, having mentioned both collective and personal horizons, we need to clarify their relation. As we shall see, strong evaluations connect our agency to cultural frameworks of significance in a specific, non-contingent manner. The key issue here is 'articulation.'

8   ARTICULATION

The concept of strong evaluations helped us understand how our whole-hearted engagement in undertakings involves engagement with collective values and norms. We evaluate our desires and commitments in the light of values, which we take our aspirations to embody. When we come to acquire the wholehearted engagements (through strong evaluations) that constitute our personal horizons, we *articulate* the background of choice-transcendent values upon which they are based. This idea is present in Heidegger's work (1927/1962: 168), and he notes that "authentic Being-one's-Self does not rest upon an exceptional condition of the subject, a condition that has been detached from the 'they;' it is rather an existential modification of the 'they'." Also, he notes (Ibid.: 167, also 312) that our commitments "articulate" the context of their intelligibility or their "referential context of significance." A more recent and complex way of putting this is with Taylor's notion of 'articulation,' which is clearly indebted to Heidegger and which departs further from Frankfurt's exclusive focus on individual aspects.

Thinking through our commitments as articulations allows us to understand why we sometimes feel overwhelmed by them, and why we sometimes have the sense that while pursuing our projects we respond to something 'higher' that is beyond our own desires. We can accommodate the fact that our strong evaluations make claims on us, and show that their authority over us cannot be reduced to our bestowing that authority upon them (see also Abbey 2000: 24). Their normative 'pull,' which claims our allegiance, does not alone derive from subjective choices and commitments but from being affirmative articulations of non-choice-dependent goods. In order for our commitments to have a normative grip on us in the full sense, they must be seen as articulations of choice-transcendent values, thus values that we recognize as not stemming from our choices. While this point will be made clearer in the following, we can for now maintain that strong evaluations that underlie our wholehearted commitments entail a component of 'articulation' that transcends the level of purely subjective reflections, establishing a dialogue between the individual evaluations and choice-transcendent norms (Taylor 1985).

As we shall see in greater detail when discussing the *structure* of wholehearted commitments, such embeddedness is not merely a contingent issue, but really constitutive of our engagements. Authenticity is not merely about wholehearted commitments, but also about embeddedness in the intersubjectively constituted horizon of a larger community that ultimately is the source of the normative pull that our commitments have on us. Our practice of authenticity, of defining identifications and commitments and of making evaluations about them as worthy of pursuing, requires not only having some epistemic familiarity with the more or less 'locally' constituted good. It also involves being responsive to their normative force.

In such a view, we need to subscribe to neither the view that goodness is a matter of a correspondence to our desires, nor the view that our values are based on Sartrean fundamental choices. Instead, we evaluate our desires and commitments in light of values, which we take our aspirations to embody. In our practice of practical reasoning through strong evaluations we articulate our relation to the good that makes claims on us (Pinkard 2004: 198). We constitute ourselves via the aggregation of such evaluations that reveal and realize our orientation toward the good. It is this kind of compass in a moral space of qualitative distinctions (concerning what is worth pursuing) that provides orientation in life.

9   EMBEDDEDNESS AND THE STRUCTURE OF WHOLEHEARTED COMMITMENT

Recalling our earlier discussion, wholehearted identifications and indeed the practice of authenticity cannot be separated from responsiveness to background contexts of significance, which we explore through interaction with others. Simply speaking, our ability to make choices that shape our lives as a whole depends on our being responsive to inter-subjective contexts of significance. The aim is now to develop this account further by investigating the structure of wholehearted caring, which will ultimately allow us to challenge a widely held antagonism between authenticity and public values. In what follows I reject the widely held view that authenticity and public values must either be antagonistic (Rousseau; Sartre) or at best a pleasant coincidence. The latter view, represented by Williams (1981b; 1981c) and Frankfurt (2006), holds that the normative grip of any public value on a person is contingent on whether this person happens to care about it. In the following I shall dig deeper into the structure of wholehearted caring, in order to shed light on how our commitments involve such constitutive values and how we tap their normative sources to guide our decisions. The main point will be that wholehearted caring has a certain structure that is far from hostile to public values that are beyond the object of one's wholehearted caring. In fact, wholehearted caring actually commits the caring person to such public values.[5]

Let us begin with the structure of wholehearted caring. As noted, wholehearted caring is not merely about wanting to accomplish some objective but also involves a commitment to the desire itself. As Frankfurt (2006: 18–19) has put it, we not only want for some goal to be accomplished by us, but we also want to be those kinds of persons who keep on wanting this desire to be a part of who we are. In such cases, if the strength of this desire starts to decline, we are inclined to attempt to adjust our reasoning and attempt to revive it. This means that wholeheartedly caring goes beyond the object of desire itself and involves some other commitment. Speaking with Korsgaard (2006), authenticity, via the internal structure of wholehearted caring, involves specific object-transcendent commitments. This implies that the commitment brings into being a *norm*. Not only should I act on my commitment, but I should also persistently care about continuously having this commitment. Briefly put, the structure of wholehearted caring is such that it entails the inauguration of a norm, which is ultimately what motivates me to invigorate my commitment should it begin to fade.

Clearly, maintaining that our commitment to continuing to desire something is constitutive of caring about that thing does not in itself resolve whether one is committed to anything like a public value. So far, we have not provided reasons why wholehearted caring involves any such additional commitment, and therefore we cannot yet reject the default position that it is merely my caring about a commitment that renders it normative to me, giving me a reason to act. However, when we think 'continuity' through, we arrive at a different position.

The question that pushes us to think further is this: if it is exclusively my wholehearted caring that renders a commitment normative to me, then why *should* I (and indeed how *could* I) motivate myself in attempting to restore my engagement in that commitment when it starts to grow fainter? What is it that gives me reason to attempt such refreshment if my project no longer has a normative grip on me? If it were the case that it is merely my wholehearted commitment that gives me a reason, then I would be in lack of any reason to engage in refreshing a fading commitment. It cannot only be my wholehearted caring that renders my commitment normative to me. What does then?

The core feature of wholehearted caring is its two-level structure and its constitutive relations to public values. When wholeheartedly committed, I assign the object of my commitment a distinctive public value that does not emanate from my caring about it. I see it as the articulation of that value. When Luther finds himself wholeheartedly engaged in his project of revealing crucial truths that religious institutions have neglected, the value of that commitment does not merely spring out of his own caring about it. Instead, and here we touch upon the issue of transparency, he must think of it as possessing a public value independently of his caring about it. This may well involve him thinking that if he did not take this task upon himself, then somebody else should.

We now begin to uncover the two-level structure of wholehearted caring. When wholeheartedly engaged, Luther grants his commitment to rethink the teachings of the Bible a public value, which means considering it as valuable for reasons that are shareable and that can be located in a web of public reasons. Korsgaard (2009: 211) hints at such a two-level structure when she maintains that "to have a personal project or ambition is not to desire a special object that you think is good for you privately, but rather to want to stand in a special relationship to something you think is good publicly." Not only does Luther's wholehearted caring go beyond the commitment itself, it also generalizes the value of what he cares about. His wholehearted caring is expressive of his longing to stand in a special and close relation to the public value that he takes his commitment to articulate. His motivation for 'standing up' and defending his standpoint does not only emerge from his simple desire to do so. This just would not do the job. Rather, he also thinks that such a commitment is a truthful articulation of honorable biblical scholarship that is of public value. At the same time, he desires that it should be *him* who acts this way, expressing his desire to stand in a close relation to this public value through his choices and acts. This then may result not only in caring about a project but also in achieving a self-conception under which he values himself (see Korsgaard 1996: 102).

Now with this two-level structure of wholehearted commitments in mind, we can return to the issue I called the 'irritating question': if we take only our wholehearted commitments to render goals normative to us, then what motivates us to refresh our commitments when they start to fade? Without the normative grip that our commitments have on us, how do we find the motivation to attempt to refresh? When taking into account the two-level structure discussed earlier, this aspect becomes intelligible. We have seen that understanding the normativity of commitment involves taking into consideration not only one's commitments, but also that through one's commitments one expresses a desire to stand in a special relationship to something that has public value, independent of one's caring about it.

Therefore, in cases when a wholehearted commitment starts to lose its normative grip, in order to refresh my commitment I cannot tap into the normative sources that arise out of my caring about this commitment (this is what is fading), but I must turn to the normativity embodied in the public value that I take my commitment to articulate. It is by turning to reasons that stem from this agent-transcendent normative force, and by tapping from the normativity embodied in the public value (that my commitment is articulating), that I can attempt to refresh my commitment.

10   BOUNDARIES OF WHOLEHEARTED ENGAGEMENT

The two-level structure of wholehearted commitments provides an answer to the 'irritating question.' We can bridge our motivational gaps and refresh our commitment to our projects by considering them worthy articulations of public goods. In this sense, it is constitutive that we understand our commitments as articulations. This constitutive relation has further repercussions for our practice of wholehearted caring. What I want to show in the following is that this feature of our commitments places important restrictions on both (a) the *selection* of the things we can be committed to, and (b) the *manner* in which we can commit to them.

(a) As to the *selection* of our wholehearted commitments, the Frankfurt-Sartrean default position comes down to maintaining that what I can wholeheartedly commit to is entirely up to me. According to this account, it makes perfect sense for me to care wholeheartedly about my collection of buttons rather than anything else in the world. However, when recalling the two-level structure of wholehearted caring, this cannot be entirely correct. We can easily imagine a case in which I cannot establish any sort of robust connection or relation of articulation between a project of mine and some public value. To illustrate this, we can use an example provided by Taylor. It may be that someone maintains that having exactly 3,732 hairs on his head is constitutive of his personality (Taylor 1991: 36). The point is that in order for this property to have significance for him an additional story is needed that embeds this property in a background horizon of significance. "Perhaps the number 3,732 is a sacred one in some society; then having this number of hairs can be significant. But we get to this by linking it to the sacred." The argument is that it cannot merely be our wholehearted commitments that render goals normative for us. One needs to locate one's project in a web of public reasons and to be able to regard it as worthy and valuable for various reasons. Grasping the normativity of our commitment involves taking into consideration that through our commitment we express a desire to stand in an intimate relation to something of worth. This is what allows us to refresh this commitment if its grip on us should fade. We should immediately add two important aspects.

First, the fact that one needs to locate one's project in a web of public reasons and to see it as the articulation of a choice-transcendent value should not make us blind to the fact that we have quite a broad range of interpretative possibilities. It is possible to establish such 'link' in a variety of ways. The point here is more one of principle, emphasizing that the two-level structure of wholehearted caring places some limitation on what we wholeheartedly engage in.

Second, the fact that through our commitments we articulate or express a desire to stand in a special relationship to something of worth that is made accessible through language and culture does not mean that we simply 'reproduce' pre-existing value orientations. The instances that make horizons of worth accessible—language and culture—are simultaneously the ones that allow us to take some distance from particular goods. We are not cultural 'dopes,' but individual agents who make individual decisions and *interpret* aspects of the broader horizon of significance. The possibility for interpretations is not unlimited however. But it is inherent in the notion of articulation that we sometimes produce genuinely new articulations of goods, which may circulate in social space and eventually feed back and alter the good that is articulated. To put it differently, my wholeheartedly caring only has a normative hold on me as long as it connects me with the normative sources of a "wider whole" (Taylor 1991: 91), all the while it not only reproduces but widens the horizon of intelligibility, as Tugendhat (1979) has convincingly put it.

(b) Moving on to the second boundary, the structure of wholehearted caring places limitations on the *way* that I can coherently go about engaging in them. Let us see how. It is common sense that wholehearted commitment may sometimes make us blind or inattentive to other people's engagements. We could also imagine that Luther's wholehearted engagement and especially his wanting to stand in a close relation with some public value might have pushed him to prevent others from engaging in a similar project. The point is that in such a case Luther's acts would not only be morally despicable, but would indeed betray his very commitment by betraying the public value that he takes his commitment to be expressive of.

Let me explain. The important aspect that follows from the structure of wholehearted caring (that I am both indebted to what I care about and the public value I see articulated in my commitment) commits me at least to be thoughtful about that kind of value in general. This is clearly not the case in Frankfurt (2006), or Williams (1981a), who hold that when someone cares about a public value she insists that she should be the one who promotes the flourishing of that value. Taking into consideration the structure of wholehearted caring, we arrive at a different position. In some cases we would betray our projects if we were to promote them in certain ways. For instance, if Luther were to spread unfounded rumors about the poor or corrupt the work of another scholar involved in a similar project, he would no longer serve the value that he takes his commitment to be an articulation of. Luther would be disloyal to his own commitment if he would prevent others from promoting the public value he attaches to his commitment. Accordingly, by insisting on being the sole promoter, he would betray his own wholehearted commitment. In general terms, if one wholeheartedly engages, then the non-agent-relative component will not permit inhibiting others from also attaining that good and from contributing to its flourishing. Investigating the structure of wholehearted caring reveals that wholehearted engagement in a project may sometimes imply stepping back from it and not prioritizing it over other people's wishes and commitments (see Korsgaard 2006).

Thus, the public value that the commitment articulates places a constraint on the manner in which one can care about it. One cannot do *everything that is possible* to promote it and disregard everything and everybody else. Importantly, this limitation does not stem from the 'outside' in the legal or moral sense of the word, but flows from the 'inside'—from the very structure of the commitment. Here, the account clearly departs from Williams (1981a) and Frankfurt (2006), who hold that we only step back from our engagement in a project if we happen to care about the value of altruism, morality, etc. Such default accounts tend to overlook the important twolevel *structure* of wholehearted caring pointed out here.

Wholehearted commitments that involve strong evaluations articulate a relation to a 'field' or background of inter-subjectively constituted (and thus choice-transcendent) values and orientations upon which they are based. Evaluative vocabulary therefore has a normative grip on us, because it connects to values that we recognize as not stemming from our choices. We have now elaborated further on this, and our inquiry into the structure of wholehearted caring (that my reasons originate from both my commitment to my project *and* my longing to stand in a close relation to the public value that it articulates) further underscored that our projects involve commitments to values and that we tap from their normative sources in order be able to revitalize our commitments. These aspects are constitutive for our engagements.

We are now in a position to reject the view that authenticity and public values are either antagonistic or coincide only by accident. The structure of wholehearted commitment is far from being hostile to public values; rather, it commits the caring individual to a public value that is beyond the object of his wholehearted caring. Moreover, this structure actually places a constraint on the person. Wholehearted caring involves a commitment to some public value that places a restriction on how I go about caring about my project. This should of course not be taken to mean that our commitments are reducible to straightforward reactions to or reproductions of public values, since the practice of articulating our commitments may both realize and eventually alter the values in question.

11 CONCLUSION

Let us return to the initial dilemma. On the one hand, who we really are is not adequately captured in terms of discovery or production but has rather to do with the (wholehearted) manner in which we relate to our commitments. At the same time, we understand ourselves as human agents who are authors of our lives. An important part of who we are is constituted in the choices that concern what we truly care about. However, it seems that we are thereby embracing productionist voluntarism, which was rejected in the last chapter.

In this chapter, I have defended a position that allows us to hold on to important aspects from both models without assuming question-begging voluntarism about self and values. It is right to say that who we are is a matter of our wholehearted involvements, and that our involvements create the values that provide orientation in our lives. However, it is crucial to take into account that engagements and commitments do not take place in a void, but always in the context of a meaningfully disclosed world that provides the necessary background of inter-subjectively constituted values and orientations. These guide our engagements in the first place. Therefore, instead of speaking of a causal relation between our commitments and the collective background of values and orientations, I have tried to spell it out in terms of a *constitutive* relation.

The reinterpretation of Sartrean fundamental choice suggests that to understand how we constitute ourselves through choices, we must consider how we are embedded in horizons of significance. These are—at least partly—constituted by qualitative distinctions of worth. Our practice of authenticity is to a significant extent situated in such a context. When reflecting on who we are and what we care about, we reflect on the relation between our commitments and the goods that our qualitative distinctions of worth are based on. Authenticity, then, is far from merely being about an intra-subjective relation between us and our 'inner'; it is very much about articulating normative goods from a shared horizon through a commitment—a process that requires some prior responsiveness to these goods.

The examination of the *structure* of wholehearted caring illustrated that it is constitutive of our commitments that they articulate goods, which lastly provide their normative sources. This helped find the solution to the 'irritating question': in order to refresh our commitments we remind ourselves that with our commitment we attempted to articulate a public good. Of course, successful refreshment requires that one is still drawn towards this good and that one is still capable of understanding the commitment as a truthful articulation.

Our commitments articulate contexts of significance, and the internal structure of our commitments commits us to the public value that we take our commitments to embody and constrains the manner in which we can pursue our commitment. In articulations we do not just reproduce. The articulation inherent in our commitments does not leave unaltered what it is as articulation of. More exactly, articulation refines and widens the horizon of intelligibility through an individual interpretation. In a sense, a cultural horizon, its values, and our commitments that articulate them are interdependent: values stop existing if there is no practice of valuing. So instead of thinking that our choices confer value on our commitments, we should think of commitments as articulations. This does not deny the importance of agency. Given the relation of interdependence, our choices are constitutive for the vitality of the value in question.

I have earlier argued that authenticity is to a decisive degree about being responsive to what really matters to us. We can now supplement this and maintain that such responsiveness also involves responsiveness to inter-subjectively constituted values and orientations, which provide vital sources for our agency. While we are on track for a formal concept of authenticity, we still need to say more about the characteristics of the relevant choices. In the next chapter, we will therefore reconsider the idea of 'existential choice.' For many critics, most prominently Habermas, the Heidegger-Sartrean notion of *existential choice* is susceptible to criticism (as applied to the productionist model). While for Habermas the idea of choosing oneself clearly amounts to unfounded decisionism, I will in the following section present a reading that successfully tames the radical nature of the productionist claim while also moving beyond the passivity of inner sense.

5   Existential Choices

In the previous chapters I have argued that the inner sense and productionist models fail. Authenticity, rather than being a matter of discovery
or production, concerns the (wholehearted) manner in which one relates
to one's commitments. Drawing on the work of Frankfurt, I have defined
wholeheartedness as involving centrality (being engaged in a 'project' that
is so central to one's self-understanding that betraying it would also mean
betraying oneself) and continuity (being committed to both the actual content of a project and to entertaining the commitment itself). In the last
chapter we went beyond Frankfurt (and, in general, the range of discussion
on personal autonomy) and added a further characteristic of wholeheartedness: 'embeddedness.' This relates to being immersed in an inter-subjectively constituted background or 'field' that is (at least partly) constituted by
qualitative distinctions of worth, and that we become immersed in through
second-personal interactions. The practice of authenticity is then about
situating us in such a context through wholehearted commitments that
articulate aspects of this background. When we make up our minds about
our wholehearted commitments we consider what is truly worth pursuing
and position ourselves on this 'map' made up by qualitative *distinctions
of worth*. In practical reasoning through strong evaluations we constitute
our wholehearted commitments in relation to the goods that our commitments attempt to articulate. Thus, when acquiring wholehearted engagements that constitute our personal horizons, we *articulate* the background
of choice-transcendent values on which they are based and from which
their normativity originally springs. These, as we have seen, constrain our
commitments in important ways.

Thus, so far, we have clarified the context within which it is intelligible
and justified to speak of choices that constitute who we are, and have added
further dimensions to our account of what wholehearted commitment is
about, namely centrality, continuity, embeddedness, and articulation. We
are now in a position to further clarify the concrete situations in which
we are called upon to make choices that articulate who we are and where
we stand. I will be referring to such self-constituting choices as 'existential
choices,' and will use this term in a less volontaristic sense than one might

think on the basis of its Sartrean sound. It is not my intention to maintain that only these kinds of choices relate to the issue of authenticity. However, it is my contention that they are prominent and emblematic when expressing our selves, and that they come with a complex phenomenology. I take them to be characteristic, because in them we both discover and get in touch with who we are 'on the inside' and actively constitute (or 'produce') ourselves at the same time.

1 BEYOND CALCULATIVE CHOICES

Let us take up the example of Luther once again. "I cannot and will not recant anything, for to go against conscience is neither right nor safe." Luther's sentence was followed by the famous "Here I stand. I can do no other. God help me. Amen." Recalling the discussion in the last chapter, we have said that Luther found himself in wholehearted engagement and now we can further clarify the nature of the relevant choices involved.

Intuitively, we are inclined to describe what is at stake here as a choice between alternative options, as a piece of instrumental reasoning that aims at determining an action with the goal to achieve a given end in a given set of circumstances. It is deeply entrenched in our understanding of choices that they are motivated by the expected rewards and costs. The idea is that benefits and expenses (in terms of energy invested or even possible punishment) shape human action. In much the same way, rational choice theory understands both individual action and broader social interaction as social exchange modeled on economic action (Varga 2011c). As in numerous general economic theories, individuals are depicted as rational, utility-maximizing agents that compute the costs and benefits of the actions they plan in order to obtain the most beneficial option at the lowest cost. Such an understanding has been extensively applied to choices performed not only in markets but also in social interaction. While choices in social interactions first do not appear to conform to rationality norms, in this view they are decipherable as calculative, thus involving envisaging the plausible costs and benefits of actions relative to a set of preferences.

Within such a picture, Luther's act of choice is intelligible as an expression of his preferences given the relevant constraints in the situation: he simply anticipates the outcomes of possible courses of action and calculates the alternative that is likely to give him the greatest satisfaction. What Luther does, then, is simply reach an end in calculating two options. In this outlook, much the same way as choosing between two meals, Luther predicts the outcomes of alternative options and rationally calculates the alternatives that are likely to bring the best match relative to his preferences. In this view, Luther's choice simply expresses his stronger preference for defending his work. Such a view may be able to explain countless instances of choice but would in our case be inadequate, because the phenomenology of the choice cannot be accounted for within its framework. Let us first consider this issue in greater depth.

2   UNTHINKABILITY AND PRACTICAL NECESSITY

To understand the qualitative differences in the choice at hand, we need to look into Luther's choice of words. His report that he "can do no other"— the sense of necessity, inescapability, and the 'unthinkability of alternatives' that his words convey—must be taken seriously. Daniel C. Dennett (1984: 133) has spoken in favor of interpreting Luther's words in this way and argued that Luther's conscience "made it impossible for him to recant." This option was somehow out of the sphere of deliberation.

It is important not to forget that this experience of practical necessity is discrete and recognizable. It is resistant to explanations that involve calculating ends or matching pre-existing preferences. It denotes an experienced necessity, a 'must' that Williams (1981a; 1985; 1993a; 1993b) has referred to as 'practical necessity.' The outspoken sense of incapacity, the sense of the impossibility of alternatives that emerges from practical necessity, the sense of 'must' that characterizes this choice are all reliable indicators. Instead of dealing with a difference in degree compared to calculated choices, we are dealing with a difference in kind. We would lose all these nuances if we attempted to explain Luther's choice as the outcome of a process of calculating options guided by a list of preferences. To emphasize this difference in kind, I shall call such choices involving practical necessity 'existential choices' and understand them as outcomes of a particular manner of deliberative reasoning. Sometimes certain considerations are presented to us as practical necessities, and we should grant this aspect an important role in explaining how we make choices through which we constitute ourselves. Yet, in what sense should we understand this necessity, impossibility, or unthinkability and where does it stem from? Let us start with the issue of origin.

3   THE ORIGIN OF NECESSITY

As Williams (1981d; 1985) and Robert J. Gay (1989) have pointed out, this experienced necessity is of a recognizable type and it is not dependent upon the persons being indebted to a particular type of moral outlook. This picture is very different than the one in Kant's reflections on the sense of practical necessity. While Kant connects necessity to 'duty' and moral choices, Williams views it as a general feature of human deliberation. Williams (1985: 188, also 196) rightly challenges the view that connects practical necessity solely to moral obligation, maintaining that such sense is "in no way peculiar to ethics." The sense of 'must' may result from moral obligation but this is far from always being the case. Instead, what is of practical necessity in general is established by the projects that are vital to the agent (Williams 1995: 17; Louden 2006: 108–109) and that the agent wholeheartedly cares about. Again, while such wholeheartedly endorsed engagements can be connected to moral obligations, this need not to be the case. Instead, necessity is grasped in light of antecedent commitments, on the background of which such a situation becomes intelligible, as particularly problematic and as affording a certain, existential mode of evaluation. Recall that it is our commitments that shape our world making situations and objects intelligible as threatening or favorable, easy or full of obstacles, or more generally, as affording certain actions (Sartre 1943/1991: 489). Our engagements provide a hermeneutic structure within which our situations and motives become comprehensible and reveal themselves in the way situations appear to us, as significant, requiring our attention, etc. (Ibid.: 485). So whether we understand the situations we face as affording calculative or existential choices, we do so only in the light of being engaged in antecedent commitments that compel us to initiate a particular kind of deliberation. In the case of Luther, the afforded mode of evaluation is not calculative. The sense of necessity called upon a more fundamental, existential decision about very principles that govern his calculations.

Thus, in situations of importance, the senses of necessity and 'unthinkability' remind us that we need to go beyond the sphere of simple calculative deliberation. Such sense of necessity is highly unlikely to appear under everyday circumstances however. There is seldom a sense of 'unthinkability' in calculative choices like between two meals in a restaurant, unless of course one is an animal rights activist and vegetarian. This point leads us to the issue at hand. For the animal rights activist, the situation in the restaurant is one that affords more than a simple calculative choice. Due to his self-understanding as the person who values and fights for animal rights and who consciously sends a political message by avoiding the consumption of meat, the situation becomes 'existential' in the sense that the vocabulary of evaluation changes; it changes to qualitative distinctions of worth where something being desired is not sufficient for the ascription of goodness. This, however, would be the case if reasoning were performed solely in terms of calculative choices. Rather than in situations facing calculative choices, the sense of 'unthinkability' arises only in connection to situations that are important to our wholehearted commitments and in connection to the strong evaluations inherent in articulating a particular notion of the good. When making such choices, we simultaneously evaluate and articulate more or less explicit ambitions to be a certain kind of person.

Before going further, we need to make a correction here. While necessity for Williams, Frankfurt, and Sartre can arise from anything that a person wholeheartedly engages in, this seems inadequate in light of the last chapter. What we care about and how we go about caring is constrained by those public goods that we try to articulate in our projects.

In short, the origins of necessity cannot merely be reduced to what we wholeheartedly care about but must also take into account the good that lastly provides the crucial normative source. The view of commitments as articulations presented in the last chapter allows us to understand why we may sometimes be overwhelmed by necessity and the feeling that we respond to something that is beyond our own projects. This also squares with the claim defended in the last chapters, namely that wholehearted identification involves being committed to things that go beyond the commitment itself.

4   THE CHIPS ARE DOWN

It is on the background of these reflections that we can make sense of Sartre's somewhat mysterious sentence "When I deliberate, the chips are down ... When the will intervenes, the decision is taken, and it has no other value than that of making the announcement" (Sartre 1943/1991: 451). We can say that in Luther's case the chips are down in two senses. First, the very feeling of necessity reveals that some (however tacit) decision has been made to wholeheartedly endorse something—this is what discloses the situation to him as necessitating in the first place. Second, the chips are also down in the sense that the agent is not only necessitated by his wholehearted commitment, but is also inclined to treat the situation under a specific deliberatory angle. In other words, the sense of necessity also commits the agent to a mode of practical reasoning that is employed in situations that touch upon wholehearted commitment (in general terms, see Bratman 2002: 68). When Luther deliberates, a choice has already been made to approach the problem from a certain angle, from an 'existential' angle, where one is committed to act for reasons that go beyond those that one's list of preferences provides. Thus, when Luther deliberates, "the chips are down"; he realizes that calculating on momentary preferences would be an inadequate means of dealing with this situation. In order to avoid misunderstanding two points must be added.

First, the argument does not imply that every situation that involves a sense of necessity and unthinkability deserves the label 'existential choice.' For most people it appears unthinkable to consciously hurt a child, without being existentially committed to not hurting children. It may be the case that these particular individuals are existentially committed to being those kinds of persons who value humans and promote the welfare of children and human life in general. It is as a consequence of such an antecedent existential commitment that hurting a child does not appear as an option.

Second, the sense of impossibility should be understood in a deflated, relaxed sense, not as of logical or causal sort. We may give this point greater precision: while Luther was well aware that he had the capacity to act otherwise, he was nevertheless unable to muster the will (see Frankfurt

1988b: 86). In the words of Frankfurt (1999a: 108–116), his commitment has become a "volitional necessity." When Luther says that he 'can do no other,' he is not expressing a quantitatively stronger preference for 'standing up against the pope' and a weaker preference for retreating and living a peaceful existence without putting his existence into danger. On the contrary, he might indeed have had a robust preference for a calm, contemplative life. Luther might in fact have thought of "not standing up to the Pope," secretly wishing that there would be a way in which he could bring himself to welcome this possibility. The sense of necessity involved in Luther's situation is neither logical nor causal, but expresses that Luther felt unable to congregate the will to act otherwise. This does not preclude that he may have been simultaneously aware of possessing the capacity for such an act. What Luther reports, is that *as the person he (implicitly) understands himself to be* (committed to the articulation of some good), he really had no options. The necessity or incapacities in question are simply expressive of the agent's wholehearted engagements (see Williams 1993a: 60).

5   COMPLEX PHENOMENOLOGY

While the most important feature of such experience is the constraint, the sense of being necessitated and compelled, the relevant phenomenology is multifaceted. In everyday life, such a feeling is experienced as upsetting, possibly involving the sense of being hindered and the feeling of passivity and loss of agency, etc. Under normal circumstances, when we experience such boundaries we often attempt to overcome them and secure the widest possible set of alternatives. This is not the case with the necessity of existential choices. The necessity at stake here is not a constraint that comes to us as an alien force that leaves no room for us. Rather, coming to be aware of such a constraint means identifying something that is central to oneself. Such moments of practical necessity may often be accompanied by a more enlivening feeling of exceptional clarity about oneself and an invigorating feeling that stems from the discovery of these boundaries.

All situations characterized by necessity and 'unthinkability of alternatives' are complex and involve aspects of self-discovery, self-alienation, positivity and negativity. When Luther reports a sense of 'unthinkability' and feels unable to undertake certain actions we are inclined understand this as if constraints were put on him by an external force. However, as we have noted, there is no such alienation at stake here. There is a special sense of acquaintance with this incapacity and the boundary that it reveals, since they arise from the wholehearted engagements that define him. The necessity and incapability are genuine expressions of him—they are crystallizations of his self. According to Williams, such experience involves an understanding both of "one's own powers and incapacities and of what the world permits, and the recognition of a limit which is neither simply external to the self, nor yet a product of the will, is what can lend a special authority or dignity to such decisions" (Williams 1981c: 130–131). While the constraint of necessity might come as a surprise, as an unexpected discovery, the person in question nevertheless often endorses it. In fact, we can readily imagine that such an endorsement is unequivocal. If Luther were given the ability to exceed this limitation that was placed upon him he may very well refuse without further deliberation.[1] It is perfectly imaginable that Luther is unable to willingly act against his commitment, even if given the power to transcend this limitation of his will.

The necessity and incapability involved (as an expression of his undivided, wholehearted endorsement, not as an alien constraint) are often accompanied by a sense of harmony and liberation. Frankfurt describes this poignantly:

> Discovering how things must necessarily be enables us—indeed, it requires us—to give up the debilitating restraint that we impose upon ourselves when we are unsure what to think. Then there is no longer any obstacle to wholehearted belief. Nothing stands in the way of a steady and untroubled conviction. We are released from the blockage of irresolution and can give ourselves to an unimpeded assent (2004: 65).

The sense of necessity identifies the limits of possible actions. As Williams (1981c: 130) notes, such necessity and incapacity not only limit who one is, but partly constitute the substance of who one is. Other forms of necessity, like the intense necessity of the addict to take drugs, lack this element. So in all, the complex phenomenology of necessity suggests the simultaneous presence of harmony, a resolution of the will and the articulation of something important that does not stem purely from the will. This last aspect could not be accommodated into accounts given by Frankfurt and Williams, who argue that the source of necessity is merely the commitment of the agent. However, this is easily accommodated in the account of wholehearted engagement presented over the last chapters, which understands commitments to be articulations of goods. It has furthermore held that the normative grip of such goods on us does not merely stem from our caring about them, and that our indebtedness to them can limit how we care and what we care about. In that case, it is quite straightforward that necessity may feel like an 'external' limitation, because it does not directly arise from wholehearted commitment, but from the good that this commitment attempts to articulate. In this way, there is no paradox.

6   ARTICULATION IN EXISTENTIAL CHOICES

Korsgaard vividly describes a situation that is similar to the present case. Also, she captures the different choices at stake in such situations:

From a third-person point of view, outside of the deliberative stand-point, it may look as if what happens when someone makes a choice is that the strongest of his conflicting desires wins. But that isn't the way it is for you when you deliberate. When you deliberate, it is as if there were something over and above all of your desires, something which is you, and which chooses which desire to act on. This means that the principle or law by which you determine your actions is one that you regard as being expressive of yourself. To identify with such a principle or way of choosing is to be, in St Paul's famous phrase, a law to yourself (1996: 100).

The way Korsgaard describes deliberation captures how certain situations are recognized as being beyond the sphere of simple calculation. While she rightly notes that such choices differ from the ones based on desires and calculation, she nevertheless tends to collapse the qualitative difference between calculative and existential choice. In her account, both cases rely on explicit knowledge of something that pre-exists, in one case a strong desire and in the other a commitment or principle. Yet, in order to engage in existential choices one does not need explicit knowledge of one's whole-hearted commitment. Such situations are often the ones in which we first come to realize or have a glimpse of what we implicitly are committed to. Then we may engage in attempting to formulate what it is about.

Acknowledging such aspects may mistakenly lead us to accept the inner sense model and to assume that authenticity is about the discovery of something pre-existing. However, what really happens is that we articulate a mainly inarticulate sense of what is of good and important to us. As Taylor (1985: 38) notes, the "articulation of this 'object' tends to make it something different from what it was before." Such an account of what informs existential decisions avoids both maintaining that these are *ex nihilo*, and that they rely on stable and pre-existing entities. More precisely, while we can agree with Sartre that such choices cannot be reduced to expressions of something fixed, we should not draw the unwarranted conclusion that they must be radically free or random and consequently "the very upsurge of a freedom which is beyond causes, motives, and ends" (Sartre 1943/1991: 450). Instead, we must say that existential choices are not produced *ex nihilo* but articulate and bring into existence more or less tacit commitments. This allows us to avoid the threatening circularity. Existential choices, as defined here, neither make recourse to reasons or motivations in the customary manner nor to sets of existing preferences. The position proposed here does not imply that our reasons are simply generated by existential choices. Instead, it holds that when making those choices we anticipate an articulation of the good, but all we may have at this point of anticipation are vague orientations that need further articulation. We may not be explicitly aware of the preferences that our existential choice brings into existence. In such way, we are able to accommodate Sartre's line of reasoning about existential choices being 'beyond causes, motives, and ends,' while we both avoid maintaining that they are *ex nihilo* and assuming stably pre-existing motivations or reasons.

7   RESPONSIBILITY

If it is in such situations that we constitute ourselves, then they must be situations in which we take responsibility for who we are. Given the experience of necessity and the 'unthinkability of alternatives' that characterize such situations, some would argue that we cannot be responsible for our existential choices. Numerous theorists who buy into the so-called 'principle of alternative possibilities' maintain that there is a fundamental incompatibility between the agent's choice being causally determined and the responsibility that he has for his choice. Only if the agent could have done otherwise can he be correctly attributed responsibility for the choice. However, not only is it wrong not to ascribe responsibility in such a situation: I both maintain that Luther was describing his situation correctly and that he was responsible for his choice. In addition, such existential choices, made under constraints of necessity, are exemplary for the exercise of autonomy and authenticity. Let us see why.

Robert Kane (1996) accepts that Luther perhaps could "do no other", but argues that Luther is still free if his choice can be traced back to previous characterforming commitments. In this case, rather than avoiding responsibility for his act by saying "I can't do no other," Luther actually takes full responsibility for it. One way of putting this is that Luther was responsible for being the sort of person he had become (Ibid.: 39). Luther may have gradually shaped his wholehearted commitment and thereby the character that issued this act, and in that case one should not object to holding Luther responsible for "the final affirmation" (Ibid.). Luther's choice (as a final affirmation) is free, despite its being determined, because it was made possible through past choices and actions that were not determined and that have made him into the kind of person that he was (Ibid.: 118; similarly Williams 1981c; 1985).

8   EXISTENTIAL CHOICES AS 'ALTERNATIVELESS' CHOICES

The difference between calculative choice and existential choice is not a matter of degree, but of kind. The latter involves no calculation and the involved sense of 'unthinkability' implies that the possibilities not acted upon are excluded categorically, not gradually. Luther's situation called for a choice of the existential kind, since there were no means—such as a stable list of preferences—that could determine the right answer and since the issue. He did not face a regular calculative choice. The choice of 'not standing up against the Pope' and avoiding the risk of prosecution was not merely another option, since it would have undermined a wholehearted commitment, constitutive of the kind of person he regarded himself as. Again, we need not presuppose that Luther must have had some kind of explicit knowledge of his engagement. He may well have slowly 'drifted' into caring about certain matters, without much explicit thought.

To further clarify the difference between calculative and existential choices, I suggest thinking of existential choices as 'alternativeless choices.' As the person he comprehends himself to be, Luther had the choice to affirm himself as being wholeheartedly engaged and to choose himself in the sense of confirming a commitment that is already his own and that he may not have been explicitly aware of. The situation was about mustering the will to authenticate the wholehearted commitment that defined him as a person.

This is an 'alternativeless' choice because the other possibilities are not adequately described as options. In such a situation, the alternatives are eliminated with an unusual force; some actions—like 'not standing up against the Pope'—are categorically excluded and do not suggest themselves as real possibilities (see Luckner 2007: 24). We see that Luther's emphasis is not on what he must do; rather, he conveys that what characterizes his experience is that all alternatives are categorically excluded as 'impossibilities.' Lack of alternatives that characterize such existential choices brings out another sense in which 'the chips are down.'

9 FAILING AND INAUTHENTICITY

I have suggested that the sense of impossibility is understood in a relaxed sense, without involving logical or causal determination. This leaves open a possibility we have not considered yet: how can we describe a situation in which Luther acts differently, in a way that would not involve 'standing up against Pope'? Let us imagine that Luther acts differently. Let us suppose an alternative ending to Luther's story, in which he—possibly due to the perspective of possible punishment—moves to a remote village to contemplate and to let things calm down. There are two questions we need to confront: how should this 'choice' be conceived if it is not simply an alternative (a), and should this be counted as an instance of inauthenticity (b)?

(a) In this case, it would be imprecise to say that Luther has chosen the alternative 'moving to a remote village and not standing up to the Pope.' We would be mischaracterizing the situation if we were to maintain that Luther chose another option, in principle in the same way as in a calculative choice. We have to bear in mind what our inquiry has revealed. Rather than choosing between alternatives, Luther's choice really consisted of being able to muster the will to go through with a decision, to authenticate his wholehearted commitment that defined him as a person. Therefore, on a more correct description, Luther's 'moving to a remote village and not standing up to the Pope' constitutes a *failure* to existentially choose, a failure to go through with the act that Kane (1996: 39) referred to as a "final affirmation" (see also Luckner 2007). Instead of a calculative choice of another alternative, Luther's act is more adequately described as a failure or inability to decide existentially.

(b) We have said in Chapter 4 that when one is wholeheartedly engaged in a matter, betraying it amounts to betraying oneself (centrality). Thus, for Luther 'not standing up against the Pope' would have meant canceling out his wholehearted commitment in a way that would have precluded him from carrying on with an unchanged self-conception. Sartre describes the consequences of such a failure:

> There is no doubt that I could have done otherwise, but that is not the problem. It ought to be formulated like this: could I have done otherwise without perceptibly modifying the organic totality of the projects that make up who I am?

Sartre goes on to say that the character of the act may be such that

> instead of remaining a purely local and accidental modification of my behaviour, it could be effected only by means of a radical transformation of my being-in-the-world . . . In other words: I could have acted otherwise. Agreed. But at what price?" (Sartre 1943/1991: 454).

Acting otherwise or, more precisely, failing to authenticate one's wholehearted commitments comes at the price of transforming who one is. The question is now whether Luther's failure to decide in a negative sense implies some kind of inauthenticity. It seems that we should be more charitable to Luther. After all, our wholehearted engagements in life are not made in concrete, and they do occasionally change. Therefore, it is sometimes the case that we are unable to carry through a choice in an existential situation because what we wholeheartedly care about has changed and has lost its grip on us. Instead of conceiving it as inauthenticity, there might be a way in which Luther's failure could be understood in a more positive sense than mere self-betrayal. A failure to decide can indeed be something positive, but only in the case in which this failure is incorporated and transformed into effective self-knowledge. To return to Sartre's formulation, the 'price' of not being able to choose is a fundamental modification of what it is that we care about and who we are. This, of course, is not a matter of a simple choice.

10   CHANGING WHOLEHEARTED COMMITMENTS

This brings out the question of whether and in which sense we can modify what we wholeheartedly care about. Let us look at a possibility in which such a modification may happen and in which failure is turned into active selfknowledge. After moving to the remote village, driven by his conscience, Luther may seek to understand his failure to authenticate his wholehearted commitment. In this process, he rethinks his life, and while doing so, something like a conversion occurs. He looks into his past and comes to realize that he actually never was a person of courage who could stand up against authorities, and that he in fact always worshiped a calm life in contemplation more than everything else. While rethinking his life, Luther does not passively observe his motivations but actively reinterprets his life. He begins to see things in a whole new perspective, and now the failure to 'stand up against the Pope' comes into view as an intelligible continuation of his life story—a process that is likely to ease his psychological torment. Luther therefore re-frames the understanding of his life, in which the 'failing' of an existential choice is turned into a piece of self-knowledge that is integrated in a novel self-interpretation. In the language of Sartre (1943/1991: 464), we see "a radical conversion" or a "metamorphosis" of a project.

> These extraordinary and marvelous instants when the prior project collapses into the past in the light of a new project which rises on its ruins and which as yet exists only in outline, in which humiliation, anguish, joy, hope are delicately blended, in which we let go in order to grasp and grasp in order to let go—these have often appeared to furnish the clearest and most moving image of our freedom (Sartre 1943/1991: 476).

Now, contrary to Sartre's overall position, such reinterpretation cannot be a wholly original free choice, since it depends on a horizon of meaning and mattering, a field of meaningful possibilities that makes such re-framing possible. Luther cannot decide to re-frame his life 'from nowhere'; rather, the 'raw material' of his life that he rearranges is already disclosed to him as meaningful. It gives way to certain interpretations, while not to others. Possibly against his intentions, I think Sartre captures exactly this when saying "the prior project collapses into the past in the light of a new project." The fading 'pull' of a certain commitment is seen in the light of a new, active 'pull,' which, as Sartre says, rises out of the ruins of the old. In this case, by failing, Luther may on the one hand reinterpret his personal history and realize that he actually never was a brave person; instead, he always tended to prefer contemplation, peace, and personal safety. On the other hand, he may realize that his best way of pleasing God may lay in the quiet, contemplative life of a scholar, rather than in the life of a public person who engages in disputes. With such a realization, Luther's understanding of his past and present changes. His choice of 'not standing up against the Pope' and to withdraw now becomes intelligible to him not as a betrayal, but as the genuine articulation of his commitment. It is in such a case that the 'failing' of an existential choice can be transformed into a piece of self-knowledge that may well play a crucial role in a novel self-interpretation.

This reemplotment is not based on an arbitrary choice. Luther's failure actually brings about important self-knowledge followed by a re-examination of his life as a whole, which may lead to an essential modification of his basic commitments.

Obviously, this is not always how it goes. It is also possible that such failure does not lead to a positive outcome. We can imagine a scenario in which Luther ignores the necessity and the existential quality of the situation and treats it as one that calls for a calculation-based choice. In that case, Luther could still understand his abandonment and his refuge to the remote village as something that can be accommodated in his 'old' self-understanding. For this, Luther must deceive himself about the distinguishing quality of the situation and conceive it as calling for a choice between mere options that do not have an impact on his self-understanding. We could say that the failing to go through with an existential choice can be considered inauthentic, if it does not give rise to self-knowledge and reemplotment. In such a case, Luther would live at odds with himself, not being able to see his life as organized as a unity with past and present motives and future ends.

11 CONSCIENCE: NECESSITY *A POSTERIORI*

We have addressed the sense of necessity characteristic of existential choices but have not yet mentioned another feature that works in a similar manner, and that is mostly encountered after situations of existential choice. This is our conscience that conveys more or less explicit judgments about choices we have carried out. In everyday life, we often say that our conscience has 'told' us what to do, implying that it sometimes affords us knowledge that informs our judgments. Also, we often say that our conscience harasses us for having done something. While conscience has many guises, for instance, as good or bad conscience, I will only consider the cases where conscience works subtly and not in the explicit way as in guilt, blame, or shame.

Let us make use of the alternative ending to Luther's story. Recall that Luther appeals to his conscience, "I cannot and will not recant anything, for to go against conscience is neither right nor safe." Applying our terms, let us again take the case in which Luther failed to choose existentially and to authenticate his wholehearted commitment. Instead of standing up, Luther was not able to go through with his decision. Due to the perspective of possible punishment, he simply abandoned the whole issue and moved to a remote village to let things calm down. In that case, it is a very likely that he would have been tormented by his conscience. But what is conscience?

Kant famously conceived of conscience in terms of reflection and as an inner court. In an inner judicial proceeding, both accuser and the defender within us are understood as arguing their point. This culminates in "the conclusion of reason (the verdict), that is, the connecting of the rightful result with the action (condemnation or acquittal)" (Kant 1797/2003: 189; Wood 2008: 184–186). In Kant's judicial imagery of conscience, it seems possible to reflectively single out the wholehearted engagements one has and turn them into objects of knowledge that can be passed verdict on. With Sartre we might doubt that it is possible for us to see our whole-hearted engagements 'from nowhere.' Sartre denies this possibility because for something to become an object of knowledge it is required that one can single out this entity and make it visible against some background. How-ever, as Sartre argues, if we accept that wholehearted engagements define who we are, then such a step back is simply infeasible. Even if the whole-hearted commitment "is fully experienced by the subject and hence wholly conscious, that certainly does not mean that it must be known by him; quite the contrary" (Sartre 1943/1991: 570). The point is that one can-not single out this entity and analyze it, since it already shapes the whole of one's life (Baldwin 1979). Sartre makes an important point here, but while he takes this to prove that knowledge of wholehearted commitments is impossible, there is another, subtler way in which we can be said to have some knowledge. We have said that the sense of necessity reveals to us some kind of knowledge about ourselves and about what we are committed to, without necessarily conveying explicit content. In the same way as necessity reveals something *before the choice*, our conscience can sometimes reveal something about us *after the choice*. At this point, Heidegger's notion of conscience can help us further illustrate how this works.

For Heidegger, far from being an articulate process of arguments and counter-arguments cumulating in a verdict, conscience is silent. The call of conscience is a sort of discourse that is carried out without a specific vocal utterance and without a specific propositional content:

> What does the conscience call him to whom it appeals? Taken strictly, nothing. The call asserts nothing, offers no information about world events, has nothing to tell us. . . . Conscience discourses solely and con-stantly in the mode of keeping silent (Heidegger 1927/1962: 318).

Its function is to summon Dasein to itself "that is, to its ownmost ability to be." What does this mean? One is spoken to in a particular manner, since "the call passes over what Dasein, proximally and for the most part understands itself as" (Heidegger 1927/1962: 318–319). In all, the 'call of conscience' may be interpreted as expressive responsiveness to one's own particularity (Carman 2003: 295). The contrast to Kant's picture of con-science as a court is quite clear. Here, conscience does not involve an inner judicial proceeding that can be brought to a verdict in recourse to some explicit norm. In Heidegger conscience does not bring about substantial knowledge of our wholehearted commitments, and he is at pains to empha-size that the call of conscience is not about anything in particular, and it is not addressed to any of one's concrete understandings of oneself.[2]

Heidegger's account is on to something very similar to the necessity that we addressed above. In this view, Luther is tormented by a claim that—akin to the sense of necessity—is not laid on him by external forces, but by himself. In Heidegger's terms, Luther is called back to himself, without being called back to a substantial or determinate conception of a commitment that he wholeheartedly cares about. Even though he feels 'called upon' and knows that this call is 'from himself,' the call has no clear sense of direction. Luther is called upon to execute an existential choice, not to realize some particular and determinate self-interpretation. The call of conscience simply notifies us that we face a weightier choice; it lets us grasp the claims that situations put on us, sometimes calling for an existential decision that articulates who we are and aspire to be.

Heidegger's account of conscience helps us understand the kind of self-knowledge that is at stake here. Against Sartre's position, we can justifiably talk of some kind of self-knowledge in this situation, since his conscience is 'telling' Luther that something is wrong.[3] However, and it is here that we can confirm Sartre, we can say that such self-knowledge is not concrete and does not have substantial content. Conscience reveals that even in the lack of substantial self-knowledge, we are responsive to ourselves and understand situations as existential, as bearing import to our lives as a whole and connecting with our implicit wholehearted commitments, without us being fully aware of what those commitments are about.[4] In fact, one is rather called upon to constitute them through articulation, which involves both discovery and self-constitution.

12   DISCOVERY AND SELF-CONSTITUTION

As I said in the beginning, the focus in this chapter is on existential choices that are emblematic when expressing and constituting ourselves and that are characterized by a particularly remarkable phenomenology. The sense of necessity, the constraint Luther discovers, is not something that is felt like an alien force, but as a force that essentially belongs to him. Recalling our attempt to find alternatives to the models of inner sense (discovery) and production (active self-constitution), we see that the choice Luther made cannot be correctly described in either set of terms. Luther gets in touch with who he is 'on the inside,' his history and memories by introspective discovery, while at the same time he actively constitutes and changes himself. The introspective and 'productive' parts in which he makes up his mind about who he is co-occur. Understanding who one really is by introspectively acquiring new knowledge about past motives and actions and the realization of being committed to the articulation of a good are not two different issues. They are just two ways of describing the same phenomenon.

The focus on existential choices should however not make us ignore that other kinds of choices may be relevant to authenticity. One could object that there are situations in which strongly valued commitments come into conflict with each other. Also, the recourse to wholehearted commitments involving strong evaluations obviously does not obliterate the dilemmas that may follow from the fact of moral pluralism. Sartre's famous problem of the young man who stands before the decision of either caring for his ailing mother or joining the Resistance is such an example. Needless to say, the choice he makes will have an impact on his life and on the person he is. In spite of this, it is a very different situation that is at stake here. The fact that there is no sense of necessity or categorical exclusion of alternatives shows that this young man is not wholeheartedly committed in the first place. Sartre's line of reasoning is that it is unattainable for the young man to choose by making recourse to reasons. Instead, he must simply 'throw' himself in one direction, which Sartre takes to show the straightforwardly arbitrary nature of such a choice. While we can easily agree with Sartre that some commitments may force us to sacrifice others, it does not mean that what is chosen must be arbitrary. Again, in such a situation, one would not throw oneself in an arbitrary direction, but attempt to be wholehearted, to articulate and thereby to connect a personal motive with a non-instrumental value. If this is not attempted, then Sartre is right and the person in question may either calculate or make an arbitrary choice. The chips are down.

13 CONCLUDING REMARKS: TOWARDS AN ALTERNATIVE CONCEPT OF AUTHENTICITY

Coming to the end of the second part of the book that dealt with the issue of authenticity mainly from the perspective of moral psychology, it is time to wrap up our discussion and reflect upon the scope of what has been accomplished.

In Chapter 4 we established that the question of authenticity, the question of who we really are, is not captured satisfactorily in terms of discovery or self-production. Rather than being about the uniqueness of the self, discovered (inner sense) or created (productionism), authenticity is connected to the (wholehearted) manner in which we engage in our lives, integrating our lives through projects that we wholeheartedly endorse. With this change of perspective we were able to avoid some of the pitfalls of the inner sense and the productionist models. We were able to account for the constitutive activity of the subject, without overemphasizing it in a productionist fashion. While who we are is defined by our wholehearted commitments to what we really care about, wholeheartedness involves being engaged to such a degree that betraying it would also mean betraying oneself (centrality), and being committed to both the actual project and to entertaining the commitment itself (continuity).

Then, in Chapter 5, we confronted what looked like a dilemma. Arguing that our wholehearted commitments define who we are and concurrently claiming that we are able to choose our commitments in life seems to oblige us to embrace the voluntarist 'productionist' assumption. This basically maintains that who we are is a matter of choice. The solution to this dilemma allowed us to hold on to our claims about our constitutive agency when choosing our commitments, while avoiding voluntarist assumptions about self and values. When we emphasize our agency in choosing our wholehearted involvements that provide orientation in our lives, it is vital to acknowledge that these do not come to us from nothing. Rather, they reach us as persons who are embedded in horizons of significance that are partly constituted by qualitative *distinctions of worth*. When constituting ourselves through our choices of commitment, we are situated in such a context and understand our commitments in the light of good and qualitative distinctions of worth. While Chapter 3 mainly addressed authenticity as an intra-subjective matter, it is now clear that this picture is incomplete. This is because the relation between our commitments and the collective background of values is *constitutive* and because authenticity is above all about articulating goods from a collective horizon though our commitments. This does not mean that we simply reproduce the pre-existing values that shape the horizons within which our choices take place; instead, our articulation reinforces, refines, and widens these horizons through an individual interpretation. While our articulations widen these horizons, the inspection of the structure of wholehearted caring revealed that our commitments articulate contexts of significance that lastly provide their normative sources. Additionally, it also became clear that the internal structure of our commitments commits us to public values that we take our commitments to embody and constrains the manner in which we can pursue our commitment. Thus, thinking of our relevant choices of commitments as articulations, rather than as acts that confer value on whatever commitments are chosen, helps us solve the dilemma. While authenticity is about being responsive to what really matters, our responsiveness to ourselves is mediated by inter-subjectively constituted contexts of significance, values, and orientations. In order to carry through an existential choice that has a normative grip, the person must display a responsive and expressive self-relation that is mediated by being embedded in a horizon of significance.

The present chapter was mainly concerned with illustrating situations in which we are called upon to make 'existential' choices that articulate who we are. I have deployed this term in a non-voluntaristic sense and argued that such choices are prominent and emblematic when expressing who we are. They furthermore have an exceptionally complex phenomenology, characterized by a sense of necessity.

Existential choices were important for our overall purposes. In them, we get in touch with who we are 'on the inside' and constitute ourselves at the same time. Basically, the idea is that what we are wholeheartedly indebted to often only takes on a gestalt-like formation rather than being clearly given to us. So in a sense, we actualize, articulate, and bring them into reality through existential 'alternativeless choices.' These attempts to articulate what we are about are superficially like the descriptions in which we make an effort to be faithful to some objectively occurring entity. Looked at more closely, though, we see that in these often demanding processes of articulation, we attempt to be faithful to something that often has an inarticulate gestalt-like formation. Additionally, these inarticulate formations are neither independent of our attempts of articulations of them, nor are they left unaltered by articulation. Here, the boundaries between the aspects that preceded articulation and those formed by it tend to dissolve. Our implicit grasp of those evaluative distinctions that govern what we want to bring to articulation change upon our deliberations about them. For instance, to bring up a simple case, upon reflection we may come to the conclusion that our implicit commitments were not adequate articulations and hence not worthy of our attention. There is thus a dialectic and dynamic two-way relation between implicitly endorsed commitments and deliberation, due to which both implicit and inarticulate formations and explicit articulations can be corrected.

With this move, we can successfully formalize the question of authenticity; maintaining that a choice I undertook really expresses who I am need not imply that I was truthful to something given. *The essence of authenticity is not a harmony between something given and its expression, but the quality of particular commitments and choices.* It involves lucidity about the quality or nature of the choices that one faces and lucidity about the fact that one is always already making choices that configure one's underlying life possibilities. These aspects enable the integration of one's endeavors into a whole and result in more complex knowledge about responsibilities. With this account, being authentic, having chosen oneself is no longer connected to some pre-existing and determinate matter, nor to the consistency of a self-created style of life. Additionally, there is no lurking paternalism here, since such an account only emphasizes the *manner of commitments* rather than saying something substantial about their content.

Part III
The Paradox of Authenticity

6 The Paradox of Authenticity

While the concept of authenticity has long been restricted to the periphery of philosophy, it has recently been restored and accepted as a valuable contemporary issue. However, as already mentioned at the beginning of this investigation, the accounts presently available omit a crucial aspect: the reciprocal shaping of capitalism and the ideal of authenticity. The practice of authenticity is not immune to and independent from the capitalist modes of production that shape modern societies. This is why this chapter seeks to address authenticity in the context of contemporary capitalism.

"Reciprocal shaping" tries to convey the non-functionalist methodological approach. The claim is not that capitalism creates the subjects it requires (a view often attributed to Max Weber). But I also find myself in disagreement with those who understand capitalism as a neutral platform, upon which all kinds of ethical orientations are possible. Having said this, the main concern of this chapter will be to put the concept of authenticity to work. First, it will be used as a *critical* concept, against which problematic or even pathological developments can be identified. Second, it will be used as a critical concept of *authenticity*, which will provide an adequate critical viewpoint, against which some *paradoxes* become visible. Namely, that authenticity has become an institutionalized demand on subjects, but also that problematic and possibly pathological conditions no longer arise from the social barriers that inhibit authenticity, but from the pursuit of authenticity and self-realization itself.

I will proceed by highlighting recent and fundamental transformations within the intersection of capitalism and authenticity. As a first step, the chapter will examine the popular 'self-help' discourse that explicitly addresses this intersection and point out a recent transformation: the emergence of a *performative* model of authenticity (1 through 4). As a second step, drawing on the work of Luc Boltanski, Eve Chiapello and Axel Honneth, a framework will be constructed that renders the emergence of the *performative* model of authenticity intelligible. This change has made possible what I will call a *paradoxical turn*. Authenticity, an idea once used to question the legitimacy of hierarchical institutions and to critique the power of capitalistic requirements, now seems to function as an institutionalized demand towards subjects that matches the systemic demands of contemporary capitalism (5 through 7). As a third and closing step, a link will be identified between this development and a specific form of psychological suffering. The aim is to show that the constant activity of performing authenticity exhausts the self, which may contribute to explaining some of the preconditions that make possible a rise in the frequency of depression and in the sales of pharmaceutical anti-depressants (8 and 9).

1   SELF-HELP AS A MEDIA OF REFLECTION ON AUTHENTICITY

How should one approach the intersection of capitalism and authenticity? In order to understand contemporary capitalism, Boltanski and Chiapello examine prescriptive texts from management discourse, which for these authors "constitutes the form par excellence in which the spirit of capitalism is incorporated and received" (2005: 14). On the other hand, in order to understand the contemporary popular notion of authenticity, Taylor (1991: 44) and Guignon (2004) analyze prescriptive, spiritually oriented self-help manuals. The claim in this chapter is also sustained through a reading of prescriptive texts, but because the aim is to address the reciprocal shaping between authenticity and capitalism, I will examine a recently developed, specific self-help genre that combines elements of management literature and traditional, spiritually oriented self-help. Consequently, in order to trace recent and hitherto unseen transformations in the ideal of authenticity, I will analyze a genre that is paradigmatic for the contemporary setting and that also explicitly targets the intersection of capitalistic requirements *and* the ideal of authenticity. In this sense, this self-help discourse is located somewhere between the management literatures that Boltanski and Chiapello analyze and the spiritually orientated self-help manuals that Taylor and Guignon examine.

Addressing a vast audience at discount prices, these self-help manuals reflect upon authenticity, social needs, and offer specific techniques to reach these goals. The term "self-help" describes an individual or group-based attempt that is undertaken to achieve self-improvement—spiritually, economically, socially, or intellectually. Self-help manuals include reflection on social needs and human concerns, but unlike other popular media in which this reflection also takes place—like television—self-help manuals always recommend specific techniques for achieving happiness and wealth. Despite its social significance and its being an important part of popular culture, the self-help genre remains a neglected study object.

Self-help can be traced back to manuals of early antiquity. These manuals, many of them presented and discussed in Foucault's late work, contain advice, exercises, and techniques that aim at enabling wise decisions concerning the practice of life and self-government. Augustine's powerful *Confessions* is also representative of this literary genre (Taylor 1991; Guignon 2004). In the following investigation I will not consider these, because Greek manuals addressed only a very narrow section of the population, while in Augustine the quest for spirituality (authenticity) is contrasted to a practical, worldly life. In addition, I will neither consider purely spiritual oriented self-help books, nor purely practically-oriented ones (on economics, health, etc.). These practical self-help manuals can be dated back to the emergence of legal self-help in the eighteenth century. At that time, the available self-help publications provided a possibility of saving costs in dealing with routine legal matters (Salerno 2005). Practical self-help has since expanded to cover such diverse areas as addictions, illnesses, business, the Internet, and so on. It continues to provide an affordable alternative to professional services, sometimes even including peer-to-peer support. Another version of self-help manuals targets economically successful individuals from humble origins who have managed to ascend into social spheres without being familiar with their specific social codifications and conditions of recognition. For my purposes I will only analyze self-help books that aim to work out a balance between authenticity and practical-strategic orientations, without declaring them inherently incompatible. Fortunately, there is no shortage of these.

In the following overview of historical transformations of the idea of authenticity as it pertains to the self-help discourse, I will highlight three models of authenticity: the 'autonomy model,' the 'inner sense model,' and the recent 'performative model' of authenticity. These models are in many ways popular articulations of philosophical ideas that we assessed in Chapter 3. While sharing many features with the purely philosophical models, they are nevertheless different. The distinctions established in Chapter 3 will provide the overall orientation when grouping these models. The extracted models should be understood as Weberian ideal types, as "unified thought-constructs" (Weber 1949: 90) that draw conceptual boundaries around otherwise fuzzy phenomena.

2   SELF-HELP AND THE AUTONOMY MODEL OF AUTHENTICITY

From the Victorian age and on, self-help manuals have stressed the obligation for self-realization. This approach assumed an idea of authenticity that we could call the 'autonomy model of authenticity.' This means that realization of the inherent and authentic potential of the individual was considered achievable by the internalization of collective values. Thus, self-realization was the realization of some general human potential (Smiles 1969: 374). One of the first manuals of this sort was Samuel Smiles' tremendously successful *Self-Help* (outmatched in sales only by the Bible), published in 1859—the same year as John Stuart Mill's *On Freedom*.

In many regards, the two publications supplement each other, since both authors feared the suppression of individual character by rigid Victorian conventions and that interventionist political government would destabilize the foundation of social stability and welfare. Both stressed the obligation for self-realization, not only for reasons of stability but also for the sake of realizing something 'higher.' Mill (1867: 45) argued that self-realization brings about the "perfection of human nature," while Smiles understood a good character as "human nature in its best form" (Smiles 1969: 360). Sacrificing the "living force" of individuality for the sake of the noiseless functioning social machinery is counter-productive, because it weakens what Smiles and Mill regard as the crucial for individual and collective prosperity:

> Where, not the person's own character, but the traditions or customs of other people are the rule of conduct, there is wanting one of the principal ingredients of human happiness, and quite the chief ingredient of individual and social progress (Mill 1867: 33).

For Mill, individual differences are productive and social forces should therefore encourage individuality rather than suppress it. Mill stresses the individual obligation for self-realization (Mill 1867: 46), and while his political apology of liberty is based on a utilitarian concept of autonomy, it implicitly contains an autonomy model of authenticity: "If he is eminent in any of the qualities which conduce to his own good, he is, so far, a proper object of admiration. He is so much the nearer to the ideal perfection of human nature" (Ibid.: 45). How exactly is this ideal of authentic human nature to be reached? Besides the fairly obvious point that authenticity requires a simultaneous affirmation of impulses and the virtue of self-control, Mill remains quite unclear. One major question remains unanswered: is authenticity valuable per se, i.e., something we should be attentive to, or is it only valuable as a product of a decisive and proper use of autonomy? One can say that Smiles' book is all about filling this gap and providing an answer to this question. While Mill examines the limits of collective authority over the individual, Smiles operates from an individual perspective and on a practical level. Like Mill, Smiles does not have faith in the government, but in the individuals themselves—the trust in progress that is characteristic of the particular historic period that Mill and Smiles belong to, is transferred into the individual (Briggs 1969: 15).

Similar to Mill, Smiles wants to limit state interference, even in providential issues. They argue that political government is necessary, but also that it has negative and restrictive effects that can obstruct positive and self-induced processes of character formation, which help constitute the stability of the state. Besides, the effect of laws remains restricted to certain areas: "No laws . . . can make the idle industrious, the thriftless provident, make the drunken more sober" (Smiles 1969: 36). Too much government, even if the intention is noble, can thus prove harmful, because it prevents self-help from becoming a habit (Ibid.: 309). How does Smiles fix the criteria of an authentic character?

Smiles intakes a quasi-productionist position by stressing that character is not a stable pre-existing entity. In this perspective, there is no particular inner teleology: "character (is) not impressed upon him by nature, but formed, out of no peculiarly fine elements, by himself" (Smiles 1969: 361). Smiles admits that character is partly forged by circumstances (Ibid.: 57), but he mainly considers it to be the product of one's own work: "I am what I have made myself" (Ibid.: 340). This however is not to be understood in a Nietzschean sense. The emergence of an authentic character is intrinsically bound to internalization (rather than rejection) of a set of (Victorian) virtues. A "man of character" is "honest, truthful, upright, polite, temperate, courageous, self-respecting, and self-helping" (Ibid.: 374) and even self-denying (Ibid.: 282). Unlike recent models of authenticity, individual distinctions and talents have no immanent value; they could even be considered obstacles in the quest for character. Smiles' self-help advices are based on what we could call an "autonomy model of authenticity." The realization of inherent and authentic potential is bound to the internalization of collective values, such that self-realization is the realization of something (at least thought to be) generally human.

3   SELF-HELP AND THE INNER SENSE MODEL OF AUTHENTICITY

In the early twentieth century Protestant and Puritan values began to lose their grip, partly because they were increasingly irrelevant to the problems faced by individuals in urban and industrial contexts. It is in such a cultural context that 'New Thought' appeared as a unified movement in the 1890s and achieved extraordinary growth in the following 40 years. Reacting against the erosion of Protestant values and forces, but also against the leveling tendencies of an ever expanding capitalist development that was felt as leveling, the New Thought movement provided a balm for the turn-of-the-century ego, because it considered subjects as unique, individual manifestations of divinity (Waldo Trine 1897/1942: 176; Starker 2002: 21). While until the emergence of this movement personal success was thought of as something to be earned, New Thought suggested that communicating wishes through 'mind power' may be sufficient. For Ralph Waldo Trine, one of the central characters of New Thought, a person's success was conditioned by "the realization of his oneness with this Infinite Power" (Waldo Trine 1897/1942: 176).

The idea of a powerful universal force within and the idea of a unique, introspectively accessible immanent teleology merged in self-help manuals and popular culture. In order to secure authenticity, material success, and spiritual well-being, later best sellers such as Deepak Chopra's *The Seven Spiritual Laws of Success* (1994), Wayne Dyer's *Staying on the Path* (2004), and Thomas Moore's *Care of the Soul* (1994) gave advice on how to live in harmony with the inner core, on how to regain the ability to listen to the inner voice and on how to distinguish the authentic self from the public one. The model of self-realization, which we have seen in Smiles, becomes inverted. The task for the individual is not 'to grow up' and eventually achieve 'Bildung,' but 'to grow down.' The task is not becoming something else, but becoming the person that one already is deep inside. In this way, the 'original power' of the innate authentic core can unfold, securing authenticity and success. This also means that the relationship between character and virtue is reversed. In other words, referring back to the distinctions made in this book, the inner sense model of authenticity replaces the 'autonomy model' (Simmel 1987). Individuals now increasingly interpret their livesusing a narrative of self-discovery[1] and as we shall see this substantial change is in harmony with particular socio-economic transformations.

The change that took place cannot be interpreted as a single development. It was an intertwined, reciprocal reinforcement of several socio-economic and cultural transformations. The tremendous growth of incomes and leisure time multiplied the possible life paths open to individuals. At the same time, the normative grip that class origin had on individuals gradually dissolved, partly due to greater social mobility. These factors augmented educational and vocational opportunities, and geographical mobility swiftly led to increasing divergence between individual biographies. It is in this socio-cultural context that Ulrich Beck (1986) and Anthony Giddens (1991) detect the emergence of a new, late-modern stage of conscious individualism. Generally, the horizon of imaginable biographies widened significantly, leaving a normative gap that was filled out by experimentation and attempts at autonomous discovery of one's identity. As Honneth (2004b: 469) puts it, "members of Western societies were compelled, urged, or encouraged, for the sake of their own future, to place their very selves at the centre of their own life-planning and practice."

Of course, it is not enough to simply list these structural changes. The objective growth of life options available to individuals did not by itself evoke a new model of authenticity. Instead, this went hand in hand with another socio-cultural change in the way individuals interpreted their lives. The re-birth and popularization of romantic ideal of authenticity was paradigmatic for this change, helping to fill the interpretative gap that the socio-economic changes brought about. A new way of looking at the world emerged and made it possible for individuals to understand their lives through a narrative of self-discovery. As the self-help literature has revealed, the narrative of life that people aspired to achieve was no longer linear in the sense of a totality that is made up by a sequence of roles. Rather, the struggle to actualize the core of one's unique personality became the gravitational center of the narrative. Also, authenticity became popularized. What until then was a way of interpreting life for the upper classes now begun to have an impact on large parts of society. It is in such a context that the language of psychotherapy entered the self-help discourse. Philip Cushman's (1995) cultural history of psychotherapy nicely traces the historical impact of popularized psychotherapy and shows how the model of the 'inner' and 'true' self neatly matches the raise of consumerism.

What we see in these self-help manuals until the 1980s is the popularization of the 'inner sense' model of authenticity. In order to 'be what they are,' individuals began to see their lives as the struggle to unfold their personal core that made them into unique individuals. This went hand in hand with the emergence of experimental life forms and with a claim on social institutions to create more tolerant institutional frameworks. So the question was: how are institutions to adapt to these claims, and how are they to transform without risking efficiency? One possible answer to this question was delivered by Daniel Bell in his famous and widely read *The Cultural Contradictions of Capitalism* from 1976. The main thesis of the book is that the values of Puritanism and Protestant ethic that capitalism was founded on have from the 1960s onwards come in conflict with the culture of authenticity that emphasizes individual self-realization and uniqueness. Bearing in mind the values that fuelled the 'spirit of 68,' Bell saw an emerging hedonistic view on life that from being reserved to subcultures of the artistic avant-garde slowly became part of everyday life for many. These advances in hedonism, the search for authenticity, aesthetic creativity, and sexual liberty were for him in contradiction with the values of industry, modesty, humility, and functional requirements that are needed to maintain economic stability. Bell diagnosed a growing contradiction in capitalist societies, and predicted that the 'avant-garde' cultural values will clash with the spirit of work and stability (O'Hara 2004).

What Bell (as Weber before him) rightly acknowledges is that capitalism lacks a consistent moral or philosophical framework that could motivative individuals to actively participate. But, as far as I can see, the thesis that the authenticity-seeking lifestyle necessarily obstructs the efficacy and productivity of capitalist production relies on the questionable assumption that capitalist modes of production are inflexible. This is not to claim that such a tension between capitalistic requirements and the ideal of authenticity never existed. This is clearly the case, and the selfhelp books unmistakably reveal this. But from this fact it does not follow that the popularized authenticity-seeking lifestyle *necessarily* conflicts with the functional requirements of capitalism. As the following examination of recent self-help books will reveal, due to the reciprocal shaping of the quest for authenticity and capitalism, the ideal of authenticity has indeed been transformed into a productive force. I think that shedding light on the emergence a new kind of model of authenticity in this self-help discourse can help us understand some of these transformations.

4 SELF-HELP AND THE PERFORMATIVE MODEL OF AUTHENTICITY

In the 1990s, new self-help books emerged that combined the quest for authenticity with strategies of new management. Different underlying logical modes, or "frames" in the vocabulary of E. Goffman, hitherto considered incompatible, become intrinsically connected. Mental health, authenticity, and success in the job market are now thought to be achievable by one and the same process. The astonishing popularity of these self-help manuals could partly be explained by this holistic solution. The manuals do not fail to notice that authenticity has become a systemic demand. However, this is considered a positive characteristic, since what is required on the market is now not adapted behavior but the skillful communication of authentic singularity (e.g., Horn 2004: 59; Gierke 2005; Härter and Öttl 2005). Also, they hold that while capitalism now allows for authenticity, techniques of self-marketing and personal branding allow everyone to be an authentic self (e.g., Arruda 2003).

Creating an authentic 'personal brand' is not considered an adjustment of one's personality to external market requirements but as a part of becoming oneself. The general argument can be reconstructed as follows: authentic individuals are per se distinct, and by extension, this distinction is simultaneously the reason for their success (Arruda 2003: 11; Gierke 2005: 16). Thus, manuals often start with an exercise called "taking stock of your personal assets" (Horn 2004: 146), which detects authentic features that—due to their distinctive quality—constitute a "unique personal value" to the market. The next task is putting this difference to work by consciously—and continuously—communicating it through a stylistically forged, coherent pattern of appearances and actions (Sampson 2002: 1; Arruda 2003: 6).

Importantly, authenticity is no longer conceived in a solipsistic manner and no longer denotes an immanent 'internal energy,' as in the case of the inner sense model of authenticity. Instead, it denotes an 'energy' that can only be developed in (strategic) interaction with others. It is the *energy of difference*. In the performance model of authenticity, difference is not the 'by-product' of an autonomous life but the primary source of both authenticity and market value. Besides this, authenticity is bound to *performing* difference in a given situation. The introspectively detected qualities that make one unique—the so-called "assets"—serve only as a starting point and do not possess any intrinsic value. This proto-uniqueness or proto-difference must—like capital—be invested in a situation, and only by performing uniqueness in a given situation with others can one be considered authentic. What does this mean? I think this has crucial consequences and completely transforms the underlying model of authenticity.

Since individual traits (proto-uniqueness) do not in themselves possess any value, it is the *performance* of these qualities in different situations that leads to authenticity. This means reinventing these qualities depending upon the given situation. Authenticity thus no longer refers to an inner teleology but instead to a process of self-creation as a creation of difference. It is not difficult to see the slide towards the productionist model of authenticity, which contains Nietzschean elements of self-fashioning (Varga 2009). The case is not that simple however. What we see here is not just the transformation of the inner sense model of authenticity into the productionist model (described in Chapter 3). Instead, we witness a combination.

On the one hand, the performative model of authenticity holds on to some features of the inner sense model. For instance the idea of uniqueness accessed through introspection, which is at the core of the inner sense model, now serves as the starting point for achieving authenticity. On the other, we see that this uniqueness or proto-difference is not credited any intrinsic value before it is put to work and re-invented in a situation where the individual *performs* difference and uniqueness. Thus, both models of authenticity are present simultaneously.

Both the idea of being true to something given—detected by introspection—and the productionist idea of choosing different identities from a pool of possibilities have become molded into the performative model of authenticity. This means that the tension *between* these models of authenticity has become a tension *within* the performative model of authenticity. On the one hand, authentic traits are viewed as given and introspectively accessible, while, on the other hand, such traits are only conceived as authentic if they help produce difference from others in such a way that it also brings a strategic gain. As we shall see later, this inner tension in the performative model adds considerably to the exhaustiveness of the practice of authenticity.

To sum up, the models presented above represent heterogeneous conceptions, with different ideas about inner life, virtues, self-transcendence, and (economic) value. Introspection, which is crucial for the inner sense model of authenticity, is not really discussed by Smiles. Here, the subject does not have a complex inner life. It is rather the confrontation and overcoming of difficult situations that forge an authentic character. This is why, for Smiles, it is more probable that individuals from a modest background will obtain a strong authentic character. In opposition to this, the exponents of the inner sense model reject the virtues that Smiles embraces, arguing that some of them tend to alienate us from our 'inner.' Needles to say, the productionist model is even more ambivalent on virtues.

The models completely diverge on how authenticity and (economic, social) success are connected. In the autonomy model, authenticity and success come about if one succeeds in tapping the source of inter-subjective virtues and values. In the inner sense model one becomes authentic by tapping an inner source. This ensures success, because it creates a 'whole' person—one that is harmonious, motivated, and thus ready to engage in work projects. So the matrix of the first two models of authenticity is that by tapping into a force that is beyond one's own choice one becomes authentic and success will follow as a by-product. In the performative model, however, there are no sources to tap and no primary or secondary products to differentiate: *authenticity is difference is success.*

Now, how does this transformation of authenticity relate to general sociopolitical and economic developments? All three models mark a retreat into the self, which can be connected to the erosion or defeat of political utopias. The historian Robert J. Morris connects Smiles' work on self-help with a political capitulation facing a society in which social inequalities could not be eliminated by political means (Morris 1981: 108). To a certain extent this applies to all models. Authentic self-relation figures as something like a last resort that cannot be affected by political instability, economical or social inequality, and the lack of public recognition. In this view, the three different stages of self-help analysed here are signs of crisis. They can be deciphered as signs of the defeat and sublimation of political ambitions of respectively the Victorian middle class, the 1968 generation, or those involved in social struggles in the 1990s under the pressure of globalization. The problem with this reaction is that it leads to a highly contra-productive individualization and de-politization of social struggle. While this transformation and growth of self-help can be deciphered as a sign of crisis from a political perspective, from an economic perspective it may contrariwise indicate the smooth functioning of market mechanisms. Morris (Ibid.: 109) states that from an economic perspective Smiles' ethos of self-help was quite productive, providing the ideological basis for much-needed small, independent production units. The inner sense model is more ambivalent. On the one hand it is critical towards requirements in the job market; on the other hand it is productive and stabilizing in the time of Fordistic production. The core self is understood to provide a bastion that can not be captured by disciplinary power and this idea might have rendered Fordistic work more acceptable. In contrast, the performative model of authenticity completely lacks the anti-capitalistic impetus that characterizes the inner sense model and it therefore has a relatively trouble-free relation to capitalistic requirements. The production of individual authenticity as difference ties in with the so-called 'subjectivation of work' and 'aesthetic turn' of the economy where production is not to be understood in the traditional sense but, as Böhme (2003) maintains, as the 'aesthetic' production of difference. Contrary to the inner sense model of authenticity, what we begin to see here is a neat match between the ideal of authenticity and the requirements of capitalism, with consequences that we will discuss later in this chapter.

Having focused attention on this match between authenticity and the contemporary logic of capitalism, we begin to grasp how the ideal of authenticity could have evolved into something like a systemic demand towards individuals. The next step of the argument will be to explain both the emergence of the performative model of authenticity and how authenticity in a highly peculiar fashion turned into a demand. To achieve a better understanding of this turn, we will now move on to the framework of Boltanski and Chiapello, which is extremely helpful when explaining how capitalism and ethical ideals work together and shape each other. To adequately explain the reciprocal shaping of authenticity and capitalism and the emergence of the performative model of authenticity, we must however modify their account quite substantially.

5   AUTHENTICITY AND SPIRITS OF CAPITALISM

Boltanski and Chiapello understand capitalism as a system that boils down to unlimited accumulation of capital by formally peaceful means, but without reducing it to a passive form of striving. Following Weber's *The Protestant Ethics and the Spirit of Capitalism*, they argue that due to its fundamentally absurd and amoral character and its having a purpose only in itself, capitalism depends on employing various sets of ideologies through which individual commitment is secured. The kind of abstract justification that Adam Smith sees in free market welfare benefits is not sufficient. Weber effectively showed how the Protestant faith provided justification for a special ethos of work. Therefore, to obtain the devotion of individuals, capitalism is reliant on a system of justifications—a 'spirit' that connects individual involvement to an agent-transcendent idea of the good and worthy. In our contemporary societies, such justification is no longer religious, but ethical and offers "what capitalism lacks: reasons for participating in the accumulation process that are rooted in quotidian reality, and attuned to the values and concerns of those who need to be actively involved" (Boltanski and Chiapello 2005: 21). Again, this demonstrates the capacity of capitalism to incorporate and absorb criticism. In fact, there is "no ideology, however radical its principles and formulations that has not eventually proved open to assimilation" (ibid.: xv).

While alluding to Weber's study of the Protestant ethic, Boltanski and Chiapello argue that up until the present day there have been three successive 'spirits of capitalism.' The first spirit of capitalism materialized between the nineteenth century and the Great Depression and was primarily 'familial' in form with the bourgeois capitalist entrepreneur as its primary ideal figure. The second spirit of capitalism, which emerged from the depression and the general economic instability of the inter-war years, no longer had the entrepreneur as its principal figure, but rather the manager/director of the large centralized bureaucratic organization. These organizations worked through long-term planning, and the carrier possibilities for 'cadres' were more or less fixed and entailed both security and some elbowroom for self-realization. This was the spirit that confronted the generation of 1968, a confrontation that ended in discrediting its authoritarian ideals and forms of justification. From this crisis, a new spirit of capitalism evolved as responding to the criticism of the 1960s and 1970s. Through a comparative examination of prescriptive management literature from the 1960s to the 1990s, Boltanski and Chiapello detect a major shift. In the 1960s management literature criticized family capitalism and sought solutions for large corporations by limiting centralization, while introducing meritocracy and partial autonomy for managers. The objectivity of the management process was not to be endangered by patriarchal patterns and nepotism and the personal and the professional spheres were to be kept strictly separate. In the 1990s there was a much more radical and sustained condemnation of bureaucratic, top-down organizations. The organizational matrix through which social entities are comprehended, is the 'network' (as opposed to the hierarchy). Instead of striving for stability, the view is that the organization must acknowledge that change has become endemic. In the 'rhizomatic' enterprise, control is internalized in employees and sustained through their drive for self-realization. Of course, it is not difficult to see some of the disadvantages of this framework. The lesser degree of direct constraint on labor is bought at the expense of the fixed and secure career paths that were characteristic of the second spirit of capitalism.

5.1   The Role of Critique

After this general outline, we can return to the issue of authenticity. As mentioned, capitalism has always relied on its critiques. In order to secure the commitments of individuals, capitalism depends on an ethical justi-fication that is achieved by the endogenization of critique. Boltanski and Chiapello (2005) argue that two forms of critique have accompanied the history of capitalism. These can be split into several demands and sources of indignation in the face of capitalism: a claim for *liberation* and *authen-ticity* and a refusal of *egoism* and social *suffering*. These sources make up two different groups, articulated in different environments and under different circumstances: the 'artistic critique' demanding liberation and authenticity was articulated in the artistic bohemian contexts of the late nineteenth century. The 'social critique,' which condemned egoism and social suffering, emerged in the context of the labor movement. The artistic critique is a critique of inauthenticity, claiming that capitalism disenchants and standardizes the world and that the conformity of the commodities limits human creativity.

> For this critique, loss of authenticity essentially refers to a standardiza-tion or, if you prefer, a loss of difference between entities, whether these are objects or human beings (Boltanski and Chiapello 2005: 439).

The loss of difference primarily concerns mass-produced commodities. Because products are not only identical, but also afford identical usage by the consumers, the critique of standardization is also a critique of the erod-ing differences between individuals. Hence, the disappearance of singularity is two-fold. The similarity and standardization of commodities and the tri-umph of advertisement have also homogenized the desiring subject (Boltan-ski and Chiapello 2005: 438). The criticism of inauthenticity also adresses the massification of the subject at work. The Taylorist organization establishes an environment where every worker is replaceable by any other. Leading members of the Frankfurt School as Adorno, Horkheimer, and Marcuse were prominent critics of inauthenticity. In *Dialectic of the Enlightenment* Adorno and Horkheimer diagnose the erosion of differences caused by the omnipres-ent instrumental logic of market mechanisms. In *Minima Moralia*, Adorno (1974: fragment nr. 132) states that even intellectuals cannot free themselves from a standardization of their critical intellect. Marcuse's *One-dimensional Man* also contains a critique of inauthenticity and the astonishing popularity of this book also demonstrates the impact of this critique.

What makes the 1968 situation exceptional is that the social and artistic critiques flourished together resulting in a coalescence of student uprisings and a general strike. This resulted at first in significant concessions to social demands, but as the first euphoric period of the social and the artistic critiques of capitalism came to an end the two critiques not only became ever more separated from each other, but they even became antagonistic. The initial 'response' of capitalism was to introduce a series of measures that were designed to answer the social critique by lessening material inequalities, but some of these measures were abandoned in favor of measures that responded to the demands of the artistic critique. The influence of the social critique of capitalism declined by the end of the 1970s when trade unions began to lose members. While this critique became silent and was abandoned, the artistic critique—combating the constraints of bureaucratic discipline, consumer conformity and demanding authenticity, creativity, 'fluid' identity, and self-development—flourished. The demand for individuality and authenticity that emerged from the artistic criticism now also turned against the aims of social criticism. Individual negotiations replaced qualification-based salary, contracts have become individualized, part-time work, flex-time were negotiated, etc. Since the end of the 1960s, artistic criticism has become the propelling factor for change. Social criticism has become fragmented and evolved into particularistic directions. New social movements like feminism, homosexual rights groups, and environmental movements were supposed to be better equipped to oppose capitalistic accumulation (Boltanski and Chiapello 2005: 178). The fragmentation of social criticism led to the result that capitalism has only developed in a way that takes into account the artistic critique. Today it seems indisputable that the struggle for authenticity and individual self-realization has replaced the struggle for social justice (Ibid.: 217).

5.2 Endogenization of the Artistic Critique of Inauthenticity

Through a comparative examination of prescriptive management literature from the 1960s to 1990s, Boltanski and Chiapello detect the emergence of a new spirit of capitalism. This grows out of integrating anti-hierarchical and artistic critiques of inauthenticity (but not the social critique of inequality). Among other issues, the artistic critique of inauthenticity targeted the Taylorist boundary between private and working selves for splitting off intrinsically linked areas of life and hindering self-realization. The critical argument was that this separation drives a wedge not only between the working person and the private person, but also between the rational and the affective, or between 'the brain and the heart' (Boltanski and Chiapello 2005: 96–99; 85 fn). A new spirit of capitalism emerged out of the integration of the anti-hierarchical and artistic critiques of inauthenticity. Corporations set out to reshape contracts and production processes, by flexibilizing and introducing more complex teamwork, subcontracting, etc.

Pongratz and Voß (2001; 2000; 2003; 1998) have elaborated a thesis about a deep-seated alteration in the character of labor, which has led to a broad debate in industrial sociology.[2] They argue that the relationship between employer and employee is changed from a hierarchical to a market-like relation (Pongratz and Voß 2001) and that a new type of labor has replaced the typical employee.[3] The passive employee is replaced by the 'entreployee' (Arbeitskraftunternehmer), who incessantly seeks to perform in an 'entrepreneurial' style, re-transforming his capacities within the framework of the company. 'Entreployees' understand their personal and professional capacities as raw commodities that require an entrepreneurial development. In order to develop such individual resources, there is increased need for techniques and skills (Hochschild 1997; Sennett 1998) which are provided by the new self-help genre. This genre has also clearly shown that in order to actively produce and market individual resources authenticity is crucial.

This is one of the reasons why it is arguable that contrary to the widespread assumption some 20 years ago about the 'end of work,' it is rather the case that work has taken innovative forms and has permeated the capillaries of everyday life. The reduction of direct disciplinary control and the promotion of individual self-realization and responsibility also suggest the relevance of more indirect forms of work, in which the task of transformation (of the purchased right to the working potential into actual performance) is now the duty of the employee. By outsourcing this task of transformation, Pongraz and Voß (2001) argue that management simply hands the problem over to the employees, who have to sort it out while simultaneously coping with the consequences.

These changes are responses to the demands of the artistic critique and incorporate them in a manner that renders them compatible with profit-making. This is why the clash between capitalism and the culture of self-realization, as predicted by Bell, never occured. Within this new spirit, creativity-restraining hierarchy and bureaucracy are abandoned. Proving one's worth and dedication to a job is not about the correct execution of predefined tasks (in the sense of a disciplinary drill) but about the playful, autonomous and inventive creation (in the sense of artistic creation). As the result of the demands for individuality, flexibility, and authenticity, a qualification-based hierarchy is discarded. Instead, *competences* become increasingly important, since they do not allow a strict distinction between the private and the working self. This boundary is seen as alienating, because it splits off intrinsically linked areas of life and thus hinders the realization of the authentic personality. Competences are called for that involve the whole person and not only the employee (Boltanski and Chiapello 2005: 236). The view is that managers must be 'coaches' and that they must have the ability to inspire employees by visions and to motivate them to autonomous work and self-realization. Thus the coach helps employees find themselves and to unfold their uniqueness within a current work-project. The categories of artists and managers used to constitute an intrinsic opposition and were associated with idealism and instrumental thinking (Ibid.: 311–312). The 'transgressive' way of life that characterized the avant-garde artist in the nineteenth century, in which single areas of life were not separated, has become the ideal. In all, the view is that separate facets of one single existence should be unified into a single piece of art that expresses the authenticity and uniqueness of his originator.

5.3   Correction: The Endurance of Authenticity

Now what is the status of authenticity in this theoretical framework? As Boltanski and Chiapello rightly point out, authenticity has been economized, in part resulting in the growth of new markets for authentic products. This of course requires a new definition of authenticity, which was previously defined by its incommensurability with money. To stress the difference to mass products, producers increasingly aim at offering authentic products. The palette of commodities becomes more differentiated and the smaller serial production is compensated by the shorter life cycle of the products. The 'real' or 'authentic' that was defined by its incommensurability with money and by its being outside the market became included in the circulation of commodities (Boltanski and Chiapello 2005: 442). Areas like leisure, personal services, and tourism, which were until then in the periphery of the market sphere, are now integrated, extending the reach of the market. This means that new authenticity reserves must constantly be disclosed—a good example of which is found in the activity of the 'Cool-Hunters' as described by Naomi Klein (2000).[4]

Nevertheless, Boltanski and Chiapello argue that the endogenization of the ideal of authenticity has finally failed, in regarding both products and people. From the consumer's perspective, 'authentic' products and people have become disappointing and suspicious (Boltanski and Chiapello 2005: 443–444). In their view, people have become skeptical about, for instance, whether an artist is a 'real' rebel or merely the protagonist in a marketing strategy. This suspicion of inauthenticity also marks relations between people. Because the borders between work and private spheres have become blurred, people are often insecure whether their relationships are based on personal or strategic reasons. In the end, the scenario Boltanski and Chiapello depict comes down to a serious contradiction (between the imperatives of flexibility and authenticity) at the heart of the new spirit. We could call this a stalemate situation. Authenticity has become suspicious, but neither suspicion nor the critique of inauthenticity can unfold because the whole idea of authenticity is radically questioned and delegitimized by post-structuralism (Ibid.: 441).

In my view, this is both implausible and goes against Boltanski and Chiapello's own premises. If this stalemate situation really were the case, we would be experiencing a severe crisis, because the ideal of authenticity could not possibly provide sufficient motivational force. It would be difficult to explain how the new spirit of capitalism still manages to engage people. From my perspective, this is where the previously presented performative model of authenticity comes into play. Motivation is possible, because the ideal of authenticity has been transformed in a manner that matches the ubiquitous imperatives of flexibility and polyvalence—a tension that was unsolvable in the inner sense model. Also, the new model effectively disarms the hermeneutics of suspicion. Because this concept of authenticity is performative, it assumes no original and thus cannot lead to disappointment.

There are several reasons why Boltanski and Chiapello might not have been in a position to see this. It has been pointed out that the body of analyzed management texts is not large enough, does not discuss the influence of these works, and does not provide an international perspective (Budgen 2000). From the perspective given here, the problem is a different one. First, one argument would be that the self-help literature examined in this book is better suited to show the reciprocal shaping of authenticity and capitalism than managerial texts. There is also a second empirical issue: their argument is based on the examination of management texts from the period between 1989 and 1994. The present examination revealed that the performative model emerged during the last decade and thus *after* the period considered by them. It is only after that period that modern self-help literature clearly assumes that maintaining employability depends on being authentic in a specific manner. This involves acting out and performing the difference of the authentic self at work, standing out from the crowd, and investing oneself emotionally in work. This is how the performative model of authenticity solves the tension between authenticity and the ubiquitous imperative of flexibility—a tension that is unsolvable in the inner sense model. The examined self-help material demonstrates that productionist self-realization is viewed both as securing self-realization, the enhancement of personal performances, and the economic flourishing of a company.

Besides this empirical argument, I also think Boltanski and Chiapello are led astray by their systematic argument, which holds that post-modern thought has completely demolished the idea of authenticity. What really happens, and this became manifest in the previous examination of Rorty and Foucault, is not that authenticity is discredited and abandoned. Rather, it is only the inner sense model of authenticity that is shattered and replaced by the productionist model of authenticity. In reality, it is a transformation, equivalent to what was identified in new self-help books. To sum up, my argument basically continues the line of thought on endogenization that was set out by Boltanski and Chiapello. I agree with these authors that the critique of inauthenticity is endogenized, However, I also argue that the post-modernist critique of authenticity is similarly endogenized and put to work in the construction of a new spirit. The emergence of the performative model of authenticity is the result of this important second-order process that remains invisible within the framework of Boltanski and Chiapello.

So while I previously looked at the tensions within the performative model of authenticity, in this section I have clarified how the performative model of authenticity emerged as a result of the reciprocal shaping of capitalism and the ideal of authenticity. It has also become clearer how authenticity has become something like a systemic demand. Taking these two points together, the internal tension and the simultaneous development into a demand bring us a little closer to the next step of the argument. This aims at demonstrating the exhaustive and potentially pathological quality of an institutionalized practice of authenticity that builds on the performative model. In order to be able to do this, we must go beyond the framework of Boltanski and Chiapello.

This is because when it comes to addressing the relation between authenticity and capitalism, Boltanski and Chiapello speak of ongoing antagonism and contradiction. However, the inquiry into the emergence of the performative model of authenticity has shown that this need not be the case. Thus, if the relation cannot be adequately described in terms of antagonism, and if the practice of authenticity based on the performative model is exhaustive and potentially pathologic (until now only assumed), then we need a theoretical framework that can address the relationship between capitalism and the ideal of authenticity in terms that go beyond the notion of contradiction. This is what I will attempt in the next section.

5.4   From Contradiction to Paradox

The concept of contradiction in Boltanski and Chiapello's work has since Marx been a classical hermeneutic model for understanding and assessing the growing individualization in modern societies. The question that has guided many social-philosophical investigations was how to assess the quantitative growth in freedom of choice that resulted from loosening traditional ties and obligations. From the start there was a deep-seated ambiguity when assessing the growing opportunities for self-realization, simply because it is unwarranted to assume that the growth of accessible possibilities for individuals to shape their own lives, the growing multiplicity of individual roles and the decreasing importance of traditions automatically bring along a growth of personal autonomy. Georg Simmel takes this ambivalence seriously and his thoughts on urban life reveal his awareness of the ambiguities of individualization. He maintains that the same processes that have suspended social dependence and brought about an increase of possibilities have also led to a greater anonymity in social relationships, to more indifference and to growing loneliness. Scientific rationalization, money economy, and the social acceleration of urban life have brought about more than merely a release from premodern life. First, through the increasing popularity of the scientific perspective, the world has become 'disenchanted,' turning into a meaningless space of causal interaction of objects that are accessible for observation. In this setting, individuals show up as just "one more piece of information, one more object among countless others that can be explained rationally on the basis of specific calculative procedures" (Aho 2007: 448). Second, due to the increasing intensity of urban life, the nervous system is overstimulated by having to relate to myriads of factors. As a paradoxical result, "the mere quantitative intensification of the same conditioning factors this achievement is transformed into its opposite and appears in the peculiar adjustment of the blasé attitude" (Simmel 1950: 418). The reaction to the overstimulation is a kind of breakdown of the nervous system, in which the subject protects itself and responds by emotional detachment and by exclusively relying on the intellect.

Simmel thus not only separates individualization from a mere quantitative growth of freedom, but also the individualization of people's biographies from the growth of possibilities for self-realization. He also points out a contradiction. The factors that enable the growth of possibilities of individual freedom might at the same time also undermine the foundation of such freedom. This idea of contradiction is clearly present in the work of contemporary social theorists such as Anthony Giddens, Zygmunt Bauman, and Ulrich Beck, who focus on the connection between the modernization of Western societies and the process of individualization. In the 'tradition of contradiction,' Giddens (1991: 142) notes that the independency gained by way of being set free from the constraints of traditions also means that individuals now depend on fragile and shifting expert knowledge in order to structure their activities and to answer the question of how to achieve a good life in a world of seemingly endless options. Parallel to Simmel, Sennett (1998) argues that the general acceleration of life and increased physical and psychological mobility results in the diminished capability of forming the kind of lasting ties that provide individuals with a meaningful social context. Also, for Bauman the increasing importance of individuality and self-realization goes hand in hand with the decreasing importance of reciprocal dependencies, the lack of mutual engagements, and indifference. As a result, the 'private' colonizes the public sphere, which is then reduced to providing the stage for the public display of private affairs and confessions of private sentiments (Bauman 2001: 49). Due to such decline, it has become increasingly difficult to provide collective political solutions to social problems, leading to a situation of contradiction. The unprecedented freedom is bought at "the price of similarly unprecedented insecurity" (Ibid.: 159).

When we look closer at these accounts there are two different models of contradiction. The first pattern is roughly this. Capitalism rationalizes spheres of action, sets free from archaic constraints, but also tends to restrain emancipatory processes due to its immanent colonizing tendencies, in which economic laws take on a life of their own and enter other areas that were previously based on a different logic of integration. This builds on the supposition that within capitalist societies several different forms of logic contradict each other, and, as a result, the attempt to realize a goal within a specific sphere of rationality decreases the possibility to attain another goal in another sphere. Nonetheless, there is also a second and less conspicuous model in Simmel, which can be more adequately described in terms of a paradox. A contradiction turns paradoxical when the very attempt to realize an intention creates conditions under which the probability of the realization of this intention is reduced (Giddens 1984: 313; Honneth and Hartmann 2006).[5] Paradoxical effects are produced when different spheres of action are affected such that "a potentiality for further rationality is blocked, misshaped, and repressed by the very social organization that emerged with the new rationality potential" (Deranty forthcoming). In this sense, the notion of paradox denotes a specific case of contradiction: a paradoxical development is one that sets out to realize what it normatively contains, while the same process undermines this realization. In the same vein, seeking a more plausible model of explanation, Honneth and Hartmann (2006: 48) replace the concept of contradiction with the stronger concept of the paradox and hold that "the structure of contemporary capitalism produces paradoxical contradictions to a significant extent, so that the concept is a suitable instrument of general explanation." What characterizes this approach is nonetheless that the ability of capitalism for self-transformation "arises not only out of the imperatives of the constant realization of capital, but also from the institutionalized normative surplus that stems from its new, emerging spheres of recognition" (Ibid.: 42). The concept of paradox is problematic from a formal point of view,[6] and this is why it is important to emphasize that the term is an explication of a *specific* structure of contradiction. Also, in opposition to first generation critical theorists like Adorno and Horkheimer, the notion of paradox does not lead to a pessimistic narrative of history. It makes it possible to identify social pathologies and inversions of the normative potential of modern institutions, but does so without denying the historical fact of normative progress and its future possibility. In addition, the concept of paradox seems adequate to analyze contemporary processes. It refers to the conversion of normative intentions in contexts, where—unlike in the case of contradiction—a clear juxtaposition of progressive and regressive dimensions no longer seems possible as these dimensions become increasingly amalgamated.

For our inquiry, the idea of paradox is more appealing when it comes to explaining the relation between authenticity and capitalism beyond antagonism and contradiction as in Boltanski and Chiapello. If the practice of authenticity based on the performative model is exhaustive and potentially pathological, then we need the stronger term of paradox to adequately describe the relationship between capitalism and the ideal of authenticity.

6 THE PARADOX OF AUTHENTICITY

As Honneth and Hartmann (2006) point out, the talk about paradoxical developments must refer to some normative underpinning. Loosely following Parsons, in their recognition-theoretical approach, the normative backbone is provided by the idea of 'normative spheres': spheres of social struggles with open-ended results that frame the subject's struggle for the recognition of their personal characteristics, rights, and achievements. These spheres are constituted by implicit moral ideals, in the name of which individuals can put forth demands that may run against existing social norms. In particular, this means that subjects can:

1. Assert the normative promise of institutionalized individualism by experimentally referring to aspects of their autonomy or facets of their authenticity that have not so far found appropriate recognition in the social culture;
2. Enforce the modern legal order's idea of equality by pointing to their membership or structural aspects of their life circumstances in order to be treated as equals among equals;
3. Assert the normative implications of the modern achievement principle by referring the actual value of their labor for social reproduction in order to attain greater social esteem and the material compensation connected to it; and finally,
4. Enforce the moral promise of romantic love by calling attention to needs or wishes that the institutionalized practice of intimate relationships has hitherto failed to meet with appropriate sensitivity and responsiveness (Honneth and Hartmann 2006: 42–43).

Outlining a recognition-theoretical reconstruction of Parson's theory about the development of modern societies, Honneth and Hartmann argue that the normative integration of capitalism succeeded to some extent, because several principles were implemented in institutions: "individualism" as a personal ideal; an egalitarian concept of justice; the idea of achievement as the basis for assigning status; and the romantic idea of the emotional transcendence of love. In these spheres of recognition, subjects can, on the basis of these underlying ideas, criticize social settings as discriminating and unjustified. The spheres continue to have normative potential, since they always hold more legitimate claims than what finds realization in reality.

The historical thesis that serves as a background for the diagnosis of a paradox is that in the age of the emerging welfare state Western capitalist societies experienced a hitherto unseen expansion of the respective recognition norms in all spheres. Under the changed structural conditions of contemporary neoliberalism and the expansion of market mechanisms, the struggles for recognition and the models of individualism, law, and achievement are substantially modified to the extent that they increasingly produce paradoxical effects.

Now clearly the view that I defend here, that the ideal of authenticity has altered so that it now produces paradoxical effects, is linked to Honneth's first realm of recognition. When striving for authenticity, individuals may assert the normative promise of institutionalized individualism and refer to aspects of their authenticity that have not yet been suitably recognized (Honneth and Hartmann 2006: 43). So if my thesis is correct, and there is a link between the practice of *performative* authenticity and psychological suffering, then we can argue that authenticity exemplifies a contradiction turned paradox, undermining its own foundation. The development would be paradoxical because the same intentional process of institutional realization that has led to normative progress now runs counter to its original aim (see Honneth 2002: 9). This also means that recognition, hitherto representing the opposite of domination, may in certain contexts have lost its 'innocence' (Honneth: 2007b). The public recognition of personal uniqueness and authenticity seems to encourage subjects to adopt attitudes that conform to capitalist requirements. This development is paradoxical, because the ideal of authenticity—once critical of hierarchical institutions and capitalistic requirements—now functions as an institutionalized requirement that legitimates de-institutionalization and promotes the very kind of logic that it originally opposed.

While I find the framework of paradox fruitful for explaining the emergence and functioning of the performative model of authenticity, I tend to disagree with Honneth and Hartmann on the question of what transforms these praxes in a paradoxical manner. For them it is the neoliberal "pressure" (2006: 48) on the spheres of recognition that causes the paradoxical effects. While it is not completely clear what this means, I think it is crucial not to understand neoliberal "pressure" as something coming from the 'outside.' In my view, we should regard paradoxical effects of authenticity not exclusively as results of external factors but also as products of the internal tensions of this changed performative model of authenticity—a tension that arises from the reciprocal shaping of capitalism and the ideal of authenticity.

To sum up, what I have done so far has been to combine the approaches of Boltanski and Chiapello with that of Honneth and Hartmann into a framework that renders intelligible the transformation of authenticity. The concept of paradox proves helpful as an analytical tool, because it is able to capture two problematic dimensions in the practice of authenticity: that authenticity has become an institutionalized demand towards subjects and that the very attempt to realize it creates conditions under which the probability of its realization is reduced. These two paradoxical aspects already render arguable that seeking authenticity might be exhaustive. More evidence for this position will be provided by adding a third paradoxical aspect. Pathological conditions no longer arise from the societal barriers that inhibit authenticity and self-realization but from the process of seeking for authenticity and self-realization itself.

Drawing on the work of Alain Ehrenberg, I will spell out what these paradoxical effects can be by establishing a link between the ideal of authenticity and psychological suffering.

7   FROM PARADOX TO PATHOLOGY: DEPRESSION

Before attempting to link the transformations of authenticity with the epidemic rise of depression, we must direct our attention to some theoretical reservations. In a theoretical climate in sociology and social philosophy, in which a growing variety of psychological sufferings are considered as instances of social pathology, it is indispensable to reflect on the difficulties that such an approach faces. Two crucial aspects have to be mentioned here. First, we have to make sure that the talk of 'pathology' neither implies the all too easy schema of a genuine discontent-free society that used to be, nor the narrative of the disciplinary society in which we were oppressed, but somehow protected (Ehrenberg 2007: 129). Second, it is crucial not to confuse a fuzzy development in which several factors go hand in hand and enforce each other with a relation of direct causation (Ehrenberg 2006). After calling attention to these theoretical reservations, we may begin to link the contemporary institutionalized demand for authenticity with depression as a form of psychic suffering.[7]

In the current debate, many agree on the contemporary growth of the prevalence of depression. Ehrenberg, Philippe Pignarre (2001), and David Healy (1998) all seem to concur on this. According to Pignarre (2001: 11), this development is epidemic. He shows that the depression rate in France rising sixfold between 1970 and 1996 and that no fewer than 14 million relevant prescriptions were recorded in 1994. The World Health Organization considers depression epidemic and predicts that within nine years it will become the second largest public health problem.[8] How is this rise explained?

Some theorists, such as Pignarre and Borch-Jacobsen's (2002), aim at a reductive explanation of the epidemic by focusing on the scientific innovation of a new generation of effective antidepressants (selective serotonin reuptake inhibitors, or SSRIs). The idea is that the new generation of SSRIs has altered our way of thinking about depression—a shift that ultimately explains its epidemic growth (Petersen 2009). For the sake of fairness, it should be pointed out that Pignarre does not intend to deny the existence of suffering from emptiness, fatigue, anxiety, inhibition, etc. Nevertheless, this approach is reductive because it connects the epidemic solely to a specific scientific innovation. Of course, I do not deny that the invention of SSRIs with fewer side effects had a remarkable effect on consumption. However, this cannot provide an adequate explanation of the quasi-epidemic growth without taking into account the social transformations and preconditions that have made it possible.

Trying to provide a non-reductive explanation of the growth of depression, Ehrenberg shifts the focus from individual biographies to social transformations. Ehrenberg sets out to examine depression not as a purely subjective condition but as *the* emblematic social pathology of contemporary society (Ehrenberg 2006; 2007: 129). One of his theoretical reservations is not to state a direct causation between capitalism and depression, but to point to the entanglement between normative transformations of individualism and the transforming psychiatric understanding of depression.

From his work on depression we can extract two different theses. The *otherness thesis* states that depression is 'the other' of the contemporary drive for authenticity and self-realization, just as Freudian neuroses were 'the other of the law' (pathology of a conflict between the subject and the law). He points out that depression is now described in a new language that is expressive of the process that has led to the transformation of the 'disciplinary society' during the last decades (Ehrenberg 2008). Besides this point, his work also shows that depression has become the *other* of the contemporary demand for authenticity and self-realization: that depression is "the dark side of contemporary inwardness" (Ibid.: 305).

In my reading, Ehrenberg's thesis that depression has become the other of contemporary society contains several aspects. Ehrenberg sustains his argument (that depression has become the negative 'counterpart' to the contemporary ideal of authenticity) by showing that depression has in recent times been defined more as a pathology of action than as a psychic conflict. From the 1980s and on, characteristics like inhibition, slowing down and asthenia were increasingly emphasized (Ehrenberg 2008: 24). He argues that the new psychiatric term to describe depression is now 'psychomotor retardation,' which emphasizes the lack of energy and the inability to 'perform.' In other words, in opposition to the view that Freud held (depression as a psychological conflict that leads to the emergence of a new, transformed subject), depression is now understood in terms of a 'pathology of action': an obstruction in the ability to act and perform (Ibid.: 20, 23). While the 'disciplinary' mechanisms of modern societies are abandoned and while there is an increasing demand for authenticity, individual responsibility, and initiative, our new understanding of depression as the pathology of action reflects that depression has become 'the other' of the ideals of contemporary society.

While this is a convincing point, there is another element in Ehrenberg that is of use to our endeavor. I suggest we call this the *exhaustion thesis*, because it holds that the attempt to fulfill the institutional demand of authenticity (to permanently perform and to put the self and emotions to work in order to secure employability) creates the social preconditions that lead to the exhaustion of the self. This suspicion also emerges in Eva Illouz's (2007) work on contemporary capitalism and intimacy. Ehrenberg states that depression is a *lesson* for "the sovereign individual" and for the "man who believes himself to be the author of his own life" (2008: 162). Even if Ehrenberg occasionally confuses autonomy and authenticity, one major advantage of his account is that he locates the conflict—at least partly—within the idea of authenticity itself. He states that the lesson of depression is about the constitutive alterity or 'otherness' of the self. The lesson is about the impossibility of completely bridging the distance between myself and myself (Ehrenberg 2008: 306). Thus, for Ehrenberg the practice of authenticity is exhaustive, because individuals attempt to achieve complete self-identity, which is impossible due to the constitutive alterity of the self.

This critique is of course legitimate, but simultaneously it appears too general. It applies to just about every model of authenticity studied here. One could argue that the inner sense model of authenticity has long functioned as an ideal without the exhaustive and pathological dimension that Ehrenberg depicts. Therefore, while Ehrenberg wants to claim that exhaustion is linked to authenticity, he cannot explain the *specific* exhausting qualities of the contemporary idea of authenticity.

The rest of this chapter will continue where Ehrenberg left off. In order to show that the contemporary practice of authenticity may contribute to creating the some of the preconditions under which depression develops into an epidemic, we must substantiate the (causal) connection between the performative model of authenticity and depression. So what is the *specific* exhausting or overburdening quality of performative authenticity? Ehrenberg (2008: 23) claims that the project to become oneself exhausts individuals, but what factors influence exhaustion?

8   EXHAUSTION EXPLAINED

The thesis that I am going to defend here is that specific exhaustive factors emerge when the performative model is implemented in the practice of authenticity. In the following I will put forward four arguments explaining the specific exhaustive factors.

8.1   Two Tensions

Beck and Bauman have pointed to a central and potentially exhaustive tension in contemporary Western societies. This arises because marked demands and institutionalized individualism force people to "to seek biographical solutions to systemic contradictions" (Beck and Beck-Gernsheim 2002: xxii). As our discussion of authenticity within the framework of the new 'spirit' of capitalism has revealed, the performative model of authenticity is a clear example of such a tension. Individuals are called upon to 'invent themselves' in a way that facilitates flexible production.

While a tension arises out of having to provide biographical solutions to systemic contradictions, a second one arises from within the very model of authenticity. The performative model of authenticity combines traits from both the inner sense and the productionist models of authenticity. On the one hand, the performative model of authenticity holds on to the inner sense ideas and lays weight on the importance of introspection. On the other hand, central features of the productionist model of authenticity are simultaneously present. What is detected 'inside' is not ascribed any intrinsic value before it is put to work and before it is re-invented in a situation where the individual 'performs' herself as unique. In this manner, the inner sense idea of being true to something given and the productionist idea of self-creation have been molded into the performative model of authenticity. This means that the tension between these models has become a tension *within* the performative model of authenticity. This tension turns the performative ideal of authenticity into something that—besides involving continuous work on the self—is both self-contradictory and impossible to live up to.

In all, there are at least two intertwining tensions that individuals must deal with. Taking into consideration the two tensions and their reciprocal reinforcement, it is arguable that a practice of authenticity based on such a performative model might be an exhaustive undertaking. This is not the only exhaustive aspect however.

8.2   Production-Devaluation: Emptying Out the Self

There is a second exhaustive quality to the performative model of authenticity. As revealed in the self-help manuals, it is not the introspectively detected unique features but the process of performing the authentic self (by creating difference) that ascribes value to the self. If this is correct, then the authentic self is primarily something that must be *continuously* created in order for an individual to achieve a sense of being unique, worthy, and employable. This acceleration resembles the general acceleration of the loop of production and devaluation (through consumption) of commercial products, which has led to the dramatic decrease of the lifetime of new consumer products. As we shall see, authenticity and the 'production' of the authentic self have in many ways become aligned within the production-consumption paradigm (see Rosa 1999).

This potentially exhaustive aspect is more difficult to get a grip on. Calling to mind the idea that in the performative model of authenticity the authentic self only exists in the performance of difference, the problem could be put like this: if it is the process of performing authenticity (by creating difference) that ascribes value to the self, then this also means that the 'product' (the authentic self, the performed difference) by itself holds no stable intrinsic value. In order to be able to perform authenticity in such a context of acceleration, this may even be an esteemed feature. If the 'product' (the different, authentic self) has no intrinsic value, then it can consequently easily be devaluated in order to secure the subsequent production of yet another way of being different, unique, and thus authentic. If authenticity is about the continuous production of difference, then it may be of advantage that the 'product' can quickly be replaced by a new way of performing difference.

The result is somewhat ironic and connects effortlessly to the idea of the paradox. If it is the performance of the uniqueness of the my self that confers worth to my self, and if the significance of my uniqueness comes from being performed by me at will, then my strategy of authenticity is self-defeating. This is because such an approach simply prevents me from approaching aspects of my self as significant, *independently of my will*. In other words, it prevents me from achieving a sense of self-recognition and thus from being able to approach aspects of my self as worthy and as holding some intrinsic value. Crucial aspects that constitute who I am and where I stand become degraded.

I am not saying that all aspects of who we are deserve recognition or that all of them are inherently valuable. This is clearly not the case. What I am suggesting is just that if I do not consider some aspects of who I am as *worthy in themselves*, then I will be unable to regard whatever I make of my self as something that is of intrinsic worth. This is how such a strategy becomes self-defeating and ironic, since it blocks exactly the kind of self-respect that is inherent to the idea of authenticity.

8.3   Broadening

In Chapter 5 we looked at what an existential choice amounts to, calling these 'alternativeless choices.' This proves useful for spotting aspects in the contemporary performative model of authenticity that might contribute to its exhaustive quality. With this in mind, the third argument for explaining the exhaustive qualities of the contemporary ideal of authenticity is the *broadening argument*. This maintains that the performance model of authenticity and its becoming an institutional demand enormously broaden the range of those (existential) choices that we connect to authenticity. There are two dimensions to this.

First, the inner sense model of authenticity would have been irreconcilable with the way we behave in certain situations, for example, a job interview or an Internet-dating situation, which are generally paradigmatic for an 'outer-directed' and instrumental orientation. However, with the performative model, significantly more situations can be understood to provide the possibility of *performing difference*. In fact, as Illouz (1997; 2004) has noted, situations such as a job interview or Internet dating become paradigmatic situations of authenticity and performing difference.[9]

Second, decisions involving existential choice and reflection on the wholeness of life become extended to encompass peripheral decisions. The new self-help books show that in order to achieve authenticity even small details of behavior, clothing, grooming, style of speaking, or gesture should be directly expressive of the person. It is not enough for these to be results of autonomous behaviour; they must be authentic and expressive of the person. This quantitative change may in itself make the practice of authenticity more exhaustive. But there is also a qualitative issue here. To put it in the vocabulary used earlier, first-order decisions—hitherto governed by preferences and calculative choices—become thought of as second-order articulations and existential choices. Quite simply, peripheral decisions that are governed by preferences (small details of behavior, clothing, grooming, style of speaking, gesture etc.) are now envisaged as existential choices that express identity. In such an outlook, it seems plausible that this feels like a permanently failing and an exhausting task, simply because one's ability to integrate all these aspects and create coherence is not endless.

Still, this transformation is just one side to the exhausting qualities of this broadening. Ironically, there is a simultaneous tendency that points in a conflicting direction. What our reading of contemporary self-help literature reveals is that while calculative choices are understood as of existential provenance, existential choices are reduced to calculative choices, thereby collapsing the difference between levels of decisions. Thus the very idea of what constitutes an existential choice becomes modeled on calculative choices that we perform on the basis of a list of preferences. Surely in such a case it is questionable whether any situation appears as bearing the kind of 'necessity' that is essential for an existential orientation.

Thus, as in the first argument, we have two aspects that reinforce each other and that significantly contribute to an exhaustive practice.

8.4   Wholeheartedness and Articulation

Out of this broadening and the transformation of existential choices into option-based ones modeled on calculation emerges another problem which adds to the exhaustive and overburdening dimension.

As we have seen in Part II, authenticity is connected to the wholehearted manner in which we integrate our lives by projects that we wholeheartedly endorse. 'Who we are' is defined by our wholehearted commitments. Being engaged in projects that are central to one's self-understanding means that betraying them would also mean betraying oneself (centrality). One may ask: how is one to be wholeheartedly engaged in any project if the ideal of authenticity has the performance of uniqueness and difference at its core? It seems that the performative model of authenticity, being merged with the demand of flexibility, is hostile to such deep commitments. In fact, it is difficult to see how one could ever really betray oneself while leading a life guided by the performative model of authenticity.

Additionally, as we have noted, wholeheartedness means being committed both to the actual project and to entertaining the commitment itself (continuity). Also in this case, it seems doubtful whether such continuity can be achieved while holding on to the performative model. This is simply because the continuity of a project will often be at odds with performing difference. If that is the case, the project loses its normative grip and its ability to guide our decisions. In such a situation, an existential disorientation is certainly at risk because such a project may be difficult to acknowledge as a genuine articulation. Instead of enabling a specific expressive self-relation that is embedded in a collective horizon of significance, the performative notion of authenticity disembeds the individual and thereby undercuts the normative sources necessary for any project.

Taken together, I think these arguments highlight some problematic and exhaustive qualities of the contemporary, performative model of authenticity. A twofold tension arises from having to provide biographical solutions to systemic contradictions and from having to do so on the basis of a model of authenticity that contains an internal tension. The performing of the authentic self that rests on premises that are characterized by such tension becomes exhausting in different ways. In addition, authenticity becomes an institutional demand and the field of questions about authenticity becomes enormously broad. At the same time, those existential choices and strong evaluations that concern life, as a whole, become modeled on how we normally understand choosing from a list of preferences. Moreover, several aspects reinforce each other. The process of articulation breaks off, and the constant activity of introspectively drawing raw material from the 'inner' and turning it into a difference drives individuals to exhaustion. If this is correct, then authenticity becomes paradox and self-defeating. The individual seeking authenticity is actively hindered in achieving the kind of self-relation characterized by recognition and respect that he set out to attain.

To sum up, I have tried to substantiate that the internal tensions in the performative model of authenticity and its transformation into an institutionalized demand can be seen as social stressors that may provide some of the exhausting circumstances under which depression is more likely to arise. These are all aspects that reinforce each other and that significantly contribute to the creation of an exhaustive practice. Thus, the constant activity of *performing authenticity* may at least explain some of the preconditions under which a rapid rise in the frequency of depression and sales of pharmaceutical anti-depressants becomes intelligible. In what follows I will try to make this claim stronger by drawing on a branch of psychiatry that relies on evolutionary explanations.

9   EXHAUSTION, DEPRESSION, AND ADAPTATION

Recently, there has been an 'adaptive turn' in psychology and psychiatry that seeks evolutionary explanations for psychopathologies (Nettle 2004; Varga 2011a; 2011b). In view of the fact that depression is convincingly prevalent through history, it is suitable to examine its evolutionary origins. So far, such investigations have tended to follow two opposing paths. Both start from the assumption that the mechanisms triggered in depression have evolved to actively deal with dangerous situations in which flight is not a viable option. From this common starting point, the two accounts point in very different directions. The 'dysregulation' model proposed by Nesse (2000) and Gilbert and Allan (1998) hypothesizes that in depression an inherited mechanism that evolved to help in dangerous situations becomes pathologically over-activated. Roughly, a problematic aspect for this model lies in its incapability to address both individual and social factors and to explain why some rather than others are affected. The competing account that I am going to expand on in more detail denies that depression is connected to the impairment of evolved mechanisms. The view is that depression cannot even be claimed to be fundamentally pathological; although causing grave distress, depression is viewed as helping to adopt to altered conditions. This more daring claim is held by researchers like Price et al. (1994), Hagen (1999), Watson and Andrews (2002).

Of course, depression is aversive and, in many senses, it unquestionably suspends regular functioning. This is why it first seems difficult not to regard it as some kind of maladaptation. Nonetheless, an inspection of many of our functional capacities, like experiencing fatigue, nausea, or pain, quickly reveals that it is exactly their aversive character that is crucial to their functioning. Their disruptive quality allows us to evade potentially dangerous and fitness-decreasing situations. Already Darwin has highlighted the possible adaptive function of depression: "Pain or suffering of any kind, if long continued, causes depression and lessens the power of action; yet it is well adapted to make a creature guard itself against any great or sudden evil" (Darwin 2003: 431).

Yet, the important issue in this context is whether depression can be said to provide any fitness advantages in our contemporary world. Surely, if depression has anything like an adaptive function in the contemporary setting, then adaptation is not related to the natural environment but to the social world. There is a wide agreement that contemporary stressors derive from our modern social environments, in which we face greater social expectations and are pressured to set higher goals to achieve in life—such as authenticity. In the same way, Gilbert (2006) argues that what really is depressogenic today is the loss of control in the social environment.

In the evolutionary approach defended by Stevens and Price (2000), certain forms of depression are regarded as constructive ways of dealing with situations in which the desired goal is unattainable. Supporting this line of thought, there is evidence that depression occurs more frequently in individuals who pursue unattainable goals and have difficulties in capitulating when it comes to status struggle (Nesse 2000). The idea is that the pain and the down-regulation of positive affect systems that characterize depression may help the depressed to reconsider unattainable goals and to abandon them. Consequently, depression could be seen as a defense mechanism that helps the person disengage from impossible undertakings that have become so ingrown in consciousness that it is impossible for him to abandon them under normal circumstances. In this case depression would be an adaptive response to social circumstances, enhancing our ability to deal with complex situations. David A. Hamburg (1974: 240), an early exponent of this view, summarized possible functions of depression, maintaining that in a case where the individual estimates that achieving an important goal is unlikely, "the depressive responses can be viewed as adaptive" because "feelings of sadness and discouragement may be a useful stimulus to consider ways of changing (the) situation."

Thus, the down-regulation of positive affect, pessimism, and diminished motivation are regarded as potentially enabling disengagement from unfeasible goals and tasks that may ultimately exhaust the individual and damage fitness. It is in this sense that depression can be understood as helping to preserve resources. Additionally, depression can be understood as adaptive from another, social angle. Adult depression is for some theorists understood as entailing a form of communication that is designed to manipulate others into providing resources by conveying a plea for help and generating compassion. Hagen (1999) has claimed that depressed mothers attain greater attention and care from their partners and their social network. Similarly, Watson and Andrews (2002) have in their "social navigation hypothesis" argued that depression has an evolved function of obtaining and stimulating social relations. While these theories have been contested, the main point is that a depressive individual puts a claim on the environment that somehow re-shuffles the social bonds within that social network.

But what adaptation theorists fail to call attention to is the intrinsic connection between the intra-subjective and the inter-subjective explanations, even though it might contribute to strengthening their point. Let me briefly sketch what I mean. The intra-subjective version of the adaptationist view maintains that down-regulating positive affect systems in depression might help the individual to re-examine and eventually discard unattainable or too costly projects. The inter-subjective version holds that fellow members of the social network are compelled to engage with the depressed person in new and more intense ways, which reconfigures the connectedness of the depressed within the social network. To me, there is an obvious connection between these two versions, and I think they are interrelated. Why? This is because reorienting one's life and getting involved in new projects needs recognition from others in order have a normative grip on the self. The reshaping of the social context and the re-negotiation of relationships in connection to a depressive episode might open new contexts of recognition within which new life goals worthy of pursuit can arise. Thus, the renewed relation with others might just create the context in which unachievable goals can be discarded and new goals and perspectives can emerge.

With these insights inspired by adaptationist views on depression, we can now return to the context of this chapter and lend further support to the general claim. The contemporary performative ideal of authenticity, due to its specific tensions, its turn into an institutionalized demand, and its exhaustive qualities, can be seen as a social stressor that might contribute to depressive exhaustion. After considering the adaptationist views on depression, this hypothesis becomes more convincing. If it is right that the performative model of authenticity is both immensely popular and full of tensions and exhaustive qualities, then (following the adaptationist theory) it becomes more plausible that this creates the preconditions under which self-protecting mechanism are triggered and more people fall into depression. In depression individuals increase their chances to abandon the pursuit of exhaustive ideals, while at the same time, the depressive breakdown might provide the strengthening of inter-subjective bonds on the basis on which the re-evaluation and replacement of life goals can occur. As a last point, let me emphasize that my argument does not hinge on whether the adaptationist view is right or not. The point was to show the exhaustive quality of the performative model of authenticity and its becoming a social stressor. Since it is uncontroversial and accepted by most parties that social stress increases the risk of depression, the thesis that there is a connection between the rise of this model of authenticity and the growth of depression was substantiated by showing that authenticity has become a social stressor. The adaptationist view of depression merely adds to the credibility of this thesis.

10   CONCLUSION

I begun this chapter by calling attention to the fact that even though authenticity has become a topic in contemporary philosophy, the reciprocal shaping of capitalism and authenticity has not received any sustained attention. The examination of the popular 'self-help' discourse revealed the emergence of a *performative* model of authenticity, which was then set into a theoretical framework that rendered intelligible how it became a demand towards subjects. A central issue was the diagnosis of a paradoxical turn in which authenticity becomes an institutionalized demand that matches the systemic requirements of contemporary capitalism. The paradoxical aspect is that the very attempt to realize (performative) authenticity creates conditions under which the probability of its realization is reduced. Such a practice of authenticity may lead to the pathological exhaustion of the self, and this may in turn contribute to explaining some of the preconditions for the rapid rise of depression. Taken together, these issues show that instead of arising from the social barriers that inhibit authenticity and self-realization, pathological conditions and problematic self-relations arise from the process of striving for authenticity and self-realization itself. Any critical endeavor that aims at targeting and criticizing social issues that limit self-realization needs to take this possibility into account.

7   Concluding Remarks

I started this investigation by showing that authenticity is much more than a topic in an ethical or moral philosophical debate. At least in the Western world, it is a ubiquitous *ideal*, and a way of conceptualizing the practice of the self that aims to achieve a good life. As many claim, in our contemporary cultural context the vocabulary of authenticity has replaced the vocabulary of autonomy from early modernity. Thus, in order to achieve a full grasp of authenticity, I started by providing insight into the historical scaffolding of ideas from which authenticity emerged. To shed light on its enormous appeal and impact, I have argued that we should look not only at its historical sources and moral philosophical foundation but also shed light on how it circulates in everyday culture and how it feeds into contemporary practices of capitalism.

As Benjamin has pointed out, it is only against the modern background of endless reproducibility that the concept of authenticity becomes intelligible in the first place. Therefore, it is rather unsuprising that from the beginning the idea of authenticity is accompanied by suspicion. In fact, authenticity is a characteristic locus of the modern intertwinement of desire and fear. This is especially clear in the ethical realm, which is the context within which this book addressed the issue. Because of this intertwinement, the more value-laden this ideal becomes throughout modernity, and the greater role it plays in shaping our cultural outlook, the more the suspicion grows. For this reason, while in contemporary Western societies authenticity has become one of the most influential ethical ideals, the greatest fear of man is now the "horror of finding himself to be only a copy or a *replica*" (Rorty 1989: 24).

Throughout this book I was led by the conviction that being alarmed about the 'other side' of authenticity is indeed justified, today more than ever. Such suspicion is articulated in the work of contemporary thinkers such as Taylor, Ferrara, and Guignon, who argue that authenticity tends to mutate into aestheticism and egoistic self-indulgence. However, there is reason to be even more suspicious. I have examined the popular self-help discourse, pointing out the emergence of a *performative* model of authenticity, which marks a *paradoxical turn*. From once questioning the legitimacy of hierarchical institutions and capitalistic requirements, authenticity now seems to function as an institutionalized demand towards subjects, corresponding to the systemic demands of contemporary capitalism. In addition, due to the reciprocal shaping of capitalism and the ideal of authenticity, pathological conditions no longer arise from the social barriers that inhibit authenticity but from the practice of authenticity itself. In the last chapter of the book a link was pointed out between the popularization of this exhaustive model of authenticity and the rapid rise in the frequency of depression and in the sales of pharmaceutical antidepressants. This 'attitude of suspicion,' inspired by thinkers like Adorno and Benjamin, has helped reveal not only that authenticity 'malfunctions' and cannot unfold its potential because its contemporary practices rely on a 'deformed' concept. A close look at the self-help and self-management literature revealed that authenticity, far from 'malfunctioning,' has become an important factor of production in the post-Fordist economy, helping to enable the economic utilization of subjective capacities.

While such an attitude of suspicion is fully justified, I have argued that we are not currently provided with a concept of authenticity that can serve as a critical concept against which problematic and pathological practices can be identified. Despite the impact of the ideal of authenticity and despite some philosophical interest, existing accounts fail to address the reciprocal shaping of capitalism and the ideal of authenticity. Therefore, the main aim of this book was to fill this void and construct a concept against which pathological practices of authenticity become intelligible. In this regard, the aims of the book surpassed the ambitions of earlier attempts. A concept of authenticity was developed that served to provide the normative backbone of a critical social theory that is able to identify not only aestheticism and egoistic self-indulgence, but also more complex problematic practices of the self and patterns of societal interactions shaped by contemporary capitalism. There is good reason to think that authenticity may not be the only approach possible in this regard, but it certainly remains an adequate concept to capture contemporary practices.

Throughout the book, I have argued that practical philosophy and certainly critical social philosophy cannot get off the ground without reflecting on the nature of 'the good.' Any philosophical undertaking that aims to illuminate the standards by which we pass normative judgments on the quality of self-relations and social relations, and that aims to explicate the point of social integration and of political institutions, needs some normative underpinning. I have noted that the question concerning the formal conditions of good can be answered in different ways. Among other possibilities, it can be answered in the vocabulary of autonomy and in the vocabulary of authenticity. While I share the general aim of identifying the "structural aspects of the good life" with critical social philosophers like Habermas and Honneth, I have attempted to spell it out not in the vocabulary of autonomy but of authenticity, since it is more adequate to our contemporary social world. I used critical social philosophy as a source of inspiration and in order to create a theoretical frame for a concept of authenticity. Such framing made it possible to establish a link between capitalism, authenticity, and social criticism. At the same time, the inquiry has contributed to clarifying some of the claims of contemporary critical social philosophy. I have argued that the concept of authenticity is a productive element at the center of the theory of recognition. Such a concept may help shed light on aspects that are necessary for self-realization, but that are not intelligible from within a framework of recognition. Also, I took a critical stand on the Honnethian claim regarding the possibility of establishing evaluative predicates that can attain some supra-contextual validity while not embodying a historically contingent vision of the good. Resulting from these considerations, I have argued for a relaxed universalism with a modest validity claim.

The second part of the book maintained that authenticity is neither about the congruence between detection and what is detected nor about the self-congruence of an artistically created whole. Avoiding the pitfalls of the inner sense and the productionist models, I have argued that authenticity is about wholeheartedness regarding the commitments one endorses. Who we really are is not adequately captured in terms of discovery or production. Rather, authenticity is a matter of the mode in which we relate to our commitments. With this point of departure I have accommodated useful aspects from both inner sense and productionist accounts and have held on to the constitutive activity of the subject, without overemphasizing this aspect. In this way, the account became immune to accusations of paternalism. Rather than saying something substantial about the content of projects and commitments, it only emphasized the *manner of commitment* and the formations of the will under which such commitments can emerge. Wholeheartedness means that betraying your commitment would also mean betraying yourself (centrality), and it involves being committed to both the actual project and to entertaining the commitment itself (continuity).

While steering clear of problems found in other models, the progression of the argument led to an apparent dilemma. If we both maintain that our wholehearted commitments to certain projects define who we are and that we are agents that are able to choose our projects in life, then it seems that we are pushed to accept voluntarist or productionist assumptions. However, such assumptions were rejected for several reasons. The solution to the dilemma involved a change of perspective away from the intra-subjective view of authenticity, and it involved understanding our choices of commitments as articulations, rather than as acts that confer value on whatever commitments we choose. This new perspective acknowledges that our wholehearted engagements have a grip on us as on persons embedded in horizons of significance that are partly constituted by qualitative distinctions of worth. While we constitute ourselves through our choices of commitments, these commitments are linked to ideas of the *good* that qualitative *distinctions of worth* are based on. There is a constitutive relation between our commitments and collective background horizons, and authenticity is above all about articulating goods from such horizons through our commitments. Choices of such wholehearted commitments that have a normative grip on us require a specific and *embedded* expressive self-relation. While authenticity is about being responsive to what really matters to us, such self-responsiveness goes via inter-subjectively constituted values and orientations. Far from being about an intra-subjective relation to our 'inner,' authenticity is about articulating goods from a collective horizon by way of a commitment which requires responsiveness to these more or less locally constituted goods. Rather than merely reproducing those pre-existing horizons within which our choices take place, our articulations do not leave them unaltered, but rather refine and widen them through our individual interpretations. In other words, cultural horizons and practices that articulate them are interdependent.

Additionally, the scrutiny of the *structure* of wholehearted caring further illustrated the constitutive relation between our commitments and public values. The values that we take our commitments to embody constrain the manner in which we can coherently pursue our commitment. The structure of wholehearted commitments commits us to more than what we happen to care about and restricts the manner in which we can coherently pursue our commitment and even the mode of our practical deliberation. At the same time, this structure explains how we are sometimes able to refresh those commitments when their normative grip on us is fading; in such cases we remind ourselves of those goods that we took our commitment to articulate. It is such public goods rather than the immanent force of our choices that lastly provide the decisive normative grip that our commitments have on us.

To illustrate the choices that are emblematic when expressing who we are, I have used the term 'existential choices' in a non-voluntaristic sense. I have described them as having an exceptionally complex phenomenology, characterized by a sense of necessity and lack of alternatives. These are the situations in which we actualize, articulate, and bring into reality who we are and what we wholeheartedly care about. Rather than being clearly given, our fundamental carings often only take on a gestalt-like formation. In existential choices we both discover who we are 'on the inside' and actively constitute ourselves. While making these choices we often feel compelled to be loyal to something about ourselves that pre-exists. But importantly, such a supposedly pre-existing entity is neither independent of our attempts at articulation nor is it left unaltered by articulation. Instead, the boundaries between the aspects that preceded articulation and those formed by it tend to dissolve in the dialectic between implicitly endorsed commitments and deliberation. This move completed the progression towards a concept of authenticity. In the last chapter this concept was deployed in a critical inquiry that aimed at explicating some problematic contemporary practices.

In all, the account of authenticity defended here is neither about accessing something pre-existing nor about the consistency of an aesthetically self-created style of life. It involves being sensitive to the nature of choices that one faces and about the fact that one is always already involved in making choices that articulate normative goods and that configure one's life. Such sensitivity facilitates the integration of one's endeavors into a whole and the achievement of composite knowledge about one's responsibilities.

Throughout this book I have continuously argued that authenticity—at least thus conceived—is an inherently social virtue. Additionally, one could—for instance, by drawing on similar ideas in Dewey—speculate whether authenticity may even be beneficial for maintaining the social bonds of a democratic society. While this is beyond the scope of this book, it is certainly a question that would merit careful investigation in the future.

Notes

NOTES TO CHAPTER 1

1. In the previous translation by Schadelwald, the choir talks to Antigone, saying "nach dem eigenen Gesetz gehst lebend du als einzige unter den Sterblichen." As Menke shows, Hölderlin moves focus away from the law translating the same passage as "Dein eigen Leben lebend, unter den Sterblichen einzig, gehst du hinab, in die Welt der Toten." Both cited in Menke (2005: 305).

NOTES TO CHAPTER 2

1. Another problematic issue is the overstretching of social philosophy in Germany and the fact that researchers tend to neglect the divergence between the tradition of *Gesellschaftskritik* and Anglo-Saxon traditions, and transfer the ideas and concepts directly from one to the other (Honneth 2007a: 3).
2. Cannon is critical about this approach (Cannon 2001: 172) and accuses Honneth of creating a "'supra-human' conception of self-constitution" (Ibid.: 154). If I read this right, such criticism rests on not taking seriously the formal nature of Honneth's anthropology.
3. In German "Geschäftsführer des Weltgeistes" (Hegel 1970: 46, 161). 4. His concept of reification in "Reification and the Consciousness of the Proletariat" is an attempt to show what inauthenticity amounts to—the subject and social relations become commodity-like and thereby thing-like. Subjects are experienced as the same kinds of entities as objects: "The subject of the exchange is just as abstract, formal and reified as its object" Lukács (1971: 105). The matrix of commodity exchange intrudes upon all aspects of life and serves as an epistemological model which eliminates human qualities and makes life thing-like. The rationalized, capitalist labor process corrodes "the qualitative, human and individual attributes of the worker" (Ibid.: 88). In a sense Lukács is more radical than Marx, because for him the supposedly 'natural' laws of the capitalist outlook now cover every "manifestation of life in society" (Ibid.: 92). This is why this condition extends to everybody: "Reification is, then, the necessary, immediate reality of every person living in capitalist society" (Ibid.: 197). Of course, one of the difficulties regarding Lukács' account is that by this very declaration Lukács necessarily undermines his own argument about every individual being subject to reification (Baldwin 2009). In other words, reality cannot have become completely opaque and inapprehensible as a genuinely historical moment, which cannot be intellectually transcended. Also, Lukács tends to shift the pattern of theoretical underpinnings, he does not place much emphasis on making

his anthropological presuppositions clear, but instead sometimes argues in a historical-philosophical manner (Honneth 2008).

5. Moral is understood as having the goal to protect ('Schutzvorrichtung') life forms (Habermas 1991: 14).

6. There is of course also the alternative of applying a stronger anthropological ontology. However, this must be clearly rejected on grounds of the historicity of concepts and the far-reaching metaphysics involved.

7. After the publication of the first volume of *The History of Sexuality* (1976), and inspired by his teacher and friend the historian Pierre Hadot, Foucault attempted to restore classical ideas to outline the potential for self-formation and liberty. Foucault turned to the ancient Greek and Greco-Roman practice of 'care of the self,' to thematize the self-constitution of ethical subjects.

8. A part of this project was to argue for the aesthetic dimension of our identities: "What strikes me is the fact that, in our society, art has become something that is related only to objects and not to individuals or to life. That art is something that is specialized or done by experts who are artists. But couldn't everyone's life become a work of art? Why should the lamp or the house be an art object but not our life?" (Foucault 1984a: 350).

9. For further tensions, see: Zittel (2003). Of course, one could argue that the tension that I have pointed to between the sovereign and the heteronymous subject is simply a condition of modernity, and in this case authenticity is not about the attempt to eliminate this tension but about accepting it and embracing it. But even if we accept this argument, this would also inevitably require putting forward an additional argument that shows why it is good to resist the elimination of this tension.

10. Foucault's notion of aesthetic-authentic selfhood contains (maybe against his intentions) a moral dimension that goes beyond the 'aesthetics of existence.' The aesthetic care for one's own existence and being 'modest' in his account also leads to the requirement that one respect the freedom of others and comports oneself in a righteous manner. Additionally, authenticity and sovereignty over the self are also taken to be mandatory for legitimate political leadership. But while there are indications for a defense of authenticity on moral grounds, if we take into consideration Foucault's ongoing criticism of universality this moral dimension must be understood as a by-product of aesthetic authenticity and not the basis on which it is defended.

11. With this move Tugendhat comes very close to Taylor's idea of humans as self-interpreting animals, which also makes up the fundament of Taylor's anthropological reflections.

NOTES TO CHAPTER 3

1. Of course, this only accounts for the kind of infallibility involved in these emotions. So this still allows us to agree with the view held by Shoemaker that self-knowledge (unlike perceptual knowledge) is immune to error through misidentification relative to the first-person pronoun (1968; 1994). I never doubt that it is me who is involved in the knowing.

2. I have approached Rorty's account mostly focusing on the inconsistency involved in turning irony into a context-transcending criterion. However, there is also the problem that Rorty thinks that cruelty as such can be useful as the measure against which social practices can be evaluated. It remains unclear why and how everybody could agree upon one particular definition

of cruelty. In this case, cruelty faces exactly the same difficulties that any other such measure would.
3. For a useful discussion of such a possibility, see Fahrenbach (1970).

NOTES TO CHAPTER 4

1. Sartre uses the example of counting cigarettes. When counting cigarettes I have (indeed must have) a non-thetic consciousness of my own activity of counting in order to be able to count in the first place. In counting twelve cigarettes I disclose an objective property existing in the world. Similar to Wittgenstein, Sartre argues that in most cases I do not have positional consciousness of my counting. When someone interrupts me and asks me what activity I am engaged in, I do not hesitate to answer: 'I'm counting,' and I am able to do so on the basis of my non-reflective (non-thetic) consciousness of my counting (see also Longuenesse 2008).
2. In another passage, the notion of pre-reflective self-awareness becomes more explicit: "this consciousness of consciousness—with the exception of the cases of reflected consciousness, which we will consider in a moment—is not positional, i.e., this consciousness is not to itself its own object. We will call this consciousness first-order consciousness or unreflected consciousness" (Sartre 1957: 45).
3. The original passage sounds like this: "Als je meines aber ist das Seinkönnen frei für Eigentlichkeit oder Uneigentlichkeit oder die modale Indifferenz ihrer" Martin Heidegger, *Sein und Zeit* (Tübingen: Max Niemeyer, 1963), 232.
4. Martin Heidegger, *Being and Time*, J. Macquarrie and E. Robinson, trans. (New York: Harper & Row, 1927/1962), 69. The Macquarrie and Robinson translation brings out the undifferentiated character that I think matches best Heidegger's point. Stambaugh (Heidegger 1996) translates this as "indifferent," which I think is misleading.
5. In another context (Varga 2011d) I have made a different point, arguing that there is even a sense in which we may be forced to rethink our usual commitment to thinking of the relation between authenticity and morality as hostile.

NOTES TO CHAPTER 5

1. For a useful discussion of a closely related matter, see Berofsky (2003).
2. Blattner connects death and anxiety in Heidegger with the concept of conscience, by stating that the call of conscience belongs to the extreme condition of death and anxiety (2006: 156). This of course delivers a plausible explanation of why the call must be silent: because in the extreme condition of anxiety and death, one is alienated from all self-understanding. Yet in my view the connection does not have to be this tight. This is because the call of conscience does not arise in anxiety or death. In other words, anxiety and death are not necessary conditions of conscience.
3. Due to this revealing force, it may deserve the attribute 'knowledge.' Without this Luther would have failed to comprehend his situation as existential, as bearing import to his life as a whole, and all he would have been left with would have been the third-person options of "man." Thus, there are no existential choices without some background that guides our decisions by informing us about the kind of choices (optional or non-optional) we ought to make.

Having said this, we must recall that such responsiveness is constitutively embedded.
4. Akin to anxiety, conscience also reveals to us something about the existential structure of our being-in-the-world. In anxiety, our everyday self-understandings fall away and, rather than geting us in touch with the purified person who is beneath all those self-understandings, we get us in touch with how we are (see Blattner 2006: 160). In the same way, conscience reveals that we always already enter a situation with an implicit constellation of projects that matter to us.

NOTES TO CHAPTER 6

1. In the form of the 'sexual revolution,' Honneth sees a good example of the linkage between social change and cultural transformation. He argues that the dissolution of conventional role patterns and the possibility of diversification "would of its own accord have suggested granting a greater importance to sexuality as forming a privileged field for trying out one's individuality" (2004b: 470). This can only be explained if one simultaneously takes into account the growing social acceptance of an ideal of authenticity that defined the subject as a 'desiring subject' whose style of sexual conduct somehow expresses his core personality.
2. Of course, one has to bear in mind that the 'entreployee' is not a global trend. Empirically, one can even argue that reverse tendencies take place in various sectors. Sociologists like Springer (2005) have pointed out non-participative rationalisation trends, which they have termed 're-Taylorization'. "Re-Taylorization here stands for two things: on the one hand a shifting back of planning, design and optimisation competences of industrial organisation to rationalisation experts inside and outside the company (e.g. industrial engineering, consultants) and on the other hand a forced standardisation of processes, above all in labour-intensive car assembly, where companies fully return to the flow principle and short job cycle times (< 5 minutes)" (Springer 2000).
3. The model is not only the base for liberating self-help strategies and management concepts but also for governmental approaches to reform the labor market, seen very clearly in Germany. The Hartz Commission coined the term "Me Inc." to describe the ideal entrepreneurial subject. Some evident risks are that in this picture structurally rooted problems are explained as individual failures (of self-realization). Also, for those who experience difficulties in coping with this model, the precarious security arrangements can mean a descent to an emerging class of the 'working poor'. In her widely read book Ehrenreich (2001) portrays the lifestyle of a new class of low wage workers that despite long working days have trouble getting by in a stable manner.
4. The so-called 'Cool-Hunters' seek sub-cultural forms of expression (usually in socially troubled suburbs) and use these for developing new products. They convert local expression forms and even subversive appropriations that become fed back into the circulation of commodities. With this, markets expand and their ability to convert non-capital into capital.
5. It should be pointed out that Giddens here assesses the concepts of contradiction given by Elster and Boudon, which he ends up rejecting. For Giddens, the contradiction lies in the social form of a capitalist state. The conditions that allow the existence of a state (the capital market) work through mechanisms that run counter to state power (see Giddens 1984: 315).

6. Admittedly, this is an unusual definition of paradox. In this context, paradox does not refer to a statement, from which opposing or contradictory conclusions may be drawn at one and the same time. Formally speaking, it seems more like a contradiction, since a paradox is a statement that *leads* to a contradiction, which is of itself the paradox. This notion seems to be closer to a literary paradox.

7. Generally the categories of mild, moderate, and severe depression are classified according to primary and secondary symptoms. Primary symptoms are fatigue, loss of interest, and lack of energy, while secondary symptoms are more severe, including self-blame, sleep disturbance, suicidal thoughts, lack of self-confidence, and concentration difficulties. The more secondary symptoms a patient has, the more severe the diagnosis (American Psychiatric Association 2000).

8. "Depression is the leading cause of disability as measured by years lived with disability (YLD) and the 4th leading contributor to the global burden of disease (disability adjusted life years [DALYs]) in 2000. By the year 2020, depression is projected to reach 2nd place of the ranking of DALYs calculated for all ages, both sexes. Today, depression is already the 2nd cause of DALYs in the age category 15–44 years for both sexes combined." Retrieved from: http://www.who.int/mental_health/management/depression/definition/en/.

References

Abbey, Ruth (2000) *Charles Taylor*. Princeton, NJ: Princeton University Press.

Adorno, Theodor W. (1973) *The Jargon of Authenticity*, trans. Knut Tarnowski and Frederic Will. Evanston, IL: Northwestern University Press.

Adorno, Theodor W. (1974) *Minima Moralia*: Reflections from Damaged Life, trans. E. F. N. Jephcott. London: NLB.

Adorno, Theodor W. (2001) *Aesthetic Theory*, trans. Robert Hullot-Kentor. Minneapolis, MN: Continuum.

Adorno, Theodor W. & Horkheimer, Max (2000) Dialectic of Enlightenment, trans. John Cumming. New York: Continuum.

Aho, Kevin (2007) "Simmel on Acceleration, Boredom, and Extreme Aesthesia," *Journal for the Theory of Social Behaviour* 37(4):447–462.

Allison, Henry E, (1990) *Kant's Theory of Freedom*, Cambridge: Cambridge University Press.

American Psychiatric Association (2000) *Diagnostic and Statistical Manual of Mental Disorders*, 4th Edition, Text Revision. Washington: American Psychiatric Association.

Anderson, Joel (1995a) "Review Essay: The Persistence of Authenticity," *Philosophy and Social Criticism* 21(1):101–109.

Anderson, Joel (1995b) "Translator's Introduction," in *The Struggle for Recognition*, edited by Axel Honneth, pp. x–xxi. Cambridge: Polity.

Anderson, Joel (1996) "The Personal Lives of Strong Evaluators: Identity, Pluralism, and Ontology in Charles Taylor's Value Theory," *Constellations* 3:17–38.

Anderson, Joel & Honneth, Axel (2005) "Autonomy, Vulnerability, Recognition, and Justice," in *Autonomy and the Challenges to Liberalism: New Essays*, edited by John Christman and Joel Anderson, pp. 127–149. Cambridge: Cambridge University Press.

Anderson, Joel (2008) "Disputing Autonomy. Second-Order Desires and the Dynamics of Ascribing Autonomy" *Sats—Nordic Journal of Philosophy* 9(1): 7–26.

Anscombe, Elizabeth (1958) "Modern Moral Philosophy," *Philosophy* 33:1–19.

Arendt, Hannah (1958) *The Human Condition*. Chicago: University of Chicago Press.

Arendt, Hannah (1966) *The Origins of Totalitarianism*. New York: Harcourt Brace.

Aristotle (1985) *Nicomachean Ethics*, trans. Terence Irwin. Indianapolis: Hackett.

Armstrong, David M. (1968), *A Materialist Theory of the Mind*. London: Routledge and Kegan Paul.

Armstrong, David M. (1981) *The Nature of Mind and Other Essays*. New York: Cornell University Press.

Arruda, William (2003) "An Introduction to Personal Branding. A Revolution in the Way We Manage Our Carriers," pp. 1–13. Accessed in October 2008 at www.reachcc.com.

Arthur, Christopher J. (1986) *Dialectics of Labour: Marx and His Relation to Hegel*. Oxford: Basil Blackwell. Augustine (1955) Confessions and Enchiridion. London: SCM Press.

Bainton, Roland H. (1950) Here I Stand: A Life of Martin Luther. Abingdon: Cokesbury.

Baldwin, Jon (2009) "Exchange and Subjectivity, Commodity, and Gift," *Semiotica* 173:377–396.

Baldwin, Thomas (1979) "The Original Choice in Sartre and Kant" *Proceedings of the Aristotelian Society, New Series*, 80: 31–44

Bauman, Zygmunt (2001) *The Individualized Society*. Cambridge: Polity.

Beck, Ulrich (1986) *Risikogesellschaft*. Auf dem Weg in eine andere Moderne. Frankfurt: Suhrkamp.

Beck, Ulrich & Beck-Gernsheim, Elisabeth (2002) *Individualization*. London: Sage.

Bell, Daniel (1976) *The Cultural Contradictions of Capitalism*. New York: Basic Books.

Bellah, Robert N. et al. (1985) *Habits of the Heart*. Berkeley: University of California Press.

Benjamin, Walter (1973) "The Work of Art in the Age of Mechanical Reproduction," in *Illuminations*, edited by Hannah Arendt. Glasgow: Fontana.

Berlin, Isaiah (1969) "Two Concepts of Liberty," in *Four Essays on Liberty*, by Isaiah Berlin, pp. 118–172. Oxford: Oxford University Press.

Berman, Marshall (1970) *The Politics of Authenticity*: Radical Individualism and the Emergence of Modern Society. New York: Atheneum.

Berofsky, Bernard (2003) "Identification, the Self, and Autonomy," *Social Philosophy & Policy* 20(2):199–220.

Blattner, William (2006) *Heidegger's Being and Time*. New York: Continuum.

Bloom, Allan (1987) *The Closing of the American Mind*. New York: Simon and Schuster.

Böhme, Gernot (2003) "Contribution to the Critique of The Aesthetic Economic," *Thesis Eleven* 73(1):71–82.

Boltanski, Luc & Chiapello, Eve (2005) *The New Spirit of Capitalism*. London: Verso.

Borch-Jacobsen, Mikkel (2002) "Prozac Notion," in *London Review of Books*, July 9.

Bratman, Michael E. (1999) "Identification, Decision, and Treating as a Reason," in *Faces of Intention: Selected Essays on Intention and Agency*, by Michael E. Bratman, pp. 197–198. Cambridge: Cambridge University Press.

Bratman, Michael E. (2002). Hierarchy, Circularity, and Double Reduction. In *Contours of Agency: Essays on Themes from Harry Frankfurt*. Buss, Sarah and Overton, Lee (Ed.), 65–85. Cambridge: MIT Press.

Briggs, Asa (1969) "A Centenary Introduction," in *Self-Help*, by Samuel Smiles, pp. 7–31. London: John Murray.

Budgen, Sebastian (2000) "A New Spirit of Capitalism" *New Left Review* 2(1):149–156.

Cahn, Michael (1984) "Theodore W. Adorno and the Modern Impasse of Critique," in *Mimesis in Contemporary Theory: An Interdisciplinary Approach*, Vol. I, edited by Mihai Spariosu, pp. 27–64. Philadelphia: John Benjamin's Publishing Company.

Callinicos, Alex (1996) *The Revolutionary Ideas of Karl Marx*. London: Bookmarks.

Cannon, Bobby A. (2001) *Rethinking the Normative Content of Critical Theory: Marx, Habermas and Beyond*. Gordonsville, VA: Palgrave Macmillan.

Carling, Alan (1992) *Social Divisions*. London: Verso.

Carman, Taylor (2003) *Heidegger's Analytic: Interpretation, Discourse, and Authenticity in Being and Time*. New York: Cambridge University Press.

Carnegie, Dale (1948) *How to Stop Worrying and Start Living*. New York: Simon & Schuster.

Cassirer, Ernst (1932) "Das Problem Jean-Jaques Rousseau," *Archiv für Geschichte der Philosophie* 41:29–37.

Chidester, David (2005) *Authentic Fakes: Religion and American Popular Culture*. Berkeley: University of California Press.

Chopra, Deepak (1994) *The Seven Spiritual Laws of Success*. New York: New World Library Amber-Allen Publishing.

Christman, John (1988) "Constructing the Inner Citadel: Recent Work on the Concept of Autonomy," *Ethics* 99:109–124.

Christman, John (1991) "Autonomy and Personal History," *Canadian Journal of Philosophy* 21(1):1–24.

Christman, John (2004) "Narrative Unity as a Condition of Personhood," *Metaphilosophy* 35(5):695–713.

Christman, John (2009) "Autonomy in Moral and Political Philosophy," in *Stanford Encyclopaedia of Philosophy*. Accessed September 7, 2009. URL: http://plato.stanford.edu/entries/autonomy-moral/

Cohen Andrew J. (2008) "Existentialist Voluntarism: From Radical Choice to Normativity," *Philosophical Papers* 37(1):89–129.

Coliva, Annalisa (2009) "Self.Knowledge and Commitments" *Synthese* 171: 365–375.

Cottingham, John (1998) *Philosophy and the Good Life. Reason and the Passions in Greek, Cartesian and Psychoanalytic Ethics*. Cambridge: University Press.

Cullen, Daniel E. (1993) *Freedom in Rousseau's Political Philosophy*. DeKalp: Northern Illinois University Press.

Cushman, Philip (1995) *Constructing the Self, Constructing America: A Cultural History of Psychotherapy*. Reading, MA: Addison-Wesley.

Cuypers, Stefaan E. (1998) "Harry Frankfurt on the Will, Autonomy and Necessity," *Ethical Perspectives* 5(1):44–52.

Damasio, Antonio (1999) *The Feeling of What Happens: Body and Emotion in the Making of Consciousness*. New York: Harcourt Brace.

Darnton, Robert (1984) *The Great Cat Massacre and Other Episodes in French Cultural History*. New York: Viking.

Darwin, Charles (2003) *On the Origin of Species, edited by Joseph Carroll*. Peterborough: Broadview Press.

Davis, D. Russell (1970) "Depression as Adaptation to Crisis," *British Journal of Medical Psychology* 43:109–116.

Dennett, Daniel C. (1984). Elbow Room: *The Varieties of Free Will Worth Wanting*. MIT Press.

Deranty, Jan-Philippe (forthcoming) "Reflective Critical Theory: A Systematic Reconstruction of Axel Honneth's Social Philosophy," in *The Critical Theory of Axel Honneth*, edited by Danielle Petherbridge. Leiden: Brill.

Derrida, Jacques (1997) *Of Grammatology, trans. Gayatri Chakravorty Spivak*. John Hopkins University Press.

Despland, Michel (1975) "Can Conscience Be Hypocritical? The Contrasting Analyses of Kant and Hegel," *The Harvard Theological Review* 68(3/4):357–370.

Dews, Peter (1995) "Modernity, "Self-Consciousness and the Scope of Philosophy: Jürgen Habermas and Dieter Henrich in Debate," in *The Limits of Disenchantment*, by Peter Dews, pp. 170–193. London: Verso.

Dohmen, Joep (2003) "Philosophers on the 'Art of Living'," *Journal of Happiness Studies* 4:351–371.

Dreyfus, Hubert L. (1991) *Being-in-the-World. A Commentary on Heidegger's Being and Time Division I.* Cambridge: MIT Press.

Dreyfus, Hubert L. & Rabinow, P. (1983) *Michel Foucault: Beyond Structuralism and Hermeneutics.* Chicago, IL: University of Chicago Press.

Düsing, Klaus (1997) *Selbstbewußtseinsmodelle. Moderne Kritiken und systematische Entwürfe zur konkreten Subjektivität.* München: Wilhelm Fink.

Dutton, Denis (2003) "Authenticity in Art," in *The Oxford Handbook of Aesthetics*, edited by Jerrold Levinson. New York: Oxford University Press.

Dworkin, Gerald (1981) "The Concept of Autonomy," in *Science and Ethics*, edited by Rudolf Haller, pp. 203–213. Amsterdam: Rodopi.

Dworkin, Gerald (1988) *The Theory and Practice of Autonomy.* New York: Cambridge University Press.

Dworkin, Gerald (1989) "The Concept of Autonomy," in *The Inner Citadel: Essays on Individual Autonomy*, edited by John Christman, pp. 54–62. New York and Oxford: Oxford University Press.

Dyers, Wayne (2004) *Staying on the Path.* New York: Hay House. Eagleton, Terry (1997) Marx and Freedom. London: Phoenix.

Ehrenberg, Alain (2006) "Das erschöpfte Selbst. Spätmodernes Leben zwischen Autonomie und Depression," lecture in Galerie der Heinrich-Böll-Stiftung, Berlin, January 18, 2006.

Ehrenberg, Alain (2007) "Depression: Discontent in the Civilisation Or New Style of Sociality," *Texte zur Kunst* 65:129–134.

Ehrenberg, Alain (2008) *Das erschöpfte Selbst. Depression und Gesellschaft in der Gegenwart.* Frankfurt am Main: Suhrkamp. Ehrenreich, Barbara (2001) *Nickel and Dimed.* New York: Henry Holt and Company.

Ekstrom, Laura W. (2005) "Alienation, Autonomy, and the Self," *Midwest Studies in Philosophy* 29:45–67.

Evans, Garreth (1982) *The Varieties of Reference*, edited by John McDowell. Oxford: Oxford University Press. Fahrenbach, Helmut (1970) *Existenzphilosophie und Ethik.* Frankfurt am Main: Vittoro Klostermann.

Fairlie, Henry (1978) "Too Rich for Heroes," *Harper's* 257:33–42; 97–98.

Farrell, James J. (1997) *The Spirit of the Sixties.* London: Routledge.

Feinberg, Joel (1973) *Social Philosophy.* New Jersey: Prentice Hall.

Ferrara, Alessandro (1993) *Modernity and Authenticity: A Study of the Social and Ethical Thought of Jean-Jacques Rousseau.* Albany, NY: Sunny Press.

Ferrara, Alessandro (1998) *Reflective Authenticity.* London: Routledge.

Finkelstein, David H. (2003). *Expression and the Inner.* Harvard University Press.

Forst, Rainer (2007) *Das Recht auf Rechtfertigung.* Frankfurt am Main: Suhrkamp.

Foster, Roger (2007) *Adorno: The Recovery of Experience.* Albany: State University of New York Press.

Foucault, Michel (1980) *The History of Sexuality, Vol. 3, An Introduction.* New York: Vintage Books.

Foucault, Michel (1983) "The Subject and Power," in *Michel Foucault Beyond Structuralism and Hermeneutics*, by Hubert L. Dreyfus & Paul Rabinow. Chicago: University of Chicago Press.

Foucault, Michel (1984a) "On the Genealogy of Ethics: An Overview of Work in Progress," in The Foucault Reader, edited by Paul Rabinow, pp. 340–372. New York: Pantheon.

Foucault, Michel (1984b) "What is Enlightenment?" in *The Foucault Reader*, edited by Paul Rabinow, pp. 41–42. New York: Pantheon Books.

Foucault, Michel (1985) *The Use of Pleasure, Vol. II, The History of Sexuality*, trans. Robert Hurley. New York: Vintage Books.

Foucault, Michel (1988) "An Aesthetics of Existence," in Michel Foucault: Politics, Philosophy, Culture, edited by Lawrence D. Kritzman, pp. 47–53. New York: Routledge.

Foucault, Michel (1991) *Remarks on Marx: Conversation with Duccio Trombadori*, trans. R. James Goldstein & J. Cascatio. New York: Semiotext (E).

Foucault, Michel (1994) *The Order of Things: An Archaeology of the Human Sciences.* New York: Vintage Books.

Foucault, Michel (2000) *Essential Works of Foucault 1954–1984, Vol. 3, Power.* New York: New Press.

Frankfurt, Harry G. (1987) "Identification and Wholeheartedness," in *Responsibility, Character and the Emotions*, edited by Ferdinand Schoeman, pp. 27–45. Cambridge: Cambridge University Press.

Frankfurt, Harry G. (1988a) "Freedom of the Will and the Concept of a Person," in *The Importance of What We Care About*, by Harry G. Frankfurt, pp. 11–25. Cambridge: Cambridge University Press.

Frankfurt, Harry G. (1988b) "Coercion and moral responsibility," in *The Importance of What We Care About*, by Harry G. Frankfurt, pp. 26–46. Cambridge, Cambridge University Press.

Frankfurt, Harry G. (1988c) "Identification and Wholeheartedness," in *The Importance of What We Care About*, by Harry G. Frankfurt, pp. 159–176. Cambridge, Cambridge University Press.

Frankfurt, Harry G. (1999a) "On the Necessity of Ideals," in *Necessity, Volition, and Love*, by Harry G. Frankfurt, pp. 108–116. Cambridge: Cambridge University Press.

Frankfurt, Harry G. (1999b) "Autonomy, Necessity, and Love," in *Necessity, Volition, and Love,* by Harry G. Frankfurt, pp. 129–148. Cambridge: Cambridge University Press.

Frankfurt, Harry G. (1999c) "The Faintest Passion," in *Necessity, Volition, and Love*, by Harry G. Frankfurt, pp. 95–107. Cambridge: Cambridge University Press.

Frankfurt, Harry G. (2004) *The Reasons of Love.* Princeton: Princeton University Press.

Frankfurt, Harry G. (2006) *Taking Ourselves Seriously and Getting it Right.* Stanford: Stanford University Press.

Fraser, Nancy (1989) "Foucault on Modern Power: Empirical Insights and Normative Confusions," in *Unruly Practices: Power, Discourse, and Gender in Contemporary Social Theory*, by Nancy Fraser, pp. 17–34. Minneapolis, MN: University of Minnesota Press.

Fraser, Nancy & Honneth, Axel (2003) *Redistribution or Recognition? A Political-Philosophical Exchange.* London: Verso.

Freundlieb, Dieter (2000) "Rethinking Critical Theory: Weaknesses and New Directions," *Constellations* 7(1):80–99.

Friedman, Marilyn (1986) "Autonomy and the Split-Level Self," *Southern Journal of Philosophy* 24:19–35.

Früchtl, Josef (1986) *Mimesis—Konstellation eines Zentralbegriffs bei Adorno.* Würzburg: Königshausen & Neumann.

Früchtl, Josef (1998) "Adorno and Mimesis," in *The Encyclopedia of Aesthetics, Vol. 3*, edited by Michael Kelly, pp. 23–25. Oxford: Oxford University Press.

Robert J. Gay (1989) "Bernard Williams on Practical Necessity"*Mind* 98 (392):551–569.

Geuss, Raymond (2005) *Outside Ethics.* Princeton: Princeton University Press.

Gibson, Nigel C. & Rubin, Andrew (2002) *Adorno. A Critical Reader.* London: Blackwell.

Giddens, Anthony (1984) *The Constitution of Society: Outline of the Theory of Structuration.* Cambridge: Polity.

Giddens, Anthony (1991) *Modernity and Self-Identity. Self and Society in the Late Modern Age.* Stanford: University Press.

Gierke, Christiane (2005) *Persönlichkeitsmarketing.* München: Gabal.

Gilbert, Paul (2006) "Emotion and Depression: Issues and Implications," *Psychological Medicine* 36:287–297.

Gilbert, Paul & Allan, Steven (1998) "The Role of Defeat and Entrapment (Arrested Flight) in Depression: Exploring an Evolutionary View," *Psychological Medicine* 28:585–598.

Gilmore, James & Pine, Joseph (2007) *Authenticity: What Consumers Really Want.* Harvard Business School Press, Harvard Business School Press.

Goldie, Peter (2000) *The Emotions. A Philosophical Exploration.* Oxford: Clarendon Press.

Golomb, Jacob (1990) "Nietzsche on Authenticity," Philosophy Today 34:243–258.

Golomb, Jacob (1995) *In Search of Authenticity from Kierkegaard to Camus.* London and New York: Routledge.

Gouldner, lvin W. (1980) *The Two Marxisms.* New York: Oxford University Press.

Gray, Glenn J. (1965) "Salvation on the Campus: Why Existentialism Is Capturing the Students," *Harper's* 230:53–59.

Guignon, Charles (2004) *On Being Authentic.* London: Routledge.

Guignon, Charles (2008) Authenticity, *Philosophy Compass* 3:277–290.

Guyer, Paul (2003) "Kant on the Theory and Practice of Autonomy," in *Autonomy*, edited by Ellen Frankel Paul, Fred Miller, & Jeffrey Paul, pp. 70–98. Cambridge: Cambridge University Press.

Habermas, Jürgen (1978) *The Philosophical Discourse on Modernity: Twelve Lectures*, trans. Frederick Lawrence. Cambridge: MIT.

Habermas, Jürgen (1981) *The Theory of Communicative Action, Vol. 1, Reason and the Rationalization of Society*, trans. Thomas McCarthy. Boston: Beacon Press.

Habermas, Jürgen (1989) *The Structural Transformation of the Public Sphere: An Inquiry into a Category of Bourgeois Society*, trans. Thomas Burger & Frederick Lawrence. Cambridge: MIT Press.

Habermas, Jürgen (1991) "Treffen Hegels Einwände gegen Kant auch auf die Diskursethik zu?" in *Erläuterungen zur Diskursethik*, by Jürgen Habermas, pp.9–30. Frankfurt am Main: Suhrkamp.

Habermas, Jürgen (1992) *Postmetaphysical Thinking: Philosophical Essays*, trans. William Mark Hohengarten. Cambridge: Polity Press.

Habermas, Jürgen (1996) *Between Facts and Norms: Contributions to a Discourse Theory of Law and Democracy*, translated by W. Rehg. Cambridge: Polity Press.

Habermas, Jürgen (1999) "From Kant to Hegel and Back again—The Move Towards Detranscendentalization," *European Journal of Philosophy* 7(2):129–157.

Habermas, Jürgen (2003) *The Future of Human Nature*, trans. Hella Beister, Max Pensky, & William Rehg. Cambridge: Polity.

Hadot, Pierre (1992) "Reflections on the Notion of the 'Cultivation of the Self'," in *Michel Foucault, Philosopher,* edited by Timothy J. Armstrong, pp. 225–232. New York: Routledge.

Hagen, Edward (1999) "The Functions of Post-partum Depression," *Evolution and Human Behavior* 20:325–359.

Hamburg, David A. (1974) "Coping Behavior in Life-threatening Circumstances," *Psychotherapy and Psychosomatics* 23:13–25.

Hansen, Miriam Bratu (1997) "Mass Culture as Hieroglyphic Writing: Adorno, Derrida, Kracauer," in *The Actuality of Adorno: Critical Essays on Adorno and the Postmodern,* edited by Max Pensky, pp. 83–111. Albany, NY: SUNY Press.

Hardimon, Michael O. (1997) "Review of the Struggle for Recognition," *The Journal of Philosophy* 94(1):46–54.

Härter, Gitte & Öttl, Christiane (2005) *Selbstmarketing*. München.

Healy, David (1998) *The Antidepressant Era*. Cambridge, MA: Harvard University Press.

Heath, Anthony (1976) *Rational Choice and Social Exchange*. Cambridge: Cambridge University Press.

Hegel, Georg W. F. (1963) *Lectures on the History of Philosophy, Vol. III*. London: Routledge and Kegan Paul.

Hegel, Georg W. F. (1970) *Vorlesungen über die Philosophie der Geschichte*, Werke, Vol. 12. Frankfurt am Main: Suhrkamp.

Hegel, Georg W. F. (1986) *Jenaer Systementwürfe I*. Hamburg: Felix Meiner.

Hegel, Georg W. F. (2002) *The Phenomenology of Mind*, Vol. 2. London: Routledge.

Heidegger, Martin (1927/1962) *Being and Time*, trans. J. Macquarrie & E. Robinson. New York: Harper & Row.

Heidegger, Martin (1963) *Sein und Zeit*. Tübingen: Max Niemeyer. Heidegger, Martin (1996) Being and Time, trans. Joan Stambaugh. Albany: SUNY Press.

Heidegger, Martin (1998) "Comments on Karl Jaspers's 'Psychology of Worldviews'," trans. John van Buren, in *Pathmarks*, by Martin Heidegger, pp. 1–38. edited by William McNeill. Cambridge: Cambridge University Press.

Herder, Johann (1877/1913) *Ideen, in Herder's Sämmtliche Werke, Vol. XIII*, edited by Bernhard Suphan. Berlin: Weidmann.

Hill, Christopher (1991) *Sensations: A Defence of Type Materialism*. Cambridge: Cambridge University Press.

Hobbes, Thomas (1968) *Leviathan*, edited by Crawford MacPherson. Middlesex: Penguin Books.

Hobson, Peter (2002) *The Cradle of Thought: Exploring the Origins of Thinking*. London: Pan Books.

Hochschild, Arlie Russel (1997) *The Time Bind—When Work Becomes Home and Home Becomes Work*. New York: Metropolitan Books.

Hohendahl, Peter Uwe & Fisher, Jaimey (2001) *Critical Theory: Current State and Future Prospects*. London: Berghahn Books.

Hölderlin, Johann C. F. (1946/1962) *Sämtliche Werke*, "Kleine Stuttgarter Ausgabe," Vol. 6, edited by Friedrich Beissner. Stuttgart: Cotta.

Honneth, Axel (1994) "Schwerpunkt: Autonomie Authentizität," *Deutsche Zeitschrift für Philosophie* 42(1):59–60.

Honneth, Axel (1995a) *The Struggle for Recognition*. Cambridge: Polity Press.

Honneth, Axel (1995b) "The Limits of Liberalism: On the Political-Ethical Discussion concerning Communitarianism," *The Fragmented World of the Social. Essays in Social and Political Philosophy*, edited by Charles W. Wright, pp. 231–246. New York: SUNY Press.

Honneth, Axel (2002) "Einleitung," in *Befreiung aus der Mündigkeit. Paradoxien des gegenwärtigen Kapitalismus*, by Axel Honneth, pp. 7–12. Frankfurt am Main: Campus.

Honneth, Axel (2004a) "Gerechtigkeit und kommunikative Freiheit. Überlegungen im Anschluss an Hegel," in *Subjektivität und Anerkennung, edited by Barbara Merker*, Georg Mohr, & Michael Quante, pp. 213–227. Paderborn: Mentis.

Honneth, Axel (2004b) "Organized Self-Realization. Some Paradoxes of Individualization," *European Journal of Social Theory* 7(4):463–478.

Honneth, Axel (2007a) "Pathologies of the Social: The Past and Present of Social Philosophy," in *Disrespect. The Normative Foundations of Critical Theory*, by Axel Honneth, pp. 3–48. Cambridge: Polity Press.

Honneth, Axel (2007b) "Recognition as Ideology," in *Recognition and Power. Axel Honneth and the Tradition of Critical Social Theory*, by Bert van den Brink & David Owen, pp. 323–348. New York: Cambridge University Press.

Honneth, Axel (2007c) "Between Aristotle and Kant: Recognition and Moral Obligation," in *Disrespect. The Normative Foundations of Critical Theory*, by Axel Honneth, pp. 129–143. Cambridge: Polity Press.

Honneth, Axel (2008) *Reification: A New Look at an Old Idea*. Oxford: Oxford University Press.

Honneth, Axel & Critchley, Simon (1998) "Philosophy in Germany," *Radical Philosophy* 89:27–39.

Honneth, Axel & Hartmann, Martin (2006) "Paradoxes of Capitalism," *Constellations* 13(1):41–58.

Horkheimer, Max. (1974) *Eclipse of Reason*. New York: Seabury Press.

Horn, Peter (2004) *Personal Branding*. Copenhagen: CBS.

Huhn, Tom (2004) "Introduction. Thoughts beside Themselves," in *The Cambridge Companion to Adorno*, edited by Tom Huhn. Cambridge: Cambridge University Press.

Husserl, Edmund (1973) *Experience and Judgment*, trans. James S. Churchill & Karl Ameriks. London: Routledge and Kegan Paul.

Husserl, Edmund (1970) *The Crisis of European Sciences and Transcendental Phenomenology: An Introduction to Phenomenological Philosophy*, trans. David Carr. Evanston, IL: Northwestern University Press.

Illes, Judy & Bird, Stephanie J. (2006) "Neuroethics: A Modern Context for Ethics in Neuroscience," *Trends in Neuroscience* 29(9):511–517.

Illouz, Eva (1997) *Consuming the Romantic Utopia: Love and the Cultural Contradictions of Capitalism*. Berkeley: University of California Press.

Illouz, Eva (2004) *Gefühle in Zeiten des Kapitalismus*. Frankfurt am Main: Suhrkamp.

Illouz, Eva (2007) *Cold Intimacies: The Making of Emotional Capitalism*. Oxford and Malden, MA: Polity Press.

Jaeggi, Rahel (2005) *Entfremdung. Zur Aktualität eines sozialphilosophischen Problems*. Frankfurt am Main: Campus.

Jay, Martin (2004) "Mimesis and Mimetology: Adorno and Lacoue-Labarthe," in *Critical Theory*, Vol. 4, edited by David Rasmussen & James Swindal, pp. 265–283. London: Sage.

Jopling, David (2000) *Self-Knowledge and the Self*. New York: Routledge.

Kane, Robert (1996). *The Significance of Free Will*. New York: Oxford University Press.

Kant, Immanuel (1797/2003) *Metaphysics of Morals*, edited by Mary J. Gregor. Cambridge: Cambridge University Press.

Kant, Immanuel (1998) *Religion within the Boundaries of Mere Reason and Other Writings*, trans. and edited by Allen Wood & George Di Giovanni. Cambridge: Cambridge University Press.

Klein, Naomi (2000) *No Logo: Taking Aim at the Brand Bullies*. London, Flamingo.

Korsgaard, Christine (1996) *The Sources of Normativity*, Ed. O'Neill. New York: Cambridge University Press.

Korsgaard, Christine M. (2006) "Morality and the Logic of Caring," in *Taking Ourselves Seriously and Getting it Right*, by Harry Frankfurt, pp. 55–76. Stanford: Stanford University Press.

Korsgaard, Christine M. (2009) *Self-Constitution: Agency, Identity, and Integrity*. Oxford: Oxford University Press.

Laitinen, Arto (2002) "Culturalist Moral Realism," in *Perspectives on the Philosophy of Charles Taylor*, edited by Arto Laitinen & Nicholas H. Smith, pp. 115–131. Helsinki: Societas Philosophica Fennica.

Larmore, Charles (1996) *Patterns of Moral Complexity*. Cambridge: Cambridge University Press.

Lieberman, Marcel (1997) The Limits of Comparison: Kant and Sartre on the Fundamental Project, *History of Philosophy Quarterly*, 14 (2) 207–217.

Lippert-Rasmussen, Kasper (2002) "Real-self Accounts of Freedom," *Sats—Nordic Journal of Philosophy* 3(2):50–72.

Locke, John (1689/1975) *An Essay Concerning Human Understanding*, edited by Peter H. Nidditch. Oxford: Clarendon Press. Longuenesse, Béatrice (2008) "Self-Consciousness and Self-Reference: Sartre and Wittgenstein," *European Journal of Philosophy* 16(1):1–21.

Louden, Robert B. (2006) "Williams's Critique of the Morality System," in *Bernard Williams*, edited by Alan Thomas, pp. 104–134. Cambridge: Cambridge University Press.

Löw-Beer, Martin. (1994) "Sind wir einzigartig?" *Deutsche Zeitschrift für Philosophie* 42:121–139.

Luckner, Andreas (2007) "Wie man zu sich kommt—Versuch über Authentizität," in *Freies Selbstsein*. Authentizität und Regression, by Julius Kuhl & Andreas Luckner, pp. 9–48. Göttingen: Vanderhoeck & Ruprecht.

Lukács, Georg (1971) *History and Class Consciousness*, trans. Rodney Livingstone. Cambridge: MIT Press.

Lund, William R. (1997) "Egalitarian Liberalism and Social Pathology: A Defense of Public Neutrality," *Social Theory and Practice* 23:449–478.

MacIntyre, Alasdair (1984) *After Virtue: A Study in Moral Theory*. Notre Dame: University of Notre Dame Press.

Mara, Gerald M. & Dovi, Suzanne L. (1995) "Mill, Nietzsche, and the Identity of Postmodern Liberalism," *The Journal of Politics* 57(1):1–23.

Marx, Karl (1974) *Capital, Vol. 1*. New World Paperbacks.

Marx, Karl (1975) *Early Writings*. Harmondsworth: Penguin.

Marx, Karl (1976) Theses on Feuerbach, in *Collected Works*, Vol. 5, by Karl Marx & Friedrich Engels. Moscow: Progress Publishers.

Marx, Karl (1990) *Ökonomisch-philosophische Manuskripte*, Vol. 40. Berlin: MEW.

Marx, Karl & Engels, F. (1976) *Collected Works*, Vol. 3. Moscow: Progress Publishers.

McDowell, John (1996) *Mind and World*. Cambridge: Harvard University Press.

McGraw, Phillip C. (2003) *Self Matters: Creating Your Life from the Inside Out*. New York: Simon & Schuster.

McPherson, Thomas (1970) *Social Philosophy*. London: Van Nostrand Reinhold.

Mele, Alfred R. (1991) "History and Personal Autonomy," *Canadian Journal of Philosophy* 23:271–280.

Menke, Christoph (1995) *Tragödie im Sittlichen: Gerechtigkeit und Freiheit nach Hegel*. Frankfurt am Main: Suhrkamp.

Menke, Christoph (2005) "Innere Natur und soziale Normativität: Die Idee der Selbstverwirklichung," in *Die kulturellen Werte Europas*, edited by Hans Joas & Klaus Wiegandt, pp. 304–352. Frankfurt am Main: Fischer.

Merleau-Ponty, Maurice (1945/2002) *Phenomenology of Perception*, trans. Colin Smith. New York: Routledge.

Mill, John Stuart (1867) *On Liberty*. London: Longmans, Green and Co.

Moore, Thomas (1994) *Care of the Soul*. New York: Harper Paperbacks.

Moran, Richard (2001) *Authority and Estrangement: An Essay on Self-Knowledge*. Princeton NJ: Princeton University Press.

Morris, Robert J. (1981) "Samuel Smiles and the Genesis of Self-Help," *Historical Journal* 24:89–109.

Muchnik, Pablo (2000) "An Essay on the Principles of Rousseau's Anthropology," *Philosophy & Social Criticism* 26:51–77.

Nehamas, Alexander (1985). *Nietzsche: Life as Literature*. Cambridge: Harvard University Press.

Nesse, Randolph M. (2000) "Is Depression an Adaptation?" *Archives of General Psychiatry* 57:14–20.

Nettle, Daniel (2004) "Evolutionary Origins of Depression: A Review and Reformulation," *Journal of Affective Disorders* 81:91–102.

Nietzsche, Friedrich (1974) *The Gay Science*, trans. Walter Kaufmann. New York:Vintage Books.

Nietzsche, Friedrich (1988) *Nachgelassene Fragmente*, in *Kritische Studienausgabe*, edited by Giorgio Colli & Mazzino Montinari, pp. 80–82. Munchen/Berlin/New York: dtv/de Gruyter.

Nietzsche, Friedrich (1992) *Beyond Good and Evil: Prelude to a Philosophy of the Future*, trans. Walter Kaufmann. New York: Random House.

Nietzsche, Friedrich (1997) *Untimely Meditations*, edited by Daniel Breazeale, trans. R. J. Hollingdale. Cambridge University Press.

Nietzsche, Friedrich (2006) *Thus Spoke Zarathustra*, edited by Adrian Del Caro & Robert Pippin, trans. Adrian Del Caro. Cambridge: Cambridge University Press.

Noggle, Robert (2005). "Autonomy and the Paradox of Self-Creation: Infinite Regresses, Finite Selves, and the Limits of Authenticity," in *Personal Autonomy: New Essays on Personal Autonomy and Its Role in Contemporary Moral Philosophy*, J.S. Taylor, ed., 87–108. Cambridge: Cambridge University Press.

Novak, Michael (1976) "The Family Out of Favor," *Harper's* 252:37–46.

Nussbaum, Martha (1994) *Therapy of Desire. Theory and Practice in Hellenistic Ethics*. Princeton: Princeton University Press.

O'Hara, Phillip Anthony (2004) "Cultural Contradictions of Global Capitalism," *Journal of Economic Issues* 38(2):413–420.

Oshana, Marina (2007). *Autonomy* and the Question of Authenticity. *Social Theory and Practice* 33 (3):411–429.

Orwell, Miles (1989) *The Real Thing: Imitation and Authenticity in American Culture, 1880–1940*. North Carolina: University of North Carolina Press.

Outhwaite, William (1994) *Habermas: A Critical Introduction*. Stanford, CA: Stanford University Press.

Petersen, Anders (2009) "Depression—A Social Pathology of Action," *Irish Journal of Sociology* 17(2):56–71.

Pignarre, Phillippe (2001) *Comment la Dépression est Devenue une Épidémie*. Paris: Hachette.

Pinkard, Terry (2004) "Taylor, History, and the History of Philosophy," in *Charles Taylor*, edited by Ruth Abbey, pp. 187–214. Cambridge: Cambridge University Press.

Pongratz, Hans J. & Voß, G. Guenter (1998) "Der Arbeitskraftunternehmer. Eine neue Grundform der Ware Arbeitskraft?" Kölner *Zeitschrift für Soziologie und Sozialpsychologie* 50:131–158.

Pongratz, Hans J. & Voß, G. Guenter (2000) "Vom Arbeitnehmer zum Arbeitskraftunternehmer. Zur Entgrenzung der Ware Arbeitskraft," in *Begrenzte Entgrenzungen. Wandlungen von Organization und Arbeit*, edited by Heiner Minssen, pp. 225–247. Berlin: Edition Sigma.

Pongratz, Hans J. & Voß, G. Guenter (2001) "From Employee to 'Entreployee'—Towards a 'Self-entrepreneurial' Work Force?" *SOWI—Sozialwissenschaftliche Informationen*, pp. 42–52.

Pongratz, Hans J. & Voß, G. Guenter (2003) *Arbeitskraftunternehmer. Erwerbsorientierungen in entgrenzten Arbeitsformen*. Berlin: Edition Sigma.

Price, John S. et al. (1994) "The Social Competition Hypothesis of Depression," *British Journal of Psychiatry* 164:309–315.

Putnam, Robert (2000) *Bowling Alone: The Collapse and Revival of American Community*. New York: Simon and Schuster.

Quante, Michael (2002) "Personale Autonomie und biographische Identität," in *Transitorische Identität. Der Prozesscharakter des modernen Selbst*, edited by Jürgen Staub & Joachim Renn, pp. 32–56. Frankfurt am Main: Campus.

Rasmussen, David M. (1990) *Reading Habermas*. Cambridge, MA: Basil Blackwell.

Rawls, John (1972) *A Theory of Justice*. Oxford: Oxford University Press.

Rawls, John (1985) "Justice as Fairness: Political not Metaphysical," *Philosophy and Public Affairs* 14(3):223–251.

Raz, Joseph (1986) *The Morality of Freedom*. Oxford: Clarendon Press.

Raz, Joseph (2001) *The Practice of Value*. Oxford: Clarendon Press.

Rorty, Richard (1982) "Contemporary Philosophy of Mind," *Synthese* 53:323–348.

Rorty, Richard (1989) *Contingency, Irony and Solidarity*. Cambridge: Cambridge University Press.

Rorty, Richard (1991) *Essays on Heidegger and Others: Philosophical Papers*, Vol. 2. Cambridge: Cambridge University Press.

Rosa, Hartmut (1998) *Identität und kulturelle Praxis. Politische Philosophie nach Charles Taylor*. Frankfurt am Main: Campus.

Rosa, Hartmut (1999) "Kapitalismus und Lebensführung. Perspektiven einer ethischen Kritik der liberalen Marktwirtschaft," *Deutsche Zeitschrift für Philosophie* 47:735–758.

Rosenfield, Kathrin H. (1999) "Getting Inside Sophocles' Mind Through Hölderlin's Antigone," *New Literary History* 30(1):107–127.

Rossinow, Doug (1998) *The Politics of Authenticity: Liberalism, Christianity and the New Left in America*. New York: Columbia University Press.

Rousseau, Jean-Jacques (1957) *The Confessions of Jean-Jacques Rousseau*, edited by Lester Crocker. New York: Pocket Books.

Rousseau, Jean-Jacques (1968) *Julie, Or the New Heloise*, trans. Judith McDowell. University Park: Pennsylvania State University Press.

Rousseau, Jean-Jacques (1979) *Emile*, trans. Allan Bloom. New York: Basic Books.

Rousseau, Jean-Jacques (1992) *Discourse on the Origin of Inequality*, trans. Donald A.Cress. Indianapolis: Hackett.

Ryle, Gilbert (1967) *The Concept of Mind*. New York: Barnes and Noble.

Salerno, Steve. (2005) *SHAM. How the Self-Help Movement Made America Helpless*. New York: Crown Publishers.

Sampson, Eleri (2002) *Build Your Personal Brand*. London: Kogan Page.

Sandel, Michael (1982) *Liberalism and the Limits of Justice*. Cambridge, MA: Cambridge University Press.

Sartre, Jean-Paul (1943/1991) *Being and Nothingness*, trans. Hazel Barnes. London: Routledge.

Sartre, Jean-Paul (1946/1954). *Réflexions sur la Question Juive*. Paris: Gallimard.

Sartre, Jean-Paul (1957) *The Transcendence of the Ego*, trans. Forrest Williams & Robert Kirkpatrick. New York: Noonday Press. Scanlon, Thomas (1998) *What We Owe to Each Other*. Belknap Press of Harvard University Press.

Schmid, Wilhelm (1992) "Uns Selbst Gestalten. Zur Philosophie der Lebenskunst bei Nietzsche," *Nietzsche-Studien* 21:50–62.

Schneewind, Jerome B. (1998) *The Invention of Autonomy*. Cambridge: Cambridge University Press.

Schulte, Günter (1992) *Kennen Sie Marx? Kritik der proletarischen Vernunft*. Frankfurt am Main: Campus.

Searle, John R. (1992) *The Rediscovery of the Mind*. Cambridge: MIT Press.

Seel, Martin (1991) "Die Wiederkehr der Ethik des guten Lebens," *Merkur* 45(1):42–49.

Seel, Martin (1993) "Das Gute und das Richtige," *Zur Verteidigungs der Vernunft gegen ihre Liebhaber und Verächter*, edited by Martin Seel & Christoph Menke, pp. 219–240. Frankfurt am Main: Suhrkamp.

Seel, Martin (1997) "Well-Being: On a Fundamental Concept of Practical Philosophy," *European Journal of Philosophy* 5(1):39–49.

Seel, Martin (1999) *Versuch über die Form des Glücks. Studien zur Ethik.* Frankfurt am Main: Suhrkamp.

Seel, Martin (2004) "'Jede wirklich gesättifte Anschauung'. Das positive Zentrum der negative Philosophie Adornos", in *Adronos Philosophie der Kontemplation*, by Martin Seel, pp. 9–19. Frankfurt am Main: Suhrkamp.

Sennett, Richard (1993) *The Conscience of the Eye: The Design and Social Life of Cities.* London: Faber & Faber.

Sennett, Richard (1998) *The Corrosion of Character—The Personal Consequences of Work in the New Capitalism.* New York /London: W.W. Norton & Company.

Sheldrake, Philip F. (2003) "Christian Spirituality as a Way of Living Publicly: A Dialectic of the Mystical and Prophetic," *Spiritus: A Journal of Christian Spirituality* 3(1):19–37.

Shoemaker, Sidney (1968) "Self-reference and Self-awareness," *The Journal of Philosophy* 65:555–567.

Shoemaker, Sidney (1994) "Self-knowledge and 'Inner-sense'," *Philosophy and Phenomenological Research* 54:249–314.

Shusterman, Richard (1992) *Pragmatist Aesthetics: Living Beauty, Rethinking Art.* Oxford: Blackwell.

Siep, Ludwig (2010) *Recognition in Hegel's Phenomenology and Contemporary Practical Philosophy.* In: *The Philosophy of Recognition. Historical and Contemporary Perspectives*, edited by H.-Ch. Schmidt am Busch, Ch. F. Zurn, pp. 107–127. Lanham: Lexington Books.

Simmel, Georg (1950) "The Metropolis and Mental Life," in *The Sociology of Georg Simmel*, edited by Kurt Wolff, pp. 409–424. New York: Free Press.

Simmel, Georg (1987) *Das individuelle Gesetz. Philosophische Exkurse.* Frankfurt am Main: Suhrkamp.

Sisk, John P. (1973) "On Being an Object," Harper's 247:60–64.

Slater, Philip Elliot (1970) *The Pursuit of Loneliness: American Culture at the Breaking Point.* Boston: Beacon Press.

Smiles, Samuel (1969) *Self-Help.* London: John Murray.

Smith, Nicholas H. (2004) "Taylor and the Hermeneutic Tradition," in *Charles Taylor*, edited by Ruth Abbey, pp. 29–51. Cambridge: Cambridge University Press.

Springer, Roland (2000) "Return to Taylorism? Work Organization and Labour Policy in the German Auto Industry," in *Proceedings of the 12th IIRA World Congress*, Vol. 1, Tokyo.

Starker, Steven (2002) *Oracle at the Supermarket: The American Preoccupation with Self-Help Books.* New York: Transaction Publishers.

Starobinski, Jean (1971) *Jean-Jacques Rousseau. La Transparance et l'obstacle.* Paris: Gallimard.

Steinfath, Holger (1998) "Einführung: Die Thematik des guten Lebens in der gegenwärtigen philosophischen Diskussion," in *Was ist ein gutes Leben? Philosophische Reflexionen*, edited by Holmer Steinfath, pp. 7–31. Frankfurt am Main: Suhrkamp.

Stevens, Anthony & Price, John (2000) *Evolutionary Psychiatry*, 2nd Ed. London: Routledge.

Szerszynski, Bronislaw (2003) "Technology, Performance and Life Itself: Hannah Arendt and the Fate of Nature," *Sociological Review* 51(2):203–218.

Taviss Thomson, Irene (1997) "From Conflict To Embedment: The IndividualSociety Relationship, 1920–1991," *Sociological Forum* 12(4):631–658.

Taviss Thomson, Irene (2000) *In Conflict No Longer: Self and Society in Contemporary America.* Oxford: Rowmann & Littlefield.

Taylor, Charles (1985) "What is Human Agency?" in *Human Agency and Language. Philosophical Papers*, Vol. I, by Charles Taylor, pp. 15–45. Cambridge: Cambridge University Press.

Taylor, Charles (1986) "Foucault on Freedom and Truth," in *Foucault: A Critical Reader, edited by David Hoy*, pp. 69–102. Oxford: Blackwell.

Taylor, Charles (1989) *Sources of the Self. The Making of the Modern Identity.* Cambridge: Cambridge University Press.

Taylor, Charles (1991) *The Ethics of Authenticity.* Cambridge: Harvard University Press.

Taylor, Charles (1994) "The Politics of Recognition," in *Multiculturalism: Examining the Politics of Recognition*, edited by Amy Gutmann, pp. 25–73. Princeton: Princeton University Press.

Taylor, Charles (1995) "The Politics of Recognition," in *Philosophical Arguments*, by Charles Taylor, pp. 225–257. Cambridge, MA: Harvard University Press.

Taylor, Charles (2007) *A Secular Age.* Cambridge: Harvard University Press.

Thalberg, I. (1978) 'Hierarchical Analyses of Unfree Action'. *Canadian Journal of Philosophy* 8, pp. 211–26.

Tietjens Meyers, Diana (2005) "Decentralizing Autonomy: Five Faces of Selfhood," in *Autonomy and the Challenges to Liberalism: New Essays*, edited by John Christ-man & Joel Anderson, pp. 27–55. Cambridge: Cambridge University Press.

Trilling, Lionel (1972) *Sincerity and Authenticity.* Cambridge: Harvard University Press.

Tugendhat, Ernst (1978) "Antike und Moderne Ethik," in Probleme der Ethik, by Ernst Tugendhat, pp. 33–56. Stuttgart: Reclam.

Tugendhat, Ernst (1979) *Selbstbewusstsein und Selbstbestimmung. Sprachanalytische Interpretationen.* Frankfurt am Main: Suhrkamp. Tugendhat, Ernst (1993) Vorlesungen über Ethik. Frankfurt am Main: Suhrkamp.

Tugendhat, Ernst (2006) "I would consider myself to be a naturalist." Interview with Darlei Dall'Agnol e Alessandro Pinzani, ethic@ 5(1):1–6.

Tugendhat, Ernst (2007) *Anthropologie statt Metaphysik.* München: Beck.

Varga, Somogy (2009) "Life as Art. Concerning some Paradoxes of an Ethical Idea," *Estetica. Central European Journal of Aesthetics* 46(1):49–61.

Varga, Somogy (2011a) "Defining Mental Disorder. Exploring the 'Natural Functions' Approach," *Philosophy, Ethics and Humanities in Medicine* 6:1.

Varga, Somogy (2011b—online first) "Evolutionary Psychiatry and Depression. Testing Two Hypotheses," *Medicine, Healthcare and Philosophy.*DOI: 10.1007/s11019–010–9305–9

Varga, Somogy (2011c) "Existential Choices. To What Degree is Who We a Matter of Choice?" *Continental Philosophy Review* 44:65–79.

Varga, Somogy (2011d) "Self-Realization and Owing to Others. A Morality Constrain?" *International Journal of Philosophical Studies* 19:71–82.

Velleman, J. David (1989) *Practical Reflection*, Princeton: Princeton University Press.

Velleman, J. David (2006). *Self to Self: Selected Essays.* Cambridge University Press.

Vesper, Achim (2007) "Das Gute und das Rerechte. Eine Kontroverse in Moral— und Rechtsphilosophie," Goethe University of Frankfurt am Main, unpublished manuscript.

Voßwinkel, Stephan & Kocyba, Hermann (2005) "Entgrenzung der Arbeit. Von der Entpersönlichung zum permanenten Selbstmanagement," *WestEnd. Neue Zeitschrift für Sozialforschung* 2:73–83.

Waldo Trine, Ralph (1897/1942) In *Tune with the Infinite.* New York: Bobbs-Merrill.

Watson, Gary (1975) "Free Agency," *Journal of Philosophy* 72:205–220.

Watson, Paul J. & Andrews, Paul W. (2002) "Towards a Revised Evolutionary Adaptationist Analysis of Depression: The Social Navigation Hypothesis," *Journal of Affective Disorders* 72:1–14.

Weber, Max (1949) *The Methodology of the Social Sciences*, edited and trans. by Edward Shills & Henry Finch. New York: Free Press.

Weber, Max (1968) *Economy and Society, edited by Guenther Roth & Claus Wittich*. Berkeley: University of California Press.

Wellmer, Albrecht (1993) "Wahrheit, Schein, Versöhnung. Adornos ästhetische Rettung der Modernität," in Zur *Dialektik der Moderne und Postmoderne. Vernunftkritik nach Adorno*, by A. Wellmer, pp. 9–47. Frankfurt am Main: Suhrkamp.

Whitmire, John F. Jr. (2009) "The Many and the One: The Ontological Multiplicity and Functional Unity of the Person in the Later Nietzsche," *The Pluralist* 4.1:1–14.

Williams, Bernard (1981a) "Persons, Character and Morality," in *Moral Luck*, by Bernard Williams, pp. 1–19. Cambridge: Cambridge University Press.

Williams, Bernard (1981b) "Conflicts of Values," in Moral Luck, by *Bernard Williams*, pp. 71–82. Cambridge: Cambridge U Press.

Williams, Bernard (1981c) "Internal and External Reasons," in Moral Luck, by Bernard Williams, pp. 101–113. Cambridge: Cambridge University Press.

Williams, Bernard (1981d) "Practical Necessity," in Moral Luck, by *Bernard Williams*, pp. 124–131. Cambridge: Cambridge U Press.

Williams, Bernard (1985). *Ethics and the Limits of Philosophy*. London: Fontana.

Williams, Bernard (1993a) "Moral Incapacity," *Proceedings of the Aristotelian Society* 93:59–79.

Williams, Bernard (1993b) *Shame and Necessity*. Berkeley: University of California Press.

Williams, Bernard (1995) "How Free Does the Will Need to Be?" *Making Sense of Humanity and Other Philosophical Papers, 1982–93*, pp. 3–21. New York: Cambridge University Press.

Williams, Bernard (2002) *Truth and Truthfulness*. New Jersey: Princeton University Press.

Wittgenstein, Ludwig (1969) *On Certainty*, edited by G. E. M. Anscombe & G. H. von Wright, trans. by G. E. M. Anscombe & D. Paul. Oxford: Blackwell.

Wolf, Susan (1990) *Freedom Within Reason*. Oxford: Oxford University Press.

Wood, Allen W. (2008) *Kantian Ethics*. Cambridge: Cambridge University Press.

Wright, Crispin (1998) "Self-Knowledge: The Wittgensteinian Legacy," in *Knowing our Own Minds*, edited by Crispin Wright, Barry C. Smith, & Cynthia Macdonald, pp. 15–45. Oxford: Clarendon Press.

Yankelovich, Daniel (1981) *New Rules: Searching for Self-Fulfilment in a World Turned Upside Down*. New York: Random House.

Zimmerman, Aaron (2008) "Self-Knowledge: Rationalism vs. Empiricism," *Philosophy Compass* 3(2):325–352.

Zittel, Claus (2003) "Ästhetisch fundierte Ethiken und Nietzsches Philosophie," *Nietzsche-Studien* 32:103–123.

Zurn, Christopher (2000) "Anthropology and Normativity: A Critique of Axel Honneth's Formal Conception of Ethical Life," *Philosophy and Social Criticism* 26(1):115–124.

Index